809.04
TRO   Leon Trotsky on literature
      and art.

DATE DUE

809.04
TRO   Leon Trotsky on literature
      and art.

DATE DUE	BORROWER'S NAME	

LEON TROTSKY
on Literature
and Art

Leon Trotsky

LEON TROTSKY
on Literature and Art

Edited with an introduction
by Paul N. Siegel

PATHFINDER PRESS

CONTENTS

Part II: Essays in Literary Criticism

INTRODUCTION

By Paul N. Siegel

I

A. V. Lunacharsky, the Soviet Commissar of Education under Lenin, writing in his *Revolutionary Silhouettes* of Leon Trotsky as the leader of the Red Army, spoke of "the titanic task which Trotsky took upon his shoulders, those lightning trips from place to place, those magnificent speeches, fanfares of instantaneous commands, that role of continual electrifier now at one point and now another of the weakening army. There is not a man on earth who could replace Trotsky there."[1] The whole world had indeed been amazed by the feats of Trotsky, acting as an expression of the revolution which had roused the Russian people.

Yet almost as remarkable in its way as Trotsky's military accomplishments is the fact that, as he was speeding from one front to another in his famous armored train, he was reading recently published French novels. Literature was always an absorbing interest of his. As he phrased it in the diary which he kept in 1935: "Politics and literature constitute in essence the content of my personal life." And just as his military feats won, as Lenin noted, the respect of experts in that field, so did the literary criticism of this professional revolutionist win the respect of professional men of letters. T. S. Eliot and F. R. Leavis paid tribute to his cultivation and insight while they were taking issue with his Marxism, and Edmund Wilson spoke of his *Literature and Revolution* as "a brilliant and valuable book" and as a "remarkable little study."[2]

Trotsky's ability as a literary critic may be gauged by his having hailed before they received general acclaim Malraux, Silone and Celine, the first two of whom wrote novels that affected so strongly the decade of the thirties and that are among the very few works which have survived it, and the last of whom wrote novels that have so strongly influenced subsequent European and American novelists. But a volume of Trotsky's literary criticism is justified not only by his taste and judgment as a literary critic. It is justified by the abiding value of what he has to say on the relationship between literature and society, by the fact that it is Marxist literary criticism written by one of the great Marxist thinkers. For just as Trotsky's Red Army, although it won the respect of the military experts by its achievements, was organized on revolutionary principles of which they had no understanding, so his literary criticism proceeds from a theory of literature concerning which most of the professional critics of the Western world, particularly those of the United States, have little knowledge.

II

The limited extent of this knowledge is indicated by the statement of Professor Rene Wellek in the 1952 brochure "The Aims, Methods and Materials of Research in the Modern Languages and Literatures" published by the Modern Language Association of America: "Marx and the Marxists only admit the determining influence of economic and social conditions, attempting to establish definite causal connections between technological change and the stratification of classes on the one hand, and literary creation on the other. The majority of literary historians in the United States have, however, eschewed such extreme determinism and have not, on the whole, endorsed claims for complete scientific explanation."[3]

Trotsky, however, quoted the Italian Marxist philosopher Antonio Labriola against those who would simpli-

Leon Trotsky, Commissar of War (1918-25).

fy Marxist theory into crude economic determinism: "By
this method fools could reduce the whole of history to
the level of commercial arithmetic and, finally, a new,
original interpretation of Dante's work could show us
The Divine Comedy in the light of calculations regarding
pieces of cloth which crafty Florentine merchants sold
for their maximum profit." Earlier in the same essay
Labriola had said of such vulgarizations of Marxism
that "they are a convenient assistance to the adversaries
of materialism, who use them as a bugbear."[4] Such an
adversary of historical materialism is Professor Wellek,
the eminent historian of literary criticism and coauthor of
the highly influential *Theory of Literature*, who, a half
century after Labriola wrote these words, still advanced
the bugbear that Marxists find only economic and social
conditions have a determining influence on literature —
and this in a statement of principles concerning the study
of literature prepared under the auspices of the Modern
Language Association and carefully reviewed by other
eminent personages of that scholarly organization.

The truth is that Marxist theory finds complex interactions to exist between what Marx called the economic
foundation (the sum total of the relations into which men
enter to carry on social production) and the ideological
superstructure (the legal, political, religious, aesthetic and
philosophical systems of ideas and institutions) which
may develop on the basis of that foundation. As Engels
wrote, "Political, juridical, philosophical, religious, literary,
artistic, etc., development is based on economic development. But all these react upon one another and also upon
the economic base. It is not that the economic position is
the *cause and alone active*, while everything else only has
a passive effect. There is, rather, interaction on the basis
of the economic necessity, which *ultimately* always asserts
itself."[5]

The men engaged in the various spheres of ideological
activity acquire their own special interests, their traditions,
their rationale. These conditions of activity established by
the disciplines themselves are only relatively independent,
the course of their movement being subject to the more
powerful movement of economic development, which alters

social relations and thereby the social consciousness determined by these relations. "The ruling ideas of each age," as Marx said, "have ever been the ideas of its ruling class,"[6] but the web of thought is woven by the ideologists of that class from the materials bequeathed by the past and is a result of a process of interaction between the class and its ideologists.

Trotsky, therefore, far from minimizing the role of tradition in literature, insists upon it as much as does T. S. Eliot. He adds, however, that the continuity of literary history is dialectical, proceeding by a series of reactions, each of which is united to the tradition from which it is seeking to break ("artistic creation is always a complicated turning inside out of old forms"). Nor are these reactions merely mechanical, the eternal swing of the pendulum from "classic" to "romantic." They take place under the stimuli of new artistic needs as the result of changes in the psychology of social classes attendant upon changes in the economic structure.

Thus Trotsky says of futurism, which proclaimed the necessity for a complete break with the past, "In the advance guard of literature, futurism is no less a product of the poetic past than any other literary school of the present day."[7] Nevertheless its revolt against "the old literary caste" which constituted itself as "the priests of bourgeois literary tradition" is significant and its course of development illuminating.

Trotsky finds futurism to have been generated at the turn of the century in an atmosphere of foreboding. "The armed peace, with its patches of diplomacy, the hollow parliamentary systems, the external and internal politics based on the system of safety valves and brakes, all this weighed heavily on poetry at a time when the air, charged with accumulated electricity, gave signs of impending great explosions." Futurism emanated from "bourgeois Bohemia," from the middle-class intelligentsia in revolt against middle-class hypocrisy and complacency. As such it is only one of a series of such rebellions which bourgeois society has controlled, assimilated and rendered innocuous, accepted by the very academy whose cultural authority was originally challenged by the rebellion. The futurists painted their cheeks, wore yellow blouses and broke up concerts just as the French and German romanticists delighted in shocking the bourgeoisie, wore long hair and flaunted red vests. This series of rebellions, Trotsky adds in "Art and Politics in Our Epoch," in words that are applicable to our own "beats" and hippies, with their long hair, their beards, their beads, their drugs and their disruptions, take on in the decline of bourgeois society "a more and more violent character, alternating between hope and despair."

If futurism, however, originated in "bourgeois Bohemia," it was attracted by the powerful current of the Russian Revolution which occurred before it could flow into and be lost in the mainstream of bourgeois culture. The Bolsheviks, far from seeking to set aside the past, had their own revolutionary tradition, which was foreign to the futurists, but the internal dynamics of the futurists' rebellion against the old values propelled them to the new social order. In Italy, on the other hand, the futurists were attracted to the pseudorevolution of fascism, which mobilized petty bourgeois masses and declaimed against the corruption of Italian society. Trotsky is not at all embarrassed by the contrary directions taken by the futurist movements of the two countries. In fact, he made a point of it, calling upon the Italian Communist leader, Antonio Gramsci, to write a description of the course taken by futurism in his country that was printed as an appendix to the Russian edition of *Literature and Revolution*. For the diverse directions taken by futurism illustrates, as does, for instance, the existence of the reactionary romanticism of Scott and the radical romanticism of Shelley, that a literary school is neither a mechanical contrivance constructed by a social class nor an independent entity immune to the changes in the intellectual and emotional environment created by changes in the economic structure.

III

If, however, the most eminent literary scholars and critics in the United States are ignorant of Marxism, Trotsky the Marxist, writing more than forty years ago, has much to say which is relevant for the leading scholarly and critical schools in the United States today. What are the Russian formalists, of whom Trotsky speaks in *Literature and Revolution*, if not forerunners of our own "new critics"? Trotsky points out the empty pretensions of the formalists in seeking to make literature completely autonomous and in proclaiming themselves to possess the first scientific theory of literature, but he adds: "The methods of formalism, confined within legitimate limits, may help to clarify the artistic and psychologic peculiarities of form (its economy, its movement, its contrasts, its hyperbolism, etc.). . . . But the formalists are not content to ascribe to their methods a merely subsidiary, serviceable and technical significance. . . . The social and psychologic approach which, to us, gives a meaning to the microscopic and statistical work done in connection with verbal material is, for the formalists, only alchemy." [8] So the "new critics," it has been observed by Professor Douglas Bush, have given American literary scholars a course in advanced remedial reading but have at the same time promoted an attitude of looking upon literary works as if they were specimens on microscope slides. As Trotsky long ago warned, "The effort to set art free from life, to declare it a craft self-sufficient unto itself, devitalizes and kills art."

"A work of art," says Trotsky, "should, in the first place, be judged by its own law, that is, by the law of art." But before we can judge we must understand, and before we can really understand, we must see the work in its historical context. This the various kinds of historical scholarship other than Marxism likewise seek to do. Marxism, however, claims to unite these kinds of scholarship into a single all-embracing system.

The literary historian looks at a literary work in relation to the development of literary form. But, says Trotsky, the development of literary form, like the individual literary work, is only relatively autonomous. Each literary work is the product of a living man handling the materials handed down to him by his predecessors and possessing a psychology that is the result of his social environment. "Between the physiology of sex and a poem about love there lies a complex system of psychological transmitting

mechanisms in which there are individual, racial and
social elements. The racial foundation, that is, the sexual
basis of man, changes slowly. The social forms of love
change more rapidly. They affect the psychologic substruc-
ture of love, they produce new shadings and intonations,
new spiritual demands, a need of a new vocabulary, and
so they present new demands on poetry." To understand
the love poetry of Donne, we have to understand how it
grows out of and reacts against Elizabethan love poetry,
as the orthodox literary historian tells us; we have to
understand the life of the Jack Donne who became the
clergyman John Donne, as the orthodox literary biographer tells us; we have to understand Donne, the man
living at a time of social change and uncertainty consequent upon the growth in power of the middle class, and
the way in which his expression of attitude toward love
reflected his outlook on life and caused him to make a
"revolution" in poetry, as the Marxist critic can tell us.

The other forms of literary scholarship—the study of
literature in relation to the history of ideas, to the history of science, to the history of religion, to myth and
ritual (Trotsky's discussion of the existence of enduring
themes in literature is relevant to this latest scholarly
vogue) and so forth—constitute what Trotsky called "a
crossing or combining and interacting of certain independent principles [as it seems to those engaged in this
scholarship]—the religious, political, juridical, aesthetic
substances, which find their origin and explanation in
themselves." For Trotsky, however, these spheres of ideological activity are "separate aspects of one and the
same process of social development" which "evolves the
necessary organs and functions from within itself." They
interact among themselves and react upon the economic
base from which they have evolved and upon whose development the general course of their development is finally
dependent.

Trotsky does not claim, as Wellek states Marxists claim,
that Marxism gives a "complete scientific explanation" for
a literary work. Marx had drawn a distinction between
"the material transformation of the economic conditions
of production which can be determined with the precision

of natural science" and the transformation of the cultural superstructure which follows this transformation. [9] So too Trotsky states: "To say that man's environment, including the artist's, that is, the conditions of his education and life, find expression in his art also, does not mean to say that such expression has a precise geographic, ethnographic and statistical character." If we cannot, however, construct an elaborate formula that gives "a complete scientific explanation" why this work of art was written just that day by just that man in just that way, it remains true that, in the words of Marx, "the mode of production in material life determines the social, political, and intellectual life processes in general" [10] and that a knowledge of how literature is governed in a general way by the functioning of the mode of production is essential for its fullest understanding.

IV

T. S. Eliot, discussing Trotsky's statement that "Marxism alone can explain why and how a given tendency in art has originated in a given period of history," comments, "If Marxism explains why and how a given tendency in history originated, such as the tendency for Shakespeare's plays to be written, . . . then there seems to me to be a good deal left to explain." [11] He goes on to ask how Marxism explains the fact that great works of literature, while they are an expression of their age, continue to have artistic interest for future generations: "While recognizing the interest of the work of literature as a document upon the ideas and the sensibility of its epoch, and recognizing even that the permanent work of literature is one which does not lack this interest, yet [one] cannot help valuing literary work, like philosophical work, in the end by its transcendence of the limits of its age. . . ." [12]

Trotsky, however, far from being concerned only with the historical origins of literature, speaks in "Class and Art" of the need for understanding "art as art." He attacks those who find the sole value of *The Divine Comedy* to be that it gives us "an understanding of the state of mind of certain classes in a certain epoch" and comments that such a view of it makes it "merely a historical document," not a work of art, which "must speak in some way to my feelings and moods."

How, then, does he explain the fact that Dante, "a Florentine petty bourgeois of the thirteenth century," speaks to him across the centuries? Before Eliot raised the question, Trotsky answered it. "In class society, in spite of all its changeabiiity, there are certain common features." The expression of the feeling of love or of the fear of death has changed with changes in society, but the feeling of love and the fear of death remain. Literature, by articulating such feelings with intensity and precision, refines feeling and generalizes experience. It thus helps man to become aware of himself, to understand his position in the universe. The great literature of the past continues to fulfill this function for us because its expression of basic feelings and experiences, however these feelings and experiences have differed among different social classes at different times, is so powerful that it throws into relief features in them common to men of all times of class society. It thus still has the capacity to enrich our internal life.

F. R. Leavis thinks that he finds Trotsky in a contradiction in his acceptance of the great literature of the past while condemning the culture of which it is an expression: "Like all Marxists, [he] practices, with the familiar air of scientific rigour, the familiar vague, blanketing use of essential terms. He can refer, for instance, to the 'second of August, 1914, when the maddened power of bourgeois culture let loose upon the world the blood and fire of an imperialistic war' (p. 190). This however is perhaps a salute to orthodoxy. And it would not be surprising if he had thought it wise to distract attention, if possible, from such things as the following, which uses 'culture' very differently, and is hardly orthodox: 'The proletariat is forced to take power before it has appropriated the fundamental elements of bourgeois culture; it is forced to overthrow bourgeois society by revolutionary violence, for the very reason that society does not allow it access to culture' (p. 195). The aim of revolution, it appears, is to secure this accursed bourgeois culture for the proletariat. Or, rather, Trotsky knows that behind the word 'culture' there is something that cannot be explained by the 'methods of production' and that it would be disastrous to destroy as 'bourgeois.'" [13]

Trotsky, however, defines precisely the way in which he uses the word "culture" in the very *Literature and Revolution* that the editor of *Scrutiny*, an advocate of rigorously close reading, did not scrutinize sufficiently closely: "Culture is the organic sum of knowledge and capacity which characterizes the entire society, or at least its ruling class. It embraces and penetrates all fields of human work and unifies them into a system." The victorious proletariat, in seizing "the fundamental elements" of this sum of knowledge and skill, modifies it by rejecting that which it finds useless, by adding to it and in general by putting its own stamp upon it. It serves a period of cultural apprenticeship, gradually mastering the whole of the culture before it can completely renovate it. By the time it will have left this period of apprenticeship to construct a culture of its own, it will have ceased to be a proletariat.

In "Culture and Socialism" Trotsky, in discussing the matter of the proletarian appropriation of bourgeois culture, from which it has been excluded, explicitly raises the question later raised by Leavis: "Exploiters' society has given rise to an exploiters' culture. . . . And yet we say to the working class: master all the culture of the past, otherwise you will not build socialism. How is this to be understood?" In raising the question, far from giving up the idea that culture is to be explained by the methods of production, as Leavis says he does in calling upon the workers to become the possessors of bourgeois culture, Trotsky insists upon it: "Over this contradiction many people have stumbled, and they stumble so frequently because they approach the understanding of class society superficially, semi-idealistically, forgetting that fundamentally this is the organization of production. Every class society has been formed on the basis of definite modes of struggle with nature, and these modes have changed in accordance with the development of technique. . . . On this dynamic foundation there arise classes, which by their interrelations determine the character of culture."

Trotsky's answer to the question is that the contradiction is not his but is the dialectical contradiction present in culture itself. Technique, the basis of class organization, has served as a means of exploitation, but it is also a condition for the emancipation of the exploited. The machine crushes the worker, but he can free himself only through the machine. What is true of material culture is also true of spiritual culture. After having conquered illiteracy and semiliteracy, the Russian worker must master classical Russian literature.

V

One cannot speak of a cultural revolution in the same way as one speaks of a social revolution. A social revolution is the birth of a new society. This new society grows for a prolonged period of time within the womb of the old society, but the seizure of power by the new class— the violent birth of the revolution—takes only a brief time. One cannot, however, build a new culture overnight, nor can one build a new culture without having mastered the old one.

Yet this is what the Chinese Cultural Revolution, outlawing the literature of past cultures, would do. Chiang Ching, Mao Tsetung's wife and a leader of the Cultural Revolution, has written: "If our literature and art do not correspond to the socialist economic base, they will inevitably destroy it." [14] Thus, despite her access to the thoughts of Chairman Mao, she flies in the face of the elementary Marxist tenet that it is the economic base, not the cultural superstructure, which is the chief force in the interaction between them, that the economic base will sooner transform the cultural superstructure than the cultural superstructure will transform the economic base. As a result of such thinking, Shakespeare, who was read by Marx every year, is forbidden in China, as is Pushkin, who was a favorite author of Lenin's. For Trotsky, on the other hand, fear of the effect of the literature of a previous class is a silly bogeyman: "It is childish to think that bourgeois *belles lettres* can make a breach in class solidarity. What the worker will take from Shakespeare, Goethe, Pushkin, or Dostoyevsky, will be a more complex idea of human personality, of its passions and feelings, a deeper and more profound understanding of its psychic forces and of the role of the subconscious, etc. In the final analysis, the worker will be richer."

However, while Trotsky does not fear the effect of bourgeois *belles lettres* in itself, he upholds the right of the proletarian dictatorship, when it is fighting for its life, to proscribe writing aimed at undermining the regime, even if it appears as *belles lettres*. If during a civil war the proletarian army has the right to destroy edifices of artistic value for military reasons (the same right which other armies arrogate to themselves without discussing the matter), so, he argues, the regime has the right under such or similar conditions to suppress counterrevolutionary literature. Its first obligation is to safeguard the new order, whose overthrow would mean an end to the cultural liberation of the masses. This right of the regime, however, should on no account be used against those not opposed to the revolution and should be exercised less and less as the regime consolidates its power. This was actually the policy during the first years of the Bolshevik government, as the Oxford historian of Russian literature, Max Hayward, no great friend of the Bolsheviks, testifies: "Its [the revolutionary censorship's] main function was to prevent the publication of overtly counter-revolutionary works. . . . It did not interfere with basic literary freedom in matters of form and content as long as the political interests of the new regime were not adversely affected." [15]

Trotsky formulated this policy in agreement with Lenin with regard to the relation between the state and the different literary schools in this manner in 1924, at a time when it was being increasingly threatened: "While having over them all the categorical criterion, *for* the revolution or *against* the revolution, to give them complete freedom in the sphere of artistic self-determination." Fidel Castro took this position, probably without knowing it was "Trotskyite," in a notable speech to intellectuals in 1961: "What are the rights of revolutionary writers and artists? Within the revolution, everything; against the revolution, no rights whatsoever." [16]   This was also the position of an earlier revolutionist, the poet John Milton, who, speaking in the language of his own ideology, wrote in *Areopagitica*: "This doubtless is more wholesome, more prudent, and more

Christian that many be tolerated, rather than all compelled. I mean not tolerated popery, and open superstition, which, as it extirpates all religions and civil suprem-
acies, so itself should be extirpate . . ." [17]

In his 1924 speech, here printed as "Class and Art,"
Trotsky fights for the right to publish of the "fellow travelers," the bourgeois literary intellectuals sympathetic to
the revolution, and at the same time reminds the members
of the Proletkult school that, although he opposes their
ideas about proletarian literature, he has promised them
to uphold their right to publish their magazine. He speaks
against those groups which seek to become "the monopolist representatives of the artistic interests of the proletariat." Shortly after Stalin used the monopolist aspirations
of these groups to impose his control of literature. Literature then ceased to be alive and vital, as it had been in
the energy-giving atmosphere of the early days of the
revolution. It became instead a puppet of the totalitarian
state. At a time when many literary intellectuals in the
United States and other Western capitalist countries, looking to the Soviet Union for hope in the midst of the capitalist crisis, were ignorantly acclaiming the supposed literary achievements there, Trotsky wrote his eloquent words
about the "epoch of mediocrities, laureates and toadies"
created under the auspices of the bureaucracy.

Today, however, thanks to the development of production, the extension of education and the growth of a new
intelligentisia, made possible, despite the stifling bureaucracy, by the revolution, a fresh generation of literary
rebels has grown up. In their heroic fight for creative
freedom against the bureaucracy, these rebels are con-
tinuing in the tradition of Leon Trotsky.

VI

The literary intellectuals of the United States for their
part no longer look to the Soviet bureaucracy as their
spiritual master. They have grown wiser in some ways,
less wise in others. Less deluded, they are more cynical.
Instead of writing "proletarian literature," they write short
stories and novels about the emptiness of American subur-

ban living and novels and dramas about the absurdity
of existence.

These very works, however, testify to the spiritual sick-
ness of American capitalism, the giant of the capitalist
world. Its intellectuals are increasingly alienated, its youth
increasingly disaffected, its blacks increasingly rebellious.
The dragging on of a monstrously brutal, unpopular
war, the shadow of a nuclear holocaust, the realization
of the disparity between the potential abundance made
possible by modern technology and the actual poverty of
millions—these lie heavily upon the spirit. In the militarized society of today artists and scientists become more
and more aware of the truth of the statement in "A Manifesto: Towards a Free Revolutionary Art," a manifesto
written or largely written by Trotsky, "Even in times of
'peace' the position of art and science has become absolutely intolerable."

Perhaps, however, many young artists who would subscribe to this statement would not so readily subscribe
to the statement that "the artist in a decadent capitalist
society" is "the natural ally of revolution." Proletarian revolution does not seem to be on the order of the day.
"Neocapitalism," making use of Keynesian measures and
above all of a gigantic militarization of the economy, has
succeeded in stabilizing the economy for a prolonged
period. However, monetary crises and inflation indicate
all is not well. The French general strike of May and
June 1968, the largest general strike in the history of
mankind, is a harbinger of things to come in Western
capitalism. And already many young black writers align
themselves with the forces of revolution. For them, as
will be true of others tomorrow, the flaming words of
Trotsky will not appear passé.

Does the statement that the artist is the natural ally of
revolution mean that he should make his art a propaganda art? Georg Lukacs, the renowned Hungarian
Marxist critic, writing in 1934, when he was striving to
maintain his critical independence while accommodating
himself to Stalinism, attacks Trotsky as supporting propaganda art or "'tendentious' portrayal" in order that Lu-

kacs himself may oppose it. Lukacs differentiates between partisanship, which is "not inconsistent with objectivity in reproducing and re-creating reality," and propaganda, "in which support of something means its idealist glorification, while opposition to it involves its distortion." [18] Trotsky, he charges, speaks of an impossibly pure art, separated from society, in the socialist future but upholds a propagandist art in the here and now: "Trotzky writes: 'Revolutionary literature cannot but be imbued with a spirit of social hatred . . . [thus it is merely "propaganda art" — G. L.] Under Socialism solidarity will be the basis of society' (*Literature and Revolution*, p. 230). In other words, 'pure art' and 'true culture' are attainable." [19]

But hatred of oppressors, with which the partisans of revolution must be filled, need not obscure the writer's vision so that it results in a distortion of reality, and social solidarity does not imply an art divorced from society. As a matter of fact, Trotsky had in *Literature and Revolution* dismissed the quarrels between the advocates of "pure art" and those of tendentious art as quarrels that "do not become us"— that is, that are unsuitable for Marxists to engage in because they are irrelevant, Marxism finding both supposedly pure art and frankly tendentious art to have social roots and to fulfill a social function. Those who seek to quarrel, however, will always find a reason to do so, even if they have to invent it.

Trotsky, like Engels before him, always objected to exaggerating the artistic worth of the purely propagandist literature which simplifies a complex reality in order to present an easy lesson. In 1922 he said of the French poet and dramatist Marcel Martinet: "One need neither expect nor fear from him purely propagandist activity." In 1939 he wrote of Jean Malaquais's *Les Javanais*: "Although social in its implications, this novel is in no way tendentious in character. He does not try to prove anything, he does not propagandize, as do many productions of our time, when far too many submit to orders even in the sphere of art. The Malaquais novel is 'only' a work of art."

But a literary work which has an avowed "message," if that work is deeply thought and felt so that it renders reality in all of its complexity and its "message" is organic to it, not an obtrusive appendix, rises from propaganda to art. Such is Ignazio Silone's *Fontamara*. It is, says Trotsky, "a book of passionate political propaganda," but it is "a truly artistic work" because "revolutionary passion is raised here to such heights" and because Silone sees "life as it is."

Although Trotsky calls upon the artist to become the ally of revolution, he does not guarantee that the revolution will enable him to produce masterpieces. The revolutionary view cannot be merely intellectually accepted; it must become part of the very being of the artist, if he is to give expression to it in art. "The artist," says "A Manifesto: Towards a Free Revolutionary Art," "cannot serve the struggle for freedom unless he subjectively assimilates its social content, unless he feels in his very nerves its meaning and drama and freely seeks to give his own inner world incarnation in his art."

He must freely seek to communicate his own inner world, not present a view of the world which has been dictated to him by anyone else or even by himself, not allow any internal inhibitions or external compulsions to cause him to withhold a part of his vision. Gorky, after beginning as a tramp poet, honorably turned toward the proletariat when the proletariat and the radical intelligentsia came into opposition with each other in 1905. However, he never organically assimilated the revolutionary view, and consequently his best period as an artist is that of his first days, when his work had a spontaneity it did not have when he was seeking to apply literary and political lessons. Mayakovsky, devoted to the revolutionary cause, squandered himself meeting the daily demands of newspapers and seeking to adhere to the "correct ideological line" that hack critics imposed on him. Malraux, after producing some significant works, found that his pessimism and skepticism made him need "some outside force to lean on, some established authority," and his novels about Germany and Spain became apologies for Stalinism.

These comments, written by Trotsky at different times, are crystallized in his words to Andre Breton: "The struggle for revolutionary ideas in art must begin once again with

the struggle for artistic *truth*, not in terms of any single
school, but in terms of *the immutable faith of the artist
in his own inner self*. Without this there is no art. 'You
shall not lie!' — that is the formula of salvation."

VII

Artistic truth, Trotsky states in defending his *History
of the Russian Revolution*, consists of the work of art
following its own laws in the unfolding of the chain of
events, in character development, and so on. To attain
it the artist must be true to his own vision. Historical
truth is analogous to it. Truth in history, as in art, does
not demand impartiality, which indeed is impossible. It
demands a rigorous regard for the facts and a scientific
method through which "facts combine into one whole process which, as in life, lives according to its own interior
laws . . ."

In his wittily devastating analysis of Churchill's history
of the period immediately after World War I and its por-
trait of Lenin, Trotsky demonstrates how false to historical
truth Churchill is: inaccurate in his facts, confused in his
visualization of the time and persons he is describing,
artificial even in his verbal antitheses. It is interesting
to compare Churchill as historian and biographer with
Trotsky. None of the political antagonists who attacked
the *History of the Russian Revolution* and the biography
of Stalin were able to challenge Trotsky's use of fact, for
which he had a scrupulous concern. One may add that his
attackers' attempt to hammer loose his causal connections
between facts left them undamaged.

What is true of Trotsky in the quasi-literary arts of the
historian and biographer is also true of him as a literary
critic. He does not disguise his sympathies, he is devoted
to accuracy of statement, he seeks to get at the essence of
things through the Marxist method. Committed to the cause
of revolution, he is especially interested in literature written
by those of revolutionary tendencies. To the writers of this
literature he is sympathetic and generous, but he is also
honest and judicious. Despite Gorky's friendship with the
leading Soviet bureaucrats, Trotsky pays tribute to him as
a man and as a writer of great talent, if not of the genius

for which he was uncritically lauded by the hacks in the service of the bureaucracy. In his obituary articles on Mayakovsky and Essenin he is warm and moving, yet discriminating. In writing to Jack London's daughter, he expresses his sincerely great admiration for *The Iron Heel* but refers to its artistic limitations.

Although Trotsky is especially interested in literary works written by writers of revolutionary tendencies and summons writers to the revolutionary cause, which he believes can save them from demoralization, he is appreciative of all kinds of literature. Political partisan though he is, he does not demand that writers be of his political camp or even of his general political sympathies for them to receive his acclaim. He is aware that, as Rosa Luxemburg said, "With the true artist, the social formula that he recommends is a matter of secondary importance; the source of his art, its animating spirit, is decisive." [20]

The young Trotsky probes the social roots of the art of Tolstoy, who was then still alive, finding them to spring from the soil of his aristocratic upbringing, but he finds the animating spirit of Tolstoy's art to be his "priceless talent for moral indignation" and his "unbending moral courage." The Trotsky of later years, who had suffered unprecedented blows but had retained his youthful faith in life and the revolution, only tempered by experience, finds Celine's *Journey to the End of Night* a novel of the utmost pessimism, but a novel which in its relentless honesty in confronting life strips aside the official lies concerning society. It thus helps to bring about the future already manifesting itself in the present, to which the novel itself is blind. "Exposing the lie, he instills the want for a more harmonious future. Though he himself may consider that nothing good can generally come from man, the very intensity of his pessimism bears within it a dose of the antidote."

In his literary criticism, then, as in his other writing, Trotsky's revolutionary optimism and his fighting revolutionary spirit express themselves. He does not write either in the impersonal manner of the scientist or with the genteel enthusiasm of a taster of fine wines. He writes as one for whom literature is an essential part of human life and for whom humanity, despite the degradation, sordidness and misery which surround us, is grand in the heroism of its struggles and noble in its potentiality. His literary criticism, in short, has its origin in the vision of socialist humanism that animated his whole life.

September, 1969

PART I

Critical Theory

FROM *LITERATURE AND REVOLUTION*

In Literature and Revolution *Trotsky traces the antecedents of the postrevolution literature, analyzes its trends and speculates on its future. He wrote it during his summer holidays in 1922 and 1923. It thus belongs to the period when issues related to the coming struggle against the bureaucracy were being fiercely argued in the Politbureau but not being made known to the party ranks or public. (The other two periods in Trotsky's postrevolution career were that of the Left Opposition's public struggle with the perspective of reforming the Communist International, and finally, after 1933, that of the struggle to build a new International with a perspective of revolution.)* Literature and Revolution *was highly influential in literary circles, but the official attack on Trotsky soon extended to his views on literature, which were anathematized in the same way as his political theory.*

The Social Roots and the Social Function of Literature

The quarrels about "pure art" and about art with a tendency[1] took place between the liberals and the "populists." They do not become us. Materialistic dialectics are

Originally published in Moscow, *Literature and Revolution* was translated into English by Rose Strunsky and appeared in 1925.

above this; from the point of view of an objective historical process, art is always a social servant and historically
utilitarian. It finds the necessary rhythm of words for dark
and vague moods, it brings thought and feeling closer or
contrasts them with one another, it enriches the spiritual
experience of the individual and of the community, it refines feeling, makes it more flexible, more responsive,
it enlarges the volume of thought in advance and not
through the personal method of accumulated experience,
it educates the individual, the social group, the class and
the nation. And this it does quite independently of whether
it appears in a given case under the flag of a "pure" or
of a frankly tendentious art.

In our Russian social development tendentiousness was
the banner of the intelligentsia which sought contact with
the people. The helpless intelligentsia, crushed by czarism
and deprived of a cultural environment, sought support
in the lower strata of society and tried to prove to the
"people" that it was thinking only of them, living only for
them and that it loved them "terribly." And just as the
"populists" [2] who went to the people were ready to do
without clean linen and without a comb and without a
toothbrush, so the intelligentsia was ready to sacrifice the
"subtleties" of form in its art, in order to give the most
direct and spontaneous expression to the sufferings and
hopes of the oppressed. On the other hand, "pure" art
was the banner of the rising bourgeoisie, which could not
openly declare its bourgeois character, and which at the
same time tried to keep the intelligentsia in its service.

The Marxist point of view is far removed from these
tendencies, which were historically necessary, but which
have become historically passé. Keeping on the plane
of scientific investigation, Marxism seeks with the same
assurance the social roots of the "pure" as well as of the
tendentious art. It does not at all "incriminate" a poet with
the thoughts and feelings which he expresses, but raises
questions of a much more profound significance, namely,
to which order of feelings does a given artistic work correspond in all its peculiarities? What are the social conditions of these thoughts and feelings? What place do they
occupy in the historic development of a society and of a

class? And, further, what literary heritage has entered into the elaboration of the new form? Under the influence of what historic impulse have the new complexes of feelings and thoughts broken through the shell which divides them from the sphere of poetic consciousness? The investigation may become complicated, detailed or individualized, but its fundamental idea will be that of the subsidiary role which art plays in the social process.

Each class has its own policy in art, that is, a system of presenting demands on art, which changes with time; for instance, the Maecenas-like protection of court and grand seigneur, the automatic relationship of supply and demand which is supplemented by complex methods of influencing the individual, and so forth, and so on. The social and even the personal dependence of art was not concealed, but was openly announced as long as art retained its court character. The wider, more popular, anonymous character of the rising bourgeoisie led, on the whole, to the theory of "pure art," though there were many deviations from this theory. As indicated above, the tendentious literature of the "populist" intelligentsia was imbued with a class interest; the intelligentsia could not strengthen itself and could not conquer for itself a right to play a part in history without the support of the people. But in the revolutionary struggle, the class egotism of the intelligentsia was turned inside out, and in its left wing, it assumed the form of highest self-sacrifice. That is why the intelligentsia not only did not conceal art with a tendency, but proclaimed it, thus sacrificing art, just as it sacrificed many other things.

Our Marxist conception of the objective social dependence and social utility of art, when translated into the language of politics, does not at all mean a desire to dominate art by means of decrees and orders. It is not true that we regard only that art as new and revolutionary which speaks of the worker, and it is nonsense to say that we demand that the poets should describe inevitably a factory chimney, or the uprising against capital! Of course the new art cannot but place the struggle of the proletariat in the center of its attention. But the plow of the new art is not limited to numbered strips. On the contrary, it must plow

the entire field in all directions. Personal lyrics of the
very smallest scope have an absolute right to exist within the new art. Moreover, the new man cannot be formed
without a new lyric poetry. But to create it, the poet himself must feel the world in a new way. If Christ alone
or Sabaoth himself bends over the poet's embraces (as
in the case of Akhmatova, Tsvetaeva,[3] Shkapskaya and
others), then this only goes to prove how much behind the
times his lyrics are and how socially and aesthetically
inadequate they are for the new man. Even where such
terminology is not a survival of experience so much as
of words, it shows psychologic inertia and therefore stands
in contradiction to the consciousness of the new man.

No one is going to prescribe themes to a poet or intends
to prescribe them. Please write about anything you can think
of! But allow the new class which considers itself, and with
reason, called upon to build a new world, to say to you
in any given case: It does not make new poets of you
to translate the philosophy of life of the seventeenth century into the language of the acmeists.[4] The form of
art is, to a certain and very large degree, independent,
but the artist who creates this form, and the spectator
who is enjoying it, are not empty machines, one for creating form and the other for appreciating it. They are
living people, with a crystallized psychology representing a certain unity, even if not entirely harmonious. This
psychology is the result of social conditions. The creation and perception of art forms is one of the functions
of this psychology. And no matter how wise the formalists[5]
try to be, their whole conception is simply based upon the
fact that they ignore the psychological unity of the social
man, who creates and who consumes what has been created.

The proletariat has to have in art the expression of the
new spiritual point of view which is just beginning to be
formulated within him, and to which art must help him
give form. This is not a state order, but a historic demand. Its strength lies in the objectivity of historic necessity. You cannot pass this by, nor escape its force. . . .

Victor Shklovsky, who flits lightly from verbal formalism to the most subjective valuations, assumes a very
uncompromising attitude towards the historico-material-

istic theory of art. In a booklet which he published in Berlin, under the title of *The March of the Horse*, he formulates in the course of three small pages — brevity is a fundamental and, at any rate, an undoubted merit of Shklovsky — five (not four and not six, but five) exhaustive arguments against the materialist conception of art. Let us examine these arguments, because it won't harm us to take a look and see what kind of chaff is handed out as the last word in scientific thought (with the greatest variety of scientific references on these same three microscopic pages).

"If the environment and the relations of production," says Shklovsky, "influenced art, then would not the themes of art be tied to the places which would correspond to these relations? But themes are homeless." Well, and how about butterflies? According to Darwin, they also "correspond" to definite relations, and yet they flit from place to place, just like an unweighted litterateur.

It is not easy to understand why Marxism should be supposed to condemn themes to a condition of serfdom. The fact that different peoples and different classes of the same people make use of the same themes merely shows how limited the human imagination is, and how man tries to maintain an economy of energy in every kind of creation, even in the artistic. Every class tries to utilize, to the greatest possible degree, the material and spiritual heritage of another class.

Shklovsky's argument could be easily transferred into the field of productive technique. From ancient times on, the wagon has been based on one and the same theme, namely, axles, wheels, and a shaft. However, the chariot of the Roman patrician was just as well adapted to his tastes and needs as was the carriage of Count Orlov, fitted out with inner comforts, to the tastes of this favorite of Catherine the Great. The wagon of the Russian peasant is adapted to the needs of his household, to the strength of his little horse, and to the peculiarities of the country road. The automobile, which is undoubtedly a product of the new technique, shows, nevertheless, the same "theme," namely, four wheels on two axles. Yet every time a peasant's horse shies in terror before the blinding lights

of an automobile on the Russian road at night, a conflict of two cultures is reflected in the episode.

"If environment expressed itself in novels," so runs the
second argument, "European science would not be breaking its head over the question of where the stories of *A
Thousand and One Nights* were made, whether in Egypt,
India, or Persia." To say that man's environment, including the artist's, that is, the conditions of his education
and life, find expression in his art also, does not mean
to say that such expression has a precise geographic,
ethnographic and statistical character. It is not at all
surprising that it is difficult to decide whether certain
novels were made in Egypt, India or Persia, because
the social conditions of these countries have much in
common. But the very fact that European science is "breaking its head" trying to solve this question from these novels themselves shows that these novels reflect an environment, even though unevenly. No one can jump beyond
himself. Even the ravings of an insane person contain
nothing that the sick man had not received before from
the outside world. But it would be an insanity of another
order to regard his ravings as the accurate reflection of
an external world. Only an experienced and thoughtful
psychiatrist, who knows the past of the patient, will be
able to find the reflected and distorted bits of reality in
the contents of his ravings.

Artistic creation, of course, is not a raving, though it
is also a deflection, a changing and a transformation
of reality, in accordance with the peculiar laws of art.
However fantastic art may be, it cannot have at its disposal any other material except that which is given to
it by the world of three dimensions and by the narrower
world of class society. Even when the artist creates heaven
and hell, he merely transforms the experience of his own
life into his phantasmagorias, almost to the point of his
landlady's unpaid bill.

"If the features of class and caste are deposited in art,"
continues Shklovsky, "then how does it come that the
various tales of the Great Russians about their nobleman are the same as their fairy tales about their priest?"
In essence, this is merely a paraphrase of the first ar-

gument. Why cannot the fairy tales about the nobleman and about the priest be the same, and how does this contradict Marxism? The proclamations which are written by well-known Marxists not infrequently speak of landlords, capitalists, priests, generals and other exploiters. The landlord undoubtedly differs from the capitalist, but there are cases when they are considered under one head. Why, then, cannot folk art in certain cases treat the nobleman and the priest together, as the representatives of the classes which stand above the people and which plunder them? In the cartoons of Moor and of Deni, the priest often stands side by side with the landlord, without any damage to Marxism.

"If ethnographic traits were reflected in art," Shklovsky goes on, "the folklore about the peoples beyond the border would not be interchangeable and could not be told by any one folk about another."

As you see, there is no letting up here. Marxism does not maintain at all that ethnographic traits have an independent character. On the contrary, it emphasizes the all-determining significance of natural and economic conditions in the formation of folklore. The similarity of conditions in the development of the herding and agricultural and primarily peasant peoples, and the similarity in the character of their mutual influence upon one another, cannot but lead to the creation of a similar folklore. And from the point of view of the question that interests us here, it makes absolutely no difference whether these homogeneous themes arose independently among different peoples, as the reflection of a life experience which was homogeneous in its fundamental traits and which was reflected through the homogeneous prism of a peasant imagination, or whether the seeds of these fairy tales were carried by a favorable wind from place to place, striking root wherever the ground turned out to be favorable. It is very likely that, in reality, these methods were combined.

And finally, as a separate argument — "The reason (Marxism) is incorrect in the fifth place" — Shklovsky points to the theme of abduction which goes through Greek comedy and reaches Ostrovsky.[6] In other words, our critic repeats, in a special form, his very first argument (as we see, even insofar as formal logic is concerned, all is not well with our formalist). Yes, themes migrate from people to people, from class to class, and even from author to author. This means only that the human imagination is economical. A new class does not begin to create all of culture from the beginning, but enters into possession of the past, assorts it, touches it up, rearranges it, and builds on it further. If there were no such utilization of the "secondhand" wardrobe of the ages, historic processes would have no progress at all. If the theme of Ostrovsky's drama came to him through the Egyptians and through Greece, then the paper on which Ostrovsky developed his theme came to him as a development of the Egyptian papyrus through the Greek parchment. Let us take another and closer analogy: the fact that the critical methods of the Greek Sophists, who were the pure formalists of their day, have penetrated the theoretic consciousness of Shklovsky, does not in the least change the fact that Shklovsky himself is a very picturesque product of a definite social environment and of a definite age.

Shklovsky's destruction of Marxism in five points reminds us very much of those articles which were published against Darwinism in the magazine *The Orthodox Review* in the good old days. If the doctrine of the origin of man from the monkey were true, wrote the learned Bishop Nikanor of Odessa thirty or forty years ago, then our grandfathers would have had distinct signs of a tail, or would have noticed such a characteristic in their grandfathers and grandmothers. Second, as everybody knows, monkeys can only give birth to monkeys. . . . Fifth, Darwinism is incorrect, because it contradicts formalism — I beg your pardon, I meant to say, the formal decisions of the universal church conferences. The advantage of the learned monk consisted, however, in the fact that he was a frank passéist and took his cue from the Apostle Paul and not from physics, chemistry or mathematics, as the futurist Shklovsky does. [7]

It is unquestionably true that the need for art is not created by economic conditions. But neither is the need for food created by economics. On the contrary, the need for food and warmth creates economics. It is very true that one cannot always go by the principles of Marxism in deciding whether to reject or to accept a work of art. A work of art should, in the first place, be judged by its own law, that is, by the law of art. But Marxism alone can explain why and how a given tendency in art has originated in a given period of history; in other words, who it was who made a demand for such an artistic form and not for another, and why.

It would be childish to think that every class can entirely and fully create its own art from within itself, and, particularly, that the proletariat is capable of creating a new art by means of closed art guilds or circles, or by the Organization for Proletarian Culture, etc. Generally speaking, the artistic work of man is continuous. Each new rising class places itself on the shoulders of its preceding one. But this continuity is dialectic, that is, it finds itself by means of internal repulsions and breaks. New artistic needs or demands for new literary and artistic points of view are stimulated by economics, through the development of a new class, and minor stimuli are supplied by changes in the position of the class, under the influence of the growth of its wealth and cultural power.

Artistic creation is always a complicated turning inside out of old forms, under the influence of new stimuli which originate outside of art. In this large sense of the word, art is a handmaiden. It is not a disembodied element feeding on itself, but a function of social man indissolubly tied to his life and environment. And how characteristic it is — if one were to reduce every social superstition to its absurdity — that Shklovsky has come to the idea of art's absolute independence from the social environment at a period of Russian history when art has revealed with such utter frankness its spiritual, environmental and material dependence upon definite social classes, subclasses and groups!

Materialism does not deny the significance of the element of form, either in logic, jurisprudence or art. Just as a system of jurisprudence can and must be judged by its internal logic and consistency, so art can and must be judged from the point of view of its achievements in form, because there can be no art without them. However, a juridical theory which attempted to establish the independence of law from social conditions would be defective at its very base. Its moving force lies in economics — in class contradictions. The law gives only a formal and an internally harmonized expression of these phenomena, not of their individual peculiarities, but of their general character, that is, of the elements that are repetitive and permanent in them. We can see now with a clarity which is rare in history how new law is made. It is not done by logical deduction, but by empirical measurement and by adjustment to the economic needs of the new ruling class.

Literature, whose methods and processes have their roots far back in the most distant past and represent the accumulated experience of verbal craftsmanship, expresses the thoughts, feelings, moods, points of view and hopes of the new epoch and of its new class. One cannot jump beyond this. And there is no need of making the jump, at least, for those who are not serving an epoch already past nor a class which has already outlived itself.

The methods of formal analysis are necessary, but insufficient. You may count up the alliterations in popular proverbs, classify metaphors, count up the number of vowels and consonants in a wedding song. It will undoubtedly enrich our knowledge of folk art, in one way or another; but if you don't know the peasant system of sowing, and the life that is based on it, if you don't know the part the scythe plays, and if you have not mastered the meaning of the church calendar to the peasant, of the time when the peasant marries, or when the peasant women give birth, you will have only understood the outer shell of folk art, but the kernel will not have been reached.

The architectural scheme of the Cologne cathedral can be established by measuring the base and the height of its arches, by determining the three dimensions of its naves, the dimensions and the placement of the columns, etc. But without knowing what a medieval city was like, what a guild was, or what was the Catholic Church of the Middle Ages, the Cologne cathedral will never be understood. The effort to set art free from life, to declare it a craft sufficient unto itself, devitalizes and kills art. The very need of such an operation is an unmistakable symptom of intellectual decline.

The analogy with the theological arguments against Darwinism which was made above may appear to the reader external and anecdotal. That may be true, to some extent. But a much deeper connection exists. The formalist theory inevitably reminds a Marxist who has done any reading at all of the familiar tunes of a very old philosophic melody. The jurists and the moralists (to recall at random the German Stammler, and our own subjectivist Mikhailovsky)[8] tried to prove that morality and law could not be determined by economics, because economic life was unthinkable outside of juridical and ethical norms. True, the formalists of law and morals did not go so far as to assert the complete independence of law and ethics from economics. They recognized a certain complex mutual relationship of "factors," and these "factors," while influencing one another, retained the qualities of independent substances, coming no one knew whence. The assertion of complete independence of the aesthetic "factor" from the influence of social conditions, as is made by Shklovsky, is an instance of specific hyperbole whose roots, by the way, lie in social conditions too; it is the megalomania of aesthetics turning our hard reality on its head. Apart from this peculiarity, the constructions of the formalists have the same kind of defective methodology that every other kind of idealism has.

To a materialist, religion, law, morals and art represent separate aspects of one and the same process of social development. Though they differentiate themselves from their industrial basis, become complex, strengthen and develop their special characteristics in detail, politics, religion, law, ethics and aesthetics remain, nonetheless, functions of social man and obey the laws of his social organization. The idealist, on the other hand, does not see a unified process of historic development which evolves the necessary organs and functions from within itself, but a crossing or combining and interacting of certain

independent principles — the religious, political, juridical,
aesthetic and ethical substances, which find their origin
and explanation in themselves.

The (dialectic) idealism of Hegel arranges these substances (which are the eternal categories) in some se-
quence by reducing them to a genetic unity. Regardless
of the fact that this unity with Hegel is the absolute spirit,
which divides itself in the process of its dialectic manifestation into various "factors," Hegel's system, because of
its dialectic character, not because of its idealism, gives
an idea of historic reality which is just as good as the
idea of a man's hand that a glove gives when turned
inside out.

But the formalists (and their greatest genius was Kant)
do not look at the dynamics of development, but at a
cross section of it, on the day and at the hour of their
own philosophic revelation. At the crossing of the line
they reveal the complexity and multiplicity of the object
(not of the process, because they do not think of processes). This complexity they analyze and classify. They
give names to the elements, which are at once transformed
into essences, into subabsolutes, without father or mother;
to wit, religion, politics, morals, law, art. Here we no
longer have a glove of history turned inside out, but the
skin torn from the separate fingers, dried out to a degree
of complete abstraction, and this hand of history turns
out to be the product of the "interaction" of the thumb,
the index, the middle finger, and all the other "factors."
The aesthetic "factor" is the little finger, the smallest, but
not the least beloved.

In biology, vitalism is a variation of the same fetish
of presenting the separate aspects of the world process,
without understanding its inner relation. A creator is all
that is lacking for a supersocial, absolute morality or
aesthetics, or for a superphysical absolute "vital force."
The multiplicity of independent factors, "factors" without
beginning or end, is nothing but a masked polytheism.
Just as Kantian idealism represents historically a translation of Christianity into the language of rationalistic
philosophy, so all the varieties of idealistic formaliza-

tion, either openly or secretly, lead to a god, as the cause of all causes. In comparison with the oligarchy of a dozen subabsolutes of the idealistic philosophy, a single personal creator is already an element of order. Herein lies the deeper connection between the formalist refutations of Marxism and the theological refutations of Darwinism.

The formalist school represents an abortive idealism applied to the question of art. The formalists show a fast ripening religiousness. They are followers of St. John. They believe that "in the beginning was the Word." But we believe that in the beginning was the deed. The word followed, as its phonetic shadow.

What Is Proletarian Culture, and Is It Possible?

Every ruling class creates its own culture, and consequently, its own art. History has known the slave-owning cultures of the East and of classic antiquity, the feudal culture of medieval Europe and the bourgeois culture which now rules the world. It would follow from this that the proletariat has also to create its own culture and its own art.

The question, however, is not as simple as it seems at first glance. Society in which slave owners were the ruling class, existed for many and many centuries. The same is true of feudalism. Bourgeois culture, if one were to count only from the time of its open and turbulent manifestation, that is, from the period of the Renaissance, has existed five centuries, but it did not reach its greatest flowering until the nineteenth century, or, more correctly, the second half of it. History shows that the formation of a new culture which centers around a ruling class demands considerable time and reaches completion only at the period preceding the political decadence of that class.

Will the proletariat have enough time to create a "proletarian" culture? In contrast to the regime of the slave owners and of the feudal lords and of the bourgeoisie, the proletariat regards its dictatorship as a brief period of transition. When we wish to denounce the all-too-optimistic views about the transition to socialism, we point out that the period of the social revolution, on a world scale, will last not months and not years, but decades — decades, but not centuries, and certainly not thousands of years. Can the proletariat in this time create a new culture? It is legitimate to doubt this, because the years of social revolution will be years of fierce class struggles in which destruction will occupy more room than new construction. At any rate the energy of the proletariat itself will be spent mainly in conquering power, in retaining and strengthening it and in applying it to the most urgent needs of existence and of further struggle. The proletariat, however, will reach its highest tension and the fullest manifestation of its class character during this revolutionary period and it will be within such narrow limits that the possibility of planful, cultural reconstruction will be confined.

On the other hand, as the new regime will be more and more protected from political and military surprises and as the conditions for cultural creation will become more favorable, the proletariat will be more and more dissolved into a socialist community and will free itself from its class characteristics and thus cease to be a proletariat. In other words, there can be no question of the creation of a new culture, that is, of construction on a large historic scale during the period of dictatorship. The cultural reconstruction, which will begin when the need of the iron clutch of a dictatorship unparalleled in history will have disappeared, will not have a class character. This seems to lead to the conclusion that there is no proletarian culture and that there never will be any and in fact there is no reason to regret this. The proletariat acquires power for the purpose of doing away forever with class culture and to make way for human culture. We frequently seem to forget this.

The formless talk about proletarian culture, in antithesis to bourgeois culture, feeds on the extremely uncritical identification of the historic destinies of the proletariat with those of the bourgeoisie. A shallow and purely liberal method of making analogies of historic forms has nothing in common with Marxism. There is no real analogy between the historic development of the bourgeoisie and of the working class.

The development of bourgeois culture began several centuries before the bourgeoisie took into its own hands the power of the state by means of a series of revolutions. Even when the bourgeoisie was a third estate, almost deprived of its rights, it played a great and continually growing part in all the fields of culture. This is especially clear in the case of architecture. The Gothic churches were not built suddenly, under the impulse of a religious inspiration. The construction of the Cologne cathedral, its architecture and its sculpture, sum up the architectural experience of mankind from the time of the cave and combine the elements of this experience in a new style which expresses the culture of its own epoch which is, in the final analysis, the social structure and technique of this epoch. The old prebourgeoisie of the guilds was the factual builder of the Gothic. When it grew and waxed strong, that is, when it became richer, the bourgeoisie passed through the Gothic stage consciously and actively and created its own architectural style, not for the church, however, but for its own palaces.

With its basis on the Gothic, it turned to antiquity, especially to Roman architecture and the Moorish, and applied all these to the conditions and needs of the new city community, thus creating the Renaissance (Italy at the end of the first quarter of the fifteenth century). Specialists may count the elements which the Renaissance owes to antiquity and those it owes to the Gothic and may argue as to which side is the stronger. But the Renaissance only begins when the new social class, already culturally satiated, feels itself strong enough to come out from under the yoke of the Gothic arch, to look at Gothic art and on all that preceded it as material for its own disposal, and to use the technique of the past for its own artistic aims. This refers also to all the other arts, but with this difference, that because of their greater flexibility, that is, of their lesser dependence upon utilitarian aims and materials, the "free" arts do not reveal the dialectics of successive styles with such firm logic as does architecture.

From the time of the Renaissance and of the Reformation, which created more favorable intellectual and political conditions for the bourgeoisie in feudal society, to the time of the revolution which transferred power to the bourgeoisie (in France), there passed three or four centuries of growth in the material and intellectual force of the bourgeoisie. The Great French Revolution and the wars which grew out of it temporarily lowered the material level of culture. But later the capitalist regime became established as the "natural" and the "eternal."

Thus the fundamental processes of the growth of bourgeois culture and of its crystallization into style were determined by the characteristics of the bourgeoisie as a possessing and exploiting class. The bourgeoisie not only developed materially within feudal society, entwining itself in various ways with the latter and attracting wealth into its own hands, but it weaned the intelligentsia to its side and created its cultural foundation (schools, universities, academies, newspapers, magazines) long before it openly took possession of the state. It is sufficient to remember that the German bourgeoisie, with its incomparable technology, philosophy, science and art, allowed the power of the state to lie in the hands of a feudal bureaucratic class as late as 1918 and decided, or, more correctly, was forced to take power into its own hands only when the material foundations of German culture began to fall to pieces.

But one may answer: It took thousands of years to create the slave-owning art and only hundreds of years for the bourgeois art. Why, then, could not proletarian art be created in tens of years? The technical bases of life are not at all the same at present and therefore the tempo is also different. This objection, which at first sight seems convincing, in reality misses the crux of the question. Undoubtedly, in the development of the new society, the time will come when economics, cultural life and art will receive the greatest impulse forward. At the present time we can only create fancies about their tempo. In a society which will have thrown off the pinching and stultifying worry about one's daily bread, in which community restaurants will prepare good, wholesome and tasteful food for all to choose, in which communal laundries will wash clean everyone's good linen, in which children, all the children, will be well-fed and strong and gay, and in which they will absorb the fundamental elements of science and art as they absorb albumen and air and the warmth of the sun, in a society in which electricity and the radio will not be the crafts they are today, but will come from inexhaustible sources of superpower at the call of a central button, in which there will be no "useless mouths," in which the liberated egotism of man — a mighty force! — will be directed wholly towards the understanding, the transformation and the betterment of the universe — in such a society the dynamic development of culture will be incomparable with anything that went on in the past. But all this will come only after a climb, prolonged and difficult, which is still ahead of us. And we are speaking only about the period of the climb.

But is not the present moment dynamic? It is in the highest degree. But its dynamics is centered in politics. The war and the revolution were dynamic, but very much at the expense of technology and culture. It is true that the war has produced a long series of technical inventions. But the poverty which it has produced has put off the practical application of these inventions for a long time and with this their possibility of revolutionizing life. This refers to radio, to aviation, and to many mechanical discoveries.

On the other hand, the revolution lays out the ground for a new society. But it does so with the methods of the old society, with the class struggle, with violence, destruction and annihilation. If the proletarian revolution had not come, mankind would have been strangled by its own contradictions. The revolution saved society and culture, but by means of the most cruel surgery. All the active forces are concentrated in politics and in the revolutionary struggle, everything else is shoved back into the background and everything which is a hindrance is cruelly trampled underfoot. In this process, of course, there is an ebb and flow; military communism gives place to the NEP,[9] which, in its turn, passes through various stages.

But in its essence, the dictatorship of the proletariat is not an organization for the production of the culture of a new society, but a revolutionary and military sys-

tem struggling for it. One must not forget this. We think
that the historian of the future will place the culminating
point of the old society on the second of August, 1914,
when the maddened power of bourgeois culture let loose
upon the world the blood and fire of an imperialistic
war. The beginning of the new history of mankind will
be dated from November 7, 1917. The fundamental stages
of the development of mankind we think will be established
somewhat as follows: prehistoric "history" of primitive
man; ancient history, whose rise was based on slavery;
the Middle Ages, based on serfdom; capitalism, with free
wage exploitation; and finally, socialist society, with, let
us hope, its painless transition to a stateless commune.
At any rate, the twenty, thirty, or fifty years of proletarian
world revolution will go down in history as the most
difficult climb from one system to another, but in no
case as an independent epoch of proletarian culture.

At present, in these years of respite, some illusions may
arise in our Soviet Republic as regards this. We have
put the cultural questions on the order of the day. By
projecting our present-day problems into the distant future, one can think himself through a long series of years
into proletarian culture. But no matter how important
and vitally necessary our culture-building may be, it is
entirely dominated by the approach of European and
world revolution. We are, as before, merely soldiers in
a campaign. We are bivouacking for a day. Our shirt
has to be washed, our hair has to be cut and combed,
and, most important of all, the rifle has to be cleaned
and oiled. Our entire present-day economic and cultural
work is nothing more than a bringing of ourselves into
order between two battles and two campaigns. The principal battles are ahead and may be not so far off. Our
epoch is not yet an epoch of new culture, but only the
entrance to it. We must, first of all, take possession, politically, of the most important elements of the old culture,
to such an extent, at least, as to be able to pave the way
for a new culture.

This becomes especially clear when one considers the
problem as one should, in its international character. The
proletariat was, and remains, a nonpossessing class. This

alone restricted it very much from acquiring those elements of bourgeois culture which have entered into the inventory of mankind forever. In a certain sense, one may truly say that the proletariat also, at least the European proletariat, had its epoch of reformation. This occurred in the second half of the nineteenth century, when, without making an attempt on the power of the state directly, it conquered for itself under the bourgeois system more favorable legal conditions for development.

But, in the first place, for this period of "reformation" (parliamentarism and social reforms) which coincides mainly with the period of the Second International history allowed the working class approximately as many decades as it allowed the bourgeoisie centuries. In the second place, the proletariat, during this preparatory period, did not at all become a richer class and did not concentrate in its hands material power. On the contrary, from a social and cultural point of view, it became more and more unfortunate. The bourgeoisie came into power fully armed with the culture of its time. The proletariat, on the other hand, comes into power fully armed only with the acute need of mastering culture. The problem of a proletariat which has conquered power consists, first of all, in taking into its own hands the apparatus of culture — the industries, schools, publications, press, theaters, etc. — which did not serve it before, and thus to open up the path of culture for itself.

Our task in Russia is complicated by the poverty of our entire cultural tradition and by the material destruction wrought by the events of the last decade. After the conquest of power and after almost six years of struggle for its retention and consolidation, our proletariat is forced to turn all its energies towards the creation of the most elementary conditions of material existence and of contact with the ABC of culture — ABC in the true and literal sense of the word. It is not for nothing that we have put to ourselves the task of having universal literacy in Russia by the tenth anniversary of the Soviet regime.

Someone may object that I take the concept of proletarian culture in too broad a sense. That if there may not be a fully and entirely developed proletarian culture,

yet the working class may succeed in putting its stamp
upon culture before it is dissolved into a communist society. Such an objection must be registered first of all as
a serious retreat from the position that there will be a proletarian culture. It is not to be questioned but that the
proletariat, during the time of its dictatorship, will put its
stamp upon culture. However, this is a far cry from a
proletarian culture in the sense of a developed and completely harmonious system of knowledge and of art in
all material and spiritual fields of work. For tens of millions of people for the first time in history to master reading and writing and arithmetic is in itself a new cultural
fact of great importance. The essence of the new culture
will be not an aristocratic one for a privileged minority,
but a mass culture, a universal and popular one. Quantity will pass into quality; with the growth of the quantity
of culture will come a rise in its level and a change in its
character. But this process will develop only through a
series of historic stages. In the degree to which it is successful, it will weaken the class character of the proletariat
and in this way it will wipe out the basis of a proletarian
culture.

But how about the upper strata of the working class?
About its intellectual vanguard? Can one not say that in
these circles, narrow though they are, a development of
proletarian culture is already taking place today? Have
we not the Socialist Academy? Red professors? Some are
guilty of putting the question in this very abstract way.
The idea seems to be that it is possible to create a proletarian culture by laboratory methods.

In fact, the texture of culture is woven at the points
where the relationships and interactions of the intelligentsia
of a class and of the class itself meet. The bourgeois culture — the technical, political, philosophical and artistic —
was developed by the interaction of the bourgeoisie and
its inventors, leaders, thinkers and poets. The reader created
the writer and the writer created the reader. This is true
in an immeasurably greater degree of the proletariat, because its economics and politics and culture can be built
only on the basis of the creative activity of the masses.
The main task of the proletarian intelligentsia in the

immediate future is not the abstract formation of a new culture regardless of the absence of a basis for it, but definite culture-bearing, that is, a systematic, planful and, of course, critical imparting to the backward masses of the essential elements of the culture which already exists. It is impossible to create a class culture behind the backs of a class. And to build culture in cooperation with the working class and in close contact with its general historic rise, one has to build socialism, even though in the rough. In this process, the class characteristics of society will not become stronger, but, on the contrary, will begin to dissolve and to disappear in direct ratio to the success of the revolution. The liberating significance of the dictatorship of the proletariat consists in the fact that it is temporary — for a brief period only — that it is a means of clearing the road and of laying the foundations of a society without classes and of a culture based upon solidarity.

In order to explain the idea of a period of culture-bearing in the development of the working class more concretely, let us consider the historic succession not of classes, but of generations. Their continuity is expressed in the fact that each one of them, given a developing and not a decadent society, adds its treasure to the past accumulations of culture. But before it can do so, each new generation must pass through a stage of apprenticeship. It appropriates existing culture and transforms it in its own way, making it more or less different from that of the older generation. But this appropriation is not, as yet, a new creation, that is, it is not a creation of new cultural values, but only a premise for them. To a certain degree, that which has been said may also be applied to the destinies of the working masses which are rising towards epoch-making creative work. One has only to add that before the proletariat will have passed out of the stage of cultural apprenticeship, it will have ceased to be a proletariat.

Let us also not forget that the upper layer of the bourgeois third estate passed its cultural apprenticeship under the roof of feudal society; that while still within the womb of feudal society it surpassed the old ruling estates cul-

turally and became the instigator of culture before it came
into power. It is different with the proletariat in general
and with the Russian proletariat in particular. The proletariat is forced to take power before it has appropriated
the fundamental elements of bourgeois culture; it is forced
to overthrow bourgeois society by revolutionary violence
for the very reason that society does not allow it access
to culture. The working class strives to transform the
state apparatus into a powerful pump for quenching the
cultural thirst of the masses. This is a task of immeasurable historic importance. But, if one is not to use words
lightly, it is not as yet a creation of a special proletarian
culture. "Proletarian culture," "proletarian art," etc., in three
cases out of ten are used uncritically to designate the culture and the art of the coming communist society, in
two cases out of ten to designate the fact that special
groups of the proletariat are acquiring separate elements
of preproletarian culture, and finally, in five cases out of
ten, it represents a jumble of concepts and words out of
which one can make neither head nor tail.

Here is a recent example, one of a hundred, where a
slovenly, uncritical and dangerous use of the term "proletarian culture" is made. "The economic basis and its corresponding system of superstructures," writes Sizov, "form
the cultural characteristics of an epoch (feudal, bourgeois
or proletarian)." Thus the epoch of proletarian culture
is placed here on the same plane as that of the bourgeois. But that which is here called the proletarian epoch
is only a brief transition from one social-cultural system
to another, from capitalism to socialism. The establishment
of the bourgeois regime was also preceded by a transitional epoch. But the bourgeois revolution tried, successfully,
to perpetuate the domination of the bourgeoisie, while the
proletarian revolution has for its aim the liquidation of
the proletariat as a class in as brief a period as possible.
The length of this period depends entirely upon the success
of the revolution. Is it not amazing that one can forget
this and place the proletarian cultural epoch on the same
plane with that of feudal and bourgeois culture?

But if this is so, does it follow that we have no proletarian science? Are we not to say that the materialistic

conception of history and the Marxist criticism of political
economy represent invaluable scientific elements of a proletarian culture?

Of course, the materialistic conception of history and the
labor theory of value have an immeasurable significance
for the arming of the proletariat as a class and for science
in general. There is more true science in the *Communist
Manifesto* alone than in all the libraries of historical and
historico-philosophical compilations, speculations and falsi-
fications of the professors. But can one say that Marxism
represents a product of proletarian culture? And can one
say that we are already making use of Marxism, not in
political battles only, but in broad scientific tasks as well?

Marx and Engels came out of the ranks of the petty
bourgeois democracy and, of course, were brought up on
its culture and not on the culture of the proletariat. If there
had been no working class, with its strikes, struggles, sufferings and revolts, there would, of course, have been no
scientific communism, because there would have been no
historical necessity for it. But its theory was formed entirely on the basis of bourgeois culture, both scientific
and political, though it declared a fight to the finish upon
that culture. Under the pressure of capitalistic contradictions, the universalizing thought of the bourgeois democracy, of its boldest, most honest, and most farsighted
representatives, rises to the heights of a marvelous renunciation, armed with all the critical weapons of bourgeois
science. Such is the origin of Marxism.

The proletariat found its weapon in Marxism not at
once, and not fully even to this day. Today this weapon
serves political aims almost primarily and exclusively. The
broad realistic application and the methodological development of dialectic materialism are still entirely in the future. Only in a socialist society will Marxism cease to be
a one-sided weapon of political struggle and become a
means of scientific creation, a most important element
and instrument of spiritual culture.

All science, in greater or lesser degree, unquestionably
reflects the tendencies of the ruling class. The more closely
science attaches itself to the practical tasks of conquering
nature (physics, chemistry, natural science in general),

the greater is its nonclass and human contribution. The more deeply science is connected with the social mechanism of exploitation (political economy), or the more abstractly it generalizes the entire experience of mankind (psychology, not in its experimental, physiological sense but in its so-called philosophic sense), the more does it obey the class egotism of the bourgeoisie and the less significant is its contribution to the general sum of human knowledge. In the domain of the experimental sciences, there exist different degrees of scientific integrity and objectivity, depending upon the scope of the generalizations made. As a general rule, the bourgeois tendencies have found a much freer place for themselves in the higher spheres of methodological philosophy, of *Weltanschauung*. It is therefore necessary to clear the structure of science from the bottom to the top, or, more correctly, from the top to the bottom, because one has to begin from the upper stories.

But it would be naive to think that the proletariat must revamp critically all science inherited from the bourgeoisie before applying it to socialist reconstruction. This is just the same as saying with the utopian moralists: before building a new society, the proletariat must rise to the heights of communist ethics. As a matter of fact, the proletarian will reconstruct ethics as well as science radically, but he will do so after he will have constructed a new society, even though in the rough.

But are we not traveling in a vicious circle? How is one to build a new society with the aid of the old science and the old morals? Here we must bring in a little dialectics, that very dialectics which we now put so uneconomically into lyric poetry and into our office bookkeeping and into our cabbage soup and into our porridge. In order to begin work, the proletarian vanguard needs certain points of departure, certain scientific methods which liberate the mind from the ideologic yoke of the bourgeoisie; it is mastering these, in part has already mastered them. It has tested its fundamental method in many battles, under various conditions. But this is a long way from proletarian science. A revolutionary class cannot stop its struggle because the party has not yet decided whether it should or should not accept the hypothesis of electrons and ions, the psychoanalytical theory of Freud, the new mathematical discoveries of relativity, etc. True, after it has conquered power, the proletariat will find a much greater opportunity for mastering science and for revising it. This is more easily said than done.

The proletariat cannot postpone socialist reconstruction until the time when its new scientists, many of whom are still running about in short trousers, will test and clean all the instruments and all the channels of knowledge. The proletariat rejects what is clearly unnecessary, false and reactionary, and in the various fields of its reconstruction makes use of the methods and conclusions of present-day science, taking them necessarily with the percentage of reactionary class-alloy which is contained in them. The practical result will justify itself generally and on the whole, because such a use when controlled by a socialist goal will gradually manage and select the methods and conclusions of the theory. And by that time there will have grown up scientists who are educated under the new conditions. At any rate, the proletariat will have to carry its socialist reconstruction to quite a high degree, that is, provide for real material security and for the satisfaction of society culturally before it will be able to carry out a general purification of science from top to bottom. I do not mean to say by this anything against the Marxist work of criticism, which many in small circles and in seminars are trying to carry through in various fields. This work is necessary and fruitful. It should be extended and deepened in every way. But one has to maintain the Marxian sense of the measure of things to count up the specific gravity of such experiments and efforts today in relation to the general scale of our historic work.

Does the foregoing exclude the possibility that even in the period of revolutionary dictatorship, there might appear eminent scientists, inventors, dramatists and poets out of the ranks of the proletariat? Not in the least. But it would be extremely light-minded to give the name of proletarian culture even to the most valuable achievements of individual representatives of the working class. One cannot turn the concept of culture into the small change of individual daily living and determine the success of a class culture by the proletarian passports of individual inventors or poets. Culture is the organic sum of knowledge and capacity which characterizes the entire society, or at least its ruling class. It embraces and penetrates all fields of human work and unifies them into a system. Individual achievements rise above this level and elevate it gradually.

Does such an organic interrelation exist between our present-day proletarian poetry and the cultural work of the working class in its entirety? It is quite evident that it does not. Individual workers or groups of workers are developing contacts with the art which was created by the bourgeois intelligentsia and are making use of its technique, for the time being, in quite an eclectic manner. But is it for the purpose of giving expression to their own internal proletarian world? The fact is that it is far from being so. The work of the proletarian poets lacks an organic quality, which is produced only by a profound interaction between art and the development of culture in general. We have the literary works of talented and gifted proletarians, but that is not proletarian literature. However, they may prove to be some of its springs.

It is possible that in the work of the present generation many germs and roots and springs will be revealed to which some future descendant will trace the various sectors of the culture of the future, just as our present-day historians of art trace the theater of Ibsen to the church mystery, or impressionism and cubism to the paintings of the monks. In the economy of art, as in the economy of nature, nothing is lost, and everything is connected in the large. But factually, concretely, vitally, the present-day work of the poets who have sprung from the proletariat is not developing at all in accordance with the plan which is behind the process of preparing the conditions of the future socialist culture, that is, the process of elevating the masses. . . .

Communist Policy Toward Art

It is untrue that revolutionary art can be created only by workers. Just because the revolution is a working-class revolution, it releases—to repeat what was said before—very little working-class energy for art. During the French Revolution, the greatest works which, directly or indirectly, reflected it, were created not by French artists, but by German, English, and others. The French bourgeoisie, which was directly concerned with making the revolution, could not give up a sufficient quantity of its strength to re-create and to perpetuate its imprint. This is still more true of the proletariat, which, though it has culture in politics, has little culture in art. The intelligentsia, aside from the advantages of its qualifications in form, has also the odious privilege of holding a passive political position, which is marked by a greater or lesser degree of hostility or friendliness towards the October Revolution.

It is not surprising, then, that this contemplative intelligentsia is able to give, and does give, a better artistic reproduction of the revolution than the proletariat which has made the revolution, though the re-creations of the intelligentsia are somewhat off line. We know very well the political limitations, the instability and the unreliability of the fellow travelers. But if we should eliminate Pilnyak, with his *The Naked Year,* the "Serapion Fraternity"[10] with Vsevolod Ivanov, Tikhonov, and Polonskaya, if we should eliminate Mayakovsky and Essenin, is there anything that will remain for us but a few unpaid promissory notes of a future proletarian literature? Especially as Demyan Byedny, who cannot be counted among the fellow travelers and who, we hope, cannot be eliminated from revolutionary literature, cannot be related to proletarian literature in the sense as defined by the manifesto of the *Kuznitsa.*[11] What will remain then?

Does that mean that the party, quite in opposition to its nature, occupies a purely eclectic position in the field of art? This argument, which seems so crushing, is, in reality, extremely childish. The Marxian method affords an opportunity to estimate the development of the new art, to trace all its sources, to help the most progressive tendencies by a critical illumination of the road, but it does not do more than that. Art must make its own way and by its own means. The Marxian methods are not the

same as the artistic. The party leads the proletariat but
not the historic processes of history. There are domains
in which the party leads, directly and imperatively. There
are domains in which it only cooperates. There are, finally, domains in which it only orients itself. The domain
of art is not one in which the party is called upon to
command. It can and must protect and help it, but it can
only lead it indirectly. It can and must give the additional
credit of its confidence to various art groups, which are
striving sincerely to approach the revolution and so help
an artistic formulation of the revolution. And at any
rate, the party cannot and will not take the position of
a literary circle which is struggling and merely competing
with other literary circles.

The party stands guard over the historic interests of
the working class in its entirety. Because it prepares consciously and step by step the ground for a new culture
and therefore for a new art, it regards the literary fellow
travelers not as the competitors of the writers of the working class, but as the real or potential helpers of the working class in the big work of reconstruction. The party
understands the episodic character of the literary groups
of a transition period and estimates them, not from the
point of view of the class passports of the individual
gentlemen literati, but from the point of view of the place
which these groups occupy and can occupy in preparing
a socialist culture. If it is not possible to determine the
place of any given group today, then the party as a party
will wait patiently and gracefully. Individual critics or
readers may sympathize with one group or another in
advance. The party, as a whole, protects the historic
interests of the working class and must be more objective
and wise. Its caution must be double-edged. If the party
does not put its stamp of approval on the *Kuznitsa*, just
because workers write for it, it does not, in advance, repel any given literary group, even from the intelligentsia,
insofar as such a group tries to approach the revolution
and tries to strengthen one of its links — a link is always
a weak point — between the city and the village, or between the party member and the nonpartisan, or between
the intelligentsia and the workers.

Does not such a policy mean, however, that the party is going to have an unprotected flank on the side of art? This is a great exaggeration. The party will repel the clearly poisonous, disintegrating tendencies of art and will guide itself by its political standards. It is true, however, that it is less protected on the flank of art than on the political front. But is this not true of science also? What are the metaphysicians of a purely proletarian science going to say about the theory of relativity? Can it be reconciled with materialism, or can it not? Has this question been decided? Where and when and by whom? It is clear to anyone, even to the uninitiated, that the work of our physiologist, Pavlov, is entirely along materialist lines. But what is one to say about the psychoanalytic theory of Freud? Can it be reconciled with materialism, as, for instance, Karl Radek thinks (and I also), or is it hostile to it? The same question can be put to all the new theories of atomic structure, etc., etc. It would be fine if a scientist would come along who could grasp all these new generalizations methodologically and introduce them into the dialectic materialist conception of the world. He could thus, at the same time, test the new theories and develop the dialectic method deeper. But I am very much afraid that this work—which is not like a newspaper or journalistic article, but a scientific and philosophic landmark, just as the *Origin of Species* and *Capital*—will not be created either today or tomorrow, or rather, if such an epoch-making book were created today, it would risk remaining uncut until the time when the proletariat will be able to lay aside its arms.

But does not the work of culture-bearing, that is, the work of acquiring the ABC of preproletarian culture, presuppose criticism, selection and a class standard? Of course it does. But the standard is a political one and not an abstract cultural one. The political standard coincides with the cultural one only in the broad sense that the revolution creates conditions for a new culture. But this does not mean that such a coinciding is secured in every given case. If the revolution has the right to destroy bridges and art monuments whenever necessary, it will stop still less from laying its hand on any tendency in art which, no matter how great its achievement in form, threatens to disintegrate the revolutionary environment or to arouse the internal forces of the revolution, that is, the proletariat, the peasantry and the intelligentsia, to a hostile opposition to one another. Our standard is, clearly, political, imperative and intolerant. But for this very reason, it must define the limits of its activity clearly. For a more precise expression of my meaning, I will say: we ought to have a watchful revolutionary censorship, and a broad and flexible policy in the field of art, free from petty partisan maliciousness. . . .

When the futurists propose to throw overboard the old literature of individualism, not only because it has become antiquated in form, but because it contradicts the collectivist nature of the proletariat, they reveal a very inadequate understanding of the dialectic nature of the contradiction between individualism and collectivism. There are no abstract truths. There are different kinds of individualism. Because of too much individualism, a section of the prerevolutionary intelligentsia threw itself into mysticism, but another section moved along the chaotic lines of futurism and, caught by the revolution — to their honor be it said — came nearer to the proletariat. But when they who came nearer because their teeth were set on edge by individualism carry their feeling over to the proletariat, they show themselves guilty of egocentrism, that is, of extreme individualism. The trouble is that the average proletarian is lacking in this very quality. In the mass, proletarian individuality has not been sufficiently formed and differentiated.

It is just such heightening of the objective quality and the subjective consciousness of individuality that is the most valuable contribution of the cultural advance at the threshold of which we stand today. It is childish to think that bourgeois *belles lettres* can make a breach in class solidarity. What the worker will take from Shakespeare, Goethe, Pushkin, or Dostoyevsky will be a more complex idea of human personality, of its passions and feelings, a deeper and profounder understanding of its psychic forces and of the role of the subconscious, etc. In the final analysis, the worker will become richer. At the beginning, Gorky was imbued with the romantic individualism of the tramp. Nevertheless, he fed the early spring revolutionism of the proletariat on the eve of 1905, because he helped to awaken individuality in that class in which individuality, once awakened, seeks contact with other awakened individualities. The proletariat is in need of artistic food and education, but that does not mean to say that the proletariat is mere clay which artists, those that have gone and those that are still to come, can fashion in their own image and in their own likeness.

Though the proletariat is spiritually, and therefore, artistically, very sensitive, it is uneducated aesthetically. It is hardly reasonable to think that it can simply begin at the point where the bourgeois intelligentsia left off on the eve of the catastrophe. Just as an individual passes biologically and psychologically through the history of the race and, to some extent, of the entire animal world in his development from the embryo, so, to a certain extent, must the overwhelming majority of a new class which has only recently come out of prehistoric life, pass through the entire history of artistic culture. This class cannot begin the construction of a new culture without absorbing and assimilating the elements of the old cultures. This does not mean in the least that it is necessary to go through step by step, slowly and systematically, the entire past history of art. Insofar as it concerns a social class and not a biologic individual, the process of absorption and transformation has a freer and more conscious character. But a new class cannot move forward without regard to the most important landmarks of the past. . . .

Revolutionary and Socialist Art

There is no revolutionary art as yet. There are the elements of this art, there are hints and attempts at it, and, what is most important, there is the revolutionary man, who is forming the new generation in his own image and who is more and more in need of this art. How long will it take for such art to reveal itself clearly? It is difficult even to guess, because the process is intangible and incalculable, and we are limited to guesswork even when we try to time more tangible social processes. But

why should not this art, at least its first big wave, come
soon as the expression of the art of the young generation
which was born in the revolution and which carries it on?

Revolutionary art which inevitably reflects all the contradictions of a revolutionary social system, should not
be confused with socialist art for which no basis has as
yet been made. On the other hand, one must not forget
that socialist art will grow out of the art of this transition
period.

In insisting on such a distinction, we are not at all
guided by a pedantic consideration of an abstract program. Not for nothing did Engels speak of the socialist
revolution as a leap from the kingdom of necessity to
the kingdom of freedom. The revolution itself is not as
yet the kingdom of freedom. On the contrary, it is developing the features of "necessity" to the greatest degree.
Socialism will abolish class antagonisms, as well as
classes, but the revolution carries the class struggle to its
highest tension. During the period of revolution, only that
literature which promotes the consolidation of the workers
in their struggle against the exploiters is necessary and
progressive. Revolutionary literature cannot but be imbued
with a spirit of social hatred, which is a creative historic
factor in an epoch of proletarian dictatorship. Under
socialism, solidarity will be the basis of society. Literature
and art will be tuned to a different key. All the emotions
which we revolutionists, at the present time, feel appre-
hensive of naming — so much have they been worn thin by
hypocrites and vulgarians — such as disinterested friendship, love for one's neighbor, sympathy, will be the mighty
ringing chords of socialist poetry.

However, does not an excess of solidarity, as the Nietz-
scheans fear, threaten to degenerate man into a sentimental, passive, herd animal? Not at all. The powerful force
of competition which, in bourgeois society, has the character of market competition, will not disappear in a socialist society, but, to use the language of psychoanalysis,
will be sublimated, that is, will assume a higher and more
fertile form. There will be the struggle for one's opinion,
for one's project, for one's taste. In the measure in which
political struggles will be eliminated — and in a society

where there will be no classes, there will be no such struggles — the liberated passions will be channelized into technique, into construction which also includes art. Art then will become more general, will mature, will become tempered, and will become the most perfect method of the progressive building of life in every field. It will not be merely "pretty" without relation to anything else.

All forms of life, such as the cultivation of land, the planning of human habitations, the building of theaters, the methods of socially educating children, the solution of scientific problems, the creation of new styles, will vitally engross all and everybody. People will divide into "parties" over the question of a new gigantic canal, or the distribution of oases in the Sahara (such a question will exist too), over the regulation of the weather and the climate, over a new theater, over chemical hypotheses, over two competing tendencies in music, and over a best system of sports. Such parties will not be poisoned by the greed of class or caste. All will be equally interested in the success of the whole. The struggle will have a purely ideologic character. It will have no running after profits, it will have nothing mean, no betrayals, no bribery, none of the things that form the soul of "competition" in a society divided into classes. But this will in no way hinder the struggle from being absorbing, dramatic and passionate.

And as all problems in a socialist society — the problems of life which formerly were solved spontaneously and automatically, and the problems of art which were in the custody of special priestly castes — will become the property of all people, one can say with certainty that collective interests and passions and individual competition will have the widest scope and the most unlimited opportunity. Art, therefore, will not suffer the lack of any such explosions of collective, nervous energy, and of such collective psychic impulses which make for the creation of new artistic tendencies and for changes in style. It will be the aesthetic schools around which "parties" will collect, that is, associations of temperaments, of tastes and of moods. In a struggle so disinterested and tense, which will take place in a culture whose foundations are steadily rising, the human personality, with its invaluable basic trait of continual discontent, will grow and become polished at all its points. In truth, we have no reason to fear that there will be a decline of individuality or an impoverishment of art in a socialist society. . . .

CLASS AND ART

This is a speech by Trotsky at a discussion meeting called by the Press Department of the Central Committee of the Communist Party on May 9, 1924. The subject of the discussion was party policy in the field of imaginative literature.

It seems to me that it is Comrade Raskolnikov who has given most distinctive expression here to the point of view of the *Na Postu* group—you can't get away from that, comrades of the *Na Postu* group! After a long absence, Raskolnikov spoke here with all the freshness of Afghanistan,[1] whereas the other *Na Postu* people, having tasted a little of the tree of knowledge, tried to cover their nakedness—except Comrade Vardin, however, who goes on living the way he was born. (Vardin: "Why, you didn't hear what I said here!") True, I arrived late. But, first, I read your article in the last issue of *Na Postu*; secondly, I have just glanced through the verbatim record of your speech; and thirdly, it must be said that one can tell beforehand, without listening to you, what you are going to say. (Laughter.)

Originally published in the book *Voprosy Kul'tury Pri Diktature Proletariate* [Problems of Culture under the Dictatorship of the Proletariat]. The first English translation, by Brian Pearce, appeared in *Fourth International* (London) July 1967.

But to return to Comrade Raskolnikov. He says: they
recommend the "fellow travelers" to us, but did the old,
prewar *Pravda* or *Zvezda* print the words of Artzybashev,
Leonid Andreyev and others whom now they would certainly call "fellow travelers"? There is an example of a
fresh approach to the question, not spoiled by any reflections. What are Artzybashev and Andreyev doing here?
So far as I know, nobody has called them "fellow travelers." Leonid Andreyev died in a state of epileptic hatred
of Soviet Russia. Artzybashev was not so long ago simply
pushed over the frontier.[2] One can't muddle things up in
such a shameless way! What is a "fellow traveler"? In
literature as in politics we call by this name someone
who, stumbling and staggering, goes up to a certain
point along the same road which we shall follow much
further. Whoever goes *against* us is not a fellow traveler
but an enemy, whom if necessary we will deport, for the
well-being of the revolution is our highest law. How can
you mix up Leonid Andreyev in this question of "fellow
travelers"? (Raskolnikov: "Well, but what about Pilnyak?")
If you are going to talk about Artzybashev when you
mean Pilnyak, there's no arguing with you. (Laughter.
A shout: "But aren't they the same thing?") What do you
mean: aren't they the same thing? If you name names,
you must stick to them. Pilnyak may be good or bad,
in this way or that he may be good or he may be bad
— but Pilnyak is Pilnyak, and you must talk about him
as Pilnyak, and not as Leonid Andreyev. Knowledge in
general bodies begins with distinguishing between things
and appearances, and not with chaotic confusion. . . .

Raskolnikov says: "We didn't invite 'fellow travelers'
into the pages of *Zvezda* and *Pravda,* but sought and
found poets and writers in the depths of the proletariat."
Sought and found! In the depths of the proletariat! But
what did you do with them? Why have you hidden them
from us? (Raskolnikov: "There is, for instance, Demyan
Byedny.") Oh, well now, that I didn't know, I must confess
— that we discovered Demyan Byedny in the depths of
the proletariat. (General laughter.) You see with what
methods we are approaching the problem of literature:
we speak of Leonid Andreyev, and we mean Pilnyak,

we boast that we have found writers and poets in the
depths of the proletariat, and then when we call the roll,
out of these "depths" there answers only Demyan Byedny.
(Laughter.) This won't do. This is frivolity. Much more
seriousness is needed in considering this matter.

Let us try, indeed, to look more seriously at those prerevolutionary workers' publications, newspapers and periodicals, which have been mentioned here. We all remember that they used to carry some verses devoted to the
struggle, to May Day, and so on. All these verses, such
as they were, constituted very important and significant
documents in the history of culture. They expressed the
revolutionary awakening and political growth of the working class. In this cultural-historical sense their importance
was no less than that of the works of all the Shakespeares,
Molieres and Pushkins in the world. In these feeble verses
was the pledge of a new and higher human culture which
the awakened masses will create when they have mastered
the elements of the old culture.

But, all the same, the workers' verses in *Zvezda* and
Pravda do not at all signify the rise of a new, proletarian
literature. Inartistic doggerel in the Derzhavin (or pre-
Derzhavin)[3] style cannot be regarded as a new literature,
although those thoughts and feelings which sought expression in these verses also belong to a writer who is
beginning to appear from the working-class milieu. It
is wrong to suppose that the development of literature is
an unbroken chain, in which the naive though sincere
doggerel of young workers at the beginning of this century
is the first link in the coming "proletarian literature." In
reality, these revolutionary verses were a political event,
not a literary one. They contributed not to the growth of
literature but to the growth of the revolution. The revolution led to the victory of the proletariat, the victory of
the proletariat is leading to the transformation of the
economy. The transformation of the economy is in process
of changing the cultural state of the working masses.
And the cultural growth of the working people will create
the real basis for a new art.

"But it is impossible to permit duality," Comrade Raskolnikov tells us. "It is necessary that in our publications

political writing and poetry should form one whole; Bolshevism is distinguished by monolithicity," and so on.
At first sight this reasoning seems irrefutable. Actually,
it is an empty abstraction. At best it is a pious but unreal
wish for something good. Of course it would be splendid
if we had, to supplement our communist political writing,
the Bolshevik world outlook expressed in artistic form.
But we haven't, and that is not accidental.

The heart of the matter is that artistic creativity, by its
very nature, lags behind the other modes of expression of
a man's spirit, and still more of the spirit of a class. It
is one thing to understand something and express it log-
ically, and quite another thing to assimilate it organically,
reconstructing the whole system of one's feelings, and to
find a new kind of artistic expression for this new entity.
The latter process is more organic, slower, more difficult
to subject to conscious influence — and in the end it will
always lag behind. The political writing of a class hastens
ahead on stilts, while its artistic creativity hobbles along
behind on crutches. Marx and Engels were great political
writers of the proletariat in the period when the class was
still not really awakened. (From the meeting: "Yes, you're
right there.") I am very grateful to you. (Laughter.)

But take the trouble to draw the necessary conclusions
from this, and understand why there is not this monolithicity between political writing and poetry, and this will
in turn help you to understand why in the old legal Marxist periodicals we always found ourselves in a bloc, or
semi-bloc, with artistic "fellow travelers," sometimes very
dubious and even plainly false ones. You remember, of
course, *Novoye Slovo*, the best of the old legal Marxist
periodicals, in which many Marxists of the older generation collaborated, including Vladimir Ilyich. [4] This peri-
odical, as everyone knows, was friendly with the decadents.
What was the reason for that? It was because the decadents
were then a young and persecuted tendency in bourgeois
literature. And this persecuted situation of theirs impelled
them to take sides with our attitude of opposition, though
the latter, of course, was quite different in character, in
spite of which the decadents were temporarily fellow travelers with us. And later Marxist periodicals (and the semi-

Marxist ones, it goes without saying), right down to *Prosveshchenie*, had no sort of "monolithic" fiction section, but set aside considerable space for the "fellow travelers." Some might be either more severe or more indulgent in this respect, but it was impossible to carry on a "monolithic" policy in the field of art, because the artistic elements needed for such a policy were lacking.

But Raskolnikov at bottom doesn't want this. In works of art he ignores that which makes them works of art. This was most vividly shown in his remarkable judgment on Dante's *The Divine Comedy*, which in his opinion is valuable to us just because it enables us to understand the psychology of a certain class at a certain time. To put the matter that way means simply to strike out *The Divine Comedy* from the realm of art. Perhaps the time has come to do that, but if so we must understand the essence of the question and not shrink from the conclusions. If I say that the importance of *The Divine Comedy* lies in the fact that it gives me an understanding of the state of mind of certain classes in a certain epoch, this means that I transform it into a mere historical document, for, as a work of art, *The Divine Comedy* must speak in some way to my feelings and moods. Dante's work may act on me in a depressing way, fostering pessimism and despondency in me, or, on the contrary, it may rouse, inspire, encourage me. . . . This is the fundamental relationship between a reader and a work of art. Nobody, of course, forbids a reader to assume the role of a researcher and approach *The Divine Comedy* as merely a historical document. It is clear, though, that these two approaches are on two different levels, which, though connected, do not overlap.

How is it thinkable that there should be not a historical but a directly aesthetic relationship between us and a medieval Italian book? This is explained by the fact that in class society, in spite of all its changeability, there are certain common features. Works of art developed in a medieval Italian city can, we find, affect us too. What does this require? A small thing: it requires that these feelings and moods shall have received such broad, intense, powerful expression as to have raised them above the limitations of the life of those days. Dante was, of

course, the product of a certain social milieu. But Dante
was a genius. He raised the experience of his epoch to a
tremendous artistic height. And if we, while today approaching other works of medieval literature merely as
objects of study, approach *The Divine Comedy* as a source
of artistic perception, this happens not because Dante
was a Florentine petty bourgeois of the thirteenth century
but, to a considerable extent, in spite of that circumstance.

Let us take, for instance, such an elementary psychological feeling as fear of death. This feeling is characteristic
not only of man but also of animals. In man it first
found simple articulate expression, and later also artistic
expression. In different ages, in different social milieus,
this expression has changed, that is to say, men have
feared death in different ways. And nevertheless what
was said on this score not only by Shakespeare, Byron,
Goethe, but also by the Psalmist, can move us. (Exclamation by Comrade Libedinsky.[5]) Yes, yes, I came in
at the very moment when you, Comrade Libedinsky,
were explaining to Comrade Voronsky in the terms of
elementary political instruction (you yourself put it like
that) about the variation in feelings and states of mind
in different classes. In that general form it is indisputable.

However, for all that, you won't deny that Shakespeare
and Byron somehow speak to your soul and mine.
(Libedinsky: "They will soon stop speaking.") Whether
it will be soon, I don't know, but undoubtedly a time
will come when people will approach the works of Shakespeare and Byron in the same way as we approach most
poets of the Middle Ages, that is, exclusively from the
standpoint of scientific-historical analysis. Even sooner,
however, will come the time when people will stop seeking
in Marx's *Capital* for precepts for their practical activity,
and *Capital* will have become merely a historical document, together with the program of our party. But at
present we do not yet intend to put Shakespeare, Byron,
Pushkin in the archives, and we will continue to recommend them to the workers.

Comrade Sosnovsky, for instance, strongly recommends
Pushkin, declaring that he will undoubtedly last another
fifty years. Let us not speak of periods of time. But in

what sense can we recommend Pushkin to a worker? There is no proletarian class viewpoint in Pushkin, not to speak of a monolithic expression of communist feelings. Of course, Pushkin's language is magnificent — that cannot be denied — but, after all, this language is used by him for expressing the world outlook of the nobility. Shall we say to the worker: read Pushkin in order to understand how a nobleman, a serfowner and gentleman of the bedchamber, encountered spring and experienced autumn? This element is, of course, present in Pushkin, for Pushkin grew up on a particular social basis. But the expression that Pushkin gave his feelings is so saturated with the artistic, and generally with the psychological, experience of centuries, is so crystallized, that it has lasted down to our times and, according to Comrade Sosnovsky, will last another fifty years.

And when people tell me that the artistic significance of Dante for us consists in his expressing the way of life of a certain epoch, that only makes one spread one's hands in helplessness. I am sure that many, like me, would, after reading Dante, have to strain their memories to remember the date and place of his birth, and yet nonetheless, this would not have prevented us from getting artistic delight, if not from the whole of *The Divine Comedy*, then at least from some parts of it. Since I am not a historian of the Middle Ages, my attitude to Dante is predominantly artistic. (Ryazanov: "That's an exaggeration. 'To read Dante is to take a bath in the sea,' said Shevyryev, who was also against history, replying to Belinsky.") I don't doubt that Shevyryev did express himself as Comrade Ryazanov says, but I am not against history — that's pointless.

Of course the historical approach to Dante is legitimate and necessary and affects our aesthetic attitude to him, but one can't substitute one for the other. I remember what Kareyev wrote on this point, in a polemic with the Marxists: let them, the Marxides (that was how they ironically spoke of the Marxists in those days) tell us, for instance, what class interests dictated *The Divine Comedy*. And from the other side, the Italian Marxist, old Antonio Labriola, wrote something like this: "only fools could try to interpret the text of *The Divine Comedy* as though it were made of the cloth that Florentine merchants provided for their customers." I remember this expression almost word for word because in the polemic with the subjectivists I had occasion to quote these words more than once, in the old days. I think that Comrade Raskolnikov's attitude not only to Dante but to art in general proceeds not from the Marxist criterion but from that of the late Shulyatikov, who provided a caricature of Marxism in this connection. Antonio Labriola also made his vigorous comment on this sort of caricature. [6]

"By proletarian literature I understand literature which looks at the world with the eyes of the vanguard," and so on, and so on. This is the opinion of Comrade Lelevich. Splendid, we are ready to accept his definition. Give us though, not only the definition but also the literature. Where is it? Show us it! (Lelevich: "*Komsomolia*—there is the best of recent times.") What times? (A voice: "The last year.") Well, all right, the last year. I don't want to speak polemically. My attitude to Bezymensky has nothing in it that can be called negative, I hope. [7] I praised *Komsomolia* highly when I read it in manuscript. But regardless of whether we can on this account proclaim the appearance of proletarian literature, I can say that Bezymensky would not exist as an artist if we did not have Mayakovsky, Pasternak [8] and even Pilnyak. (A voice: "That proves nothing.") This does prove, at least, that the artistic creativity of a given epoch is a very complex web which is not woven automatically, by discussion groups and seminars, but comes into being through complex interrelations, in the first place with the different fellow-traveling groups. You can't get away from that; Bezymensky doesn't try to, and he does well not to. In some of his works, the influence of "fellow travelers" is even too noticeable. But this is an unavoidable phenomenon of youth and growth.

And here we have Comrade Libedinsky, the enemy of "fellow travelers," and himself an imitator of Pilnyak and even Byely. Yes, yes, Comrade Averbach must excuse me; I see him shaking his head, though without much conviction. [9] Libedinsky's last story, *Zavtra* [Tomorrow] is like the diagonal of a parallelogram, one side of whicn is Pilnyak and the other Andrei Byely. In itself that's no misfortune — Libedinsky can't be born in the land of *Na Postu* as a ready-made writer. (Voice: "It's a very barren[10] land.") I have already spoken about Libedinsky, after the first appearance of his *Nedelya* [The Week]. Bukharin then, as you will recall, fervently praised it, out of the expansiveness and kindness of his nature, and this praise alarmed me. Meanwhile I was obliged to observe the extreme dependence of Comrade Libedinsky on those very writers — "fellow travelers" and semifellow travelers — whom he and his co-thinkers all curse in *Na Postu*. You see once more that art and political writing are not always monolithic.

I have no intention of giving up Comrade Libedinsky as a bad job on that account. I think that it is clear to all of us that our common duty is to show the greatest concern for every young artistic talent ideologically close to us, and all the more when it is a matter of someone who is our brother-in-arms. The first condition of such an attentive and considerate attitude is not to give premature praise, killing the young writer's self-criticism; the second condition is not to wash one's hands of the man at once if he stumbles. Comrade Libedinsky is still very young. He needs to learn and to grow. And in this connection it turns out that Pilnyak fulfills a need. (A voice: "For Libedinsky or for us?") First of all, for Libedinsky. (Libedinsky: "But this means that I've been poisoned by Pilnyak.") Alas, the human organism can be nourished only by taking poison and producing internal resources that combat the poison. That's life. If you let yourself go dry, like a Caspian roach, that won't mean you're poisoned, but you won't be nourished either; indeed, it will mean nothing at all will happen. (Laughter.)

Comrade Pletnev, speaking here in defense of his abstractions about proletarian culture and its constituent part, proletarian literature, quoted Vladimir Ilyich against me. Now there's something that's really to the point! We must give that proper consideration. Not long ago an entire booklet appeared, written by Pletnev, Tretyakov and Sizov, in which proletarian literature was defended by means of quotations from Lenin against Trotsky. This method is very fashionable nowadays. Vardin could write a whole thesis on the subject. But the fact is, Comrade Pletnev, that *you* know very well how matters stood, because you yourself appealed to me to save you from the thunders of Vladimir Ilych, who was going, you thought, on account of this very "proletarian culture" of yours, to close down *Proletkult* altogether. And I promised you that I would defend the continued existence of *Proletkult*, on certain grounds, but that as regards Bogdanov's abstractions about proletarian culture I was entirely opposed to you and your protector Bukharin, and entirely in agreement with Vladimir Ilyich.

Comrade Vardin, who speaks here as nothing less than the living embodiment of party tradition, does not shrink from trampling in the crudest way on what Lenin wrote about proletarian culture. As we know, there is plenty of empty piety around: people "firmly agree" with Lenin and then preach the absolute opposite to his views. In terms that leave room for no other interpretation, Lenin mercilessly condemned "chatter about proletarian culture." However, there is nothing simpler than getting away from this evidence: why, of course, Lenin condemned chatter about proletarian culture, but, don't you see, it was only chatter that he condemned, and we are not chattering but seriously getting down to work, and even standing with our arms akimbo. . . . They only forget that Lenin's sharp condemnation was aimed precisely at those who are now referring to him. Empty piety, I repeat, is available in plenty: refer to Lenin and do the contrary.

The comrades who have spoken here under the sign of proletarian culture approach different ideas according to the attitude of the authors of those ideas to their *Proletkult* groups. I have tested this and found it true as regards my own fate. My book on literature, which caused so much alarm among certain comrades, appeared originally, as some of you may perhaps recall, in the form of articles in *Pravda*. I wrote this book over a period of two years, during two summer breaks. This circumstance, as we see today, is of importance in relation to the question that interests us. When it appeared, in the

form of newspaper articles, the first part of the book,
dealing with "non-October" literature, with the "fellow travelers," with the "peasant-singers," and exposing the limited-
ness and contradictions of the ideological-artistic position
of the fellow travelers, the *Na Postu* comrades hailed me
with enthusiasm — everywhere you cared to look you found
quotations from my articles on the fellow travelers. At
one stage I was quite depressed by it. (Laughter.) My
estimation of the "fellow travelers," I repeat, was regarded
as practically faultless; even Vardin made no objections
to it. (Vardin: "And I don't object to it now.") That is
just what I say.

But why then do you now obliquely and insinuatingly
argue against me about the "fellow travelers"? What is
going on here? At first sight it's quite incomprehensible.
But the solution is a simple one: my crime is not that I
incorrectly defined the social nature of the fellow travelers
or their artistic significance — no, Comrade Vardin even
now, as we heard, "does not object" to that — my crime is
that I did not bow before the manifestos of *Oktyabr* or
Kuznitsa, that I did not acknowledge these groups as the
monopolist representatives of the artistic interests of the
proletariat — in short, that I did not identify the cultural-
historical interests and tasks of the class with the intentions, plans and pretensions of certain literary groups.
That was where I went wrong. And when this became
clear, then there arose the howl, unexpected by its belat-
edness: Trotsky is on the side of the petty bourgeois "fellow travelers"!

Am I for the "fellow travelers," or against them? In
what sense am I against them? You knew that nearly two
years ago, from my articles on the "fellow travelers."
But then you agreed, you praised, you quoted, you gave
your approval. And when, a year later, it turned out
that my criticism of the "fellow travelers" was not at all
just an approach to the glorification of some amateurish
literary group or other, then the writers and defenders of
this group, or rather of these groups, began to bring
forward philosophical arguments against my allegedly
incorrect attitude to the "fellow travelers." Oh, strategists!
My offense was not that I estimated incorrectly Pilnyak or

Mayakovsky—the *Na Postu* group added nothing to what
I had said, but merely repeated it in vulgarized form—
my offense was that I knocked their own literary factory!
In the whole of their peevish criticism there is not the
shadow of a class approach. What we find is the attitude
of one literary group engaged in competition with others,
and that's all.

I mentioned the "peasant-singers," and we have heard
here that the *Na Postu* group especially approved of
that chapter. It's not enough to approve, you should
understand. What is the point here regarding the "peasant-
singing" fellow travelers? It is that this is a phenomenon
which is not accidental, is not of minor importance and
is not ephemeral. In our country, please don't forget,
we have the dictatorship of the proletariat in a country
which is inhabited mainly by peasants. The intelligentsia
is placed between these two classes as between two mill-
stones, is ground up little by little and arises anew, and
cannot be ground up completely, that is, it will remain
as an 'intelligentsia' for a long time yet, until the full
development of socialism and a very considerable rise
in the cultural level of the entire population of the country.
The intelligentsia serves the workers' and peasants' state
and subordinates itself to the proletariat, partly from
fear, partly from conviction; it wavers and will continue
to waver in accordance with the course of events, and
it will seek ideological support for its waverings in the
peasantry—this is the source of the Soviet literature of
the "peasant-singers."

What are the prospects of this school? Is it basically
hostile to us? Does its path lead towards us or away
from us? All this depends on the general course of events.
The task of the proletariat consists in retaining all-round
hegemony over the peasantry and leading it to socialism.
If we were to suffer a setback on this road, that is, if there
were to be a break between the proletariat and the peasantry, then the "peasant-singing" intelligentsia, or, more
correctly, 99 percent of the entire intelligentsia, would
turn against the proletariat. But this eventuality is not
at all inevitable. We are, on the contrary, following a
course aimed at bringing the peasantry, under the leader-

ship of the proletariat, to socialism. This is a very, very long road. In the course of this process both the proletariat and the peasantry will bring forward their own intelligentsia. It need not be supposed that the intelligentsia arising from the proletariat will be a hundred percent proletarian intelligentsia. The very fact that the proletariat is obliged to promote from its ranks a special stratum of "cultural workers" inevitably means a more or less considerable cultural disconnection between the remainder of the class as a whole and the proletarians promoted from it. This applies even more in the case of the peasant intelligentsia.

The peasants' road to socialism is not at all the same as the proletariat's. And insofar as the intelligentsia, even an arch-Soviet intelligentsia, is unable to merge its road with the road of the proletarian vanguard, to that degree it tries to find a political, ideological, artistic support for itself in the peasant, whether real or imagined. This appears all the more in the sphere of fiction, where we have an old populist tradition. Is this for us or against us? I repeat: the answer entirely depends on the entire future course of development. If we draw the peasant, towed by the proletariat, to socialism — and we confidently believe that we shall draw him — then the creative work of the "peasant-singers" will evolve by complex and tortuous paths into the socialist art of the future. [11] This complexity of the problems involved, and at the same time their reality and concreteness, is completely beyond the understanding of the *Na Postu* group, and not only of them. This is their fundamental mistake. Talking about the "fellow travelers" regardless of this social basis and prospect means simply wagging one's tongue.

Allow me, comrades, to say a little more about Comrade Vardin's tactics in the field of literature, in relation to his last article in *Na Postu*. In my view this is not tactics but a disgrace! An amazingly supercilious tone, but deadly little knowledge or understanding. No understanding of art as art, that is, as a particular, specific field of human creativity; nor any Marxist understanding of the conditions and ways of development of art. Instead, an unworthy juggling of quotations from White Guard publications abroad which, do you see, have praised Comrade Voronsky for publishing the works of Pilnyak, or ought to have praised him, or said something against Vardin and, maybe, for Voronsky, and so on, and so on—in that spirit of "circumstantial evidence" which has to make up for the lack of knowledge and understanding. Comrade Vardin's last article is built on the idea that a White Guard newspaper supported Voronsky against Vardin, writing that the whole conflict came down to the point that Voronsky approached literature from the literary point of view. "Comrade Voronsky, by his political behavior," says Vardin, "has fully deserved this White Guard kiss." But this is an insinuation, not an analysis of the question! If Vardin disagrees with the multiplication table, while Voronsky finds himself in this matter on the same side as a White Guard who knows arithmetic, Voronsky's political reputation has nothing to fear from that.

Yes, art has to be approached as art, literature as literature, that is, as a quite specific field of human endeavor. Of course we have a class criterion in art too, but this class criterion must be refracted artistically, that is, in conformity with the quite specific peculiarities of that field of creativity to which we are applying our criterion. The bourgeoisie knows this very well, it likewise approaches art from its class point of view, it knows how to get from art what it needs, but only because it approaches art as art. What is there to wonder at if an artistically-literate bourgeois has a disrespectful attitude to Vardin, who approaches art from the standpoint of political "circumstantial evidence," and not with a class-artistic criterion? And if there is anything that makes me feel ashamed, it is not that in this dispute I may find myself formally in the same boat with some White Guard who understands art, but that, before the eyes of this White Guard I am obliged to explain the first letters in the alphabet of art to a party publicist who writes articles about art. What a cheapening of Marxism this is: instead of making a Marxist analysis of the question, one finds a quotation from *Rul* or *Dyen*[12] and around it piles up abuse and insinuations!

One cannot approach art as one can politics, not because artistic creation is a religious rite or something mystical, as somebody here ironically said, but because it has its own laws of development, and above all because in artistic creation an enormous role is played by subconscious processes — slower, more idle and less subjected to management and guidance, just because they are subconscious. It has been said here that those writings of Pilnyak's which are closer to communism are feebler than those which are politically farther away from us. What is the explanation? Why, just this, that on the rationalistic plane Pilnyak is ahead of himself as an artist. To consciously swing himself round on his own axis even only a few degrees is a very difficult task for an artist, often connected with a profound, sometimes fatal crisis. And what we are considering is not an individual or group change in creative endeavor, but such a change on the class, social scale. This is a long and very complicated process.

When we speak of proletarian literature not in the sense of particular more or less successful verses or stories, but in the incomparably more weighty sense in which we speak of bourgeois literature, we have no right to forget for one moment the extraordinary cultural backwardness of the overwhelming majority of the proletariat. Art is created on the basis of a continual everyday, cultural, ideological interrelationship between a class and its artists. Between the aristocracy or the bourgeoisie and their artists there was no split in daily life. The artists lived, and still live, in a bourgeois milieu; breathing the air of bourgeois salons, they received and are receiving hypodermic inspirations from their class. This nourishes the subconscious processes of their creativity.

Does the proletariat of today offer such a cultural-ideological milieu, in which the new artist may obtain, without leaving it in his day-to-day existence, all the inspiration he needs while at the same time mastering the procedures of his craft? No, the working masses are culturally extremely backward; the illiteracy or low level of literacy of the majority of the workers presents in itself a very great obstacle to this. And above all, the proletariat, insofar as it remains a proletariat, is compelled to expend

its best forces in political struggle, in restoring the economy, and in meeting elementary cultural needs, fighting
against illiteracy, lousiness, syphilis, etc. Of course, the
political methods and revolutionary customs of the proletariat can also be called its culture; but this, in any case,
is a sort of culture which is destined to die out as a new,
real culture develops. And this new culture will be culture
all the more to the extent that the proletariat has ceased
to be a proletariat, that is, the more successfully and completely socialist society develops.

Mayakovsky wrote a very powerful piece called *The
Thirteen Apostles,* the revolutionariness of which was still
rather cloudy and formless. And when this same Mayakovsky decided to swing himself round to the proletarian line,
and wrote *150 Million,* he suffered a most frightful rationalistic downfall. This means that in his logic he had
outrun his real creative condition. With Pilnyak, as we
have said already, a similar disparity is to be observed
between his conscious striving and the unconscious processes of creation. To this must be added merely this,
that archproletarian works also do not in themselves provide the writer in present-day conditions with any guaran-
tees that his creativity will prove to be organically linked
with the class. Nor do groupings of proletarian writers
provide this guarantee, precisely because the writer, by de-
voting himself to artistic work, is compelled, in existing
conditions, to separate himself from the milieu of his
own class and breathe an atmosphere which, after all,
is the same as that breathed by the "fellow travelers."
This is just one literary circle among other literary circles.

And as regards future prospects, as they are called,
I wanted to say something, but my time is long since
up. (Voices: "Please go on!") "Give us, at least, some view
of the way ahead," comrades come back at me. What
does this mean? The *Na Postu* comrades and their allied
groups are steering towards a proletarian literature created
by the circle method, in a laboratory, so to speak. This
way forward I reject absolutely. I repeat once more
that it is not possible to put in one historical category
feudal, bourgeois and proletarian literature. Such a historical classification is radically false. I spoke about this

in my book, and all the objections I have heard seem to
me unconvincing and frivolous.

Those who talk about proletarian literature seriously
and over a long period, who make a platform of proletarian culture, are thinking, where this question is concerned, along the line of a formal analogy with bourgeois culture. The bourgeoisie took power and created
its own culture; the proletariat, they think, having taken
power, will create proletarian culture. But the bourgeoisie
is a rich and therefore educated class. Bourgeois culture
existed already before the bourgeoisie had formally taken
power. The bourgeoisie took power in order to perpetuate
its rule. The proletariat in bourgeois society is a property-
less and deprived class, and so it cannot create a culture
of its own. Only after taking power does it really become
aware of its own frightful cultural backwardness. In order
to overcome this it needs to abolish those conditions which
keep it in the position of a class, the proletariat. The
more we can speak of a new culture in being, the less
this will possess a class character. This is the fundamental problem and the principal difference, insofar as we
are arguing about the way forward.

Some, starting from the principle of proletarian culture,
say: we have in mind only the epoch of transition to
socialism — those twenty, thirty, fifty years during which
the bourgeois world will be transformed. Can the literature, intended and suitable for the proletariat, which will
be created in this period, be called proletarian literature?
In any case, we are giving this term "proletarian literature" a totally different meaning from the first, broad meaning we spoke of. But this is not the main problem.

The basic feature of the transition period, taken on the
international scale, is intense class struggle. Those twenty
to thirty years of which we speak will be first and foremost a period of open civil war. And civil war, though
preparing the way for the great culture of the future, is
in itself extremely unfavorable in its effect on contemporary culture. In its immediate effect October more or
less killed literature. Poets and artists fell silent. Was this
an accident? No. Long ago it was said: when the sound
of weapons is heard, the Muses fall silent. A breathing

space was needed if literature was to revive. It began to revive in our country at the same time as NEP began. Reviving, it at once took on the coloring of the fellow travelers. It is impossible not to reckon with the facts. The tensest moments, that is, those in which our revolutionary epoch finds its highest expression, are unfavorable for literary, and in general for artistic, creation. If revolution begins tomorrow in Germany or in all Europe, will this bring an immediate flowering of proletarian literature? Certainly not. It will weaken and destroy, not expand, artistic creation, for we shall again have to mobilize and arm, one and all. And amid the clash of arms, the Muses are silent. (Cries: "Demyan wasn't silent.")

Yes, you keep harping on Demyan, but it won't do. You begin by proclaiming a new era of proletarian literature, you create circles, associations, groups for this literature, you again and again refer to Demyan. But Demyan is a product of the old, pre-October literature. He has not founded any school, nor will he found any. He was brought up on Krylov, Gogol and Nekrassov. [13] In this sense he is the revolutionary last-born child of our old literature. The very fact of your referring to him is a refutation of your theory.

What is the way forward? Fundamentally, it is the growth of literacy, education, special courses for workers, the cinema, the gradual reconstruction of everyday life, the further advance in the cultural level. This is the fundamental process, intersecting with new intensifications of civil war, on an all-European and world scale. On this basis, the line of purely literary creation will be an extremely zigzag one. *Kuznitsa, Oktyabr* and other such groups are in no sense landmarks along the road of the cultural class creativity of the proletariat, but merely episodes of a superficial nature. If from these groups a few good young poets or writers emerge, this won't give us proletarian literature, but it will be useful. But if you try to transform MAPP and VAPP into factories of proletarian literature, you will certainly fail, just as you have failed up to now. A member of one of these associations regards himself as, in one way, a representative of the proletariat in the world of art, in another way as a representative of art in the world of the proletariat. Membership of VAPP confers a sort of title.

It is objected that VAPP is only a communist circle in which a young poet obtains the necessary inspiration, and so on. Well, and what about the party? If he is a real poet and a genuine communist, the party in all its work will give him incomparably more inspiration than MAPP and VAPP. Of course, the party must and will pay very great attention to every young artistic talent that is akin or ideologically close to it. But its fundamental task in relation to literature and culture is raising the level of literacy — simple literacy, political literacy, scientific literacy — of the working masses, and thereby laying the foundation for a new art.

I know that this prospect does not satisfy you. It seems insufficiently definite. Why? Because you envisage the further development of culture in too regular, too evolutionary a way: the present shoots of proletarian literature will, you think, grow and develop, becoming continually richer, and so genuine proletarian literature will be created, which later will change into socialist literature. No, things won't develop like that. After the present breathing space, when a literature strongly colored by the "fellow travelers" is being created — not by the party, not by the state—there will come a period of new, terrible spasms of civil war. We shall inevitably be drawn into it. It is quite possible that revolutionary poets will give us martial verses, but the continuity of literary development will nevertheless be sharply broken. All forces will be concentrated on the direct struggle. Shall we then have a second breathing space? I do not know.

But the result of this new, much mightier period of civil war, if we are victorious, will be the complete securing and consolidation of the socialist basis of our economy. We shall receive fresh technical and organizational help. Our development will go forward at a different rate. And on that basis, after the zigzags and upheavals of civil war, only then will begin a real building of culture, and, consequently, also the creation of a new literature. But this will be socialist culture, built entirely on constant intercourse between the artist and the masses who will have come of age culturally, linked by ties of solidarity. You do not proceed in your thinking from *this* vision of the future: you have your own, the vision of a group. You want our party, in the name of the proletariat, to officially adopt your little artistic factory. You think that, having planted a kidney bean in a flower pot, you are capable of raising the tree of proletarian literature. That is not the way. No tree can be grown from a kidney bean.

FROM *CULTURE AND SOCIALISM*

This long essay is based on a number of lectures which Trotsky gave in 1926.

1. Technique and Culture

Let us recall first of all that culture meant originally a plowed, cultivated field, as distinct from virgin forest and virgin soil. Culture was contrasted with nature, that is, what was acquired by man's efforts was contrasted with what was given by nature. This antithesis fundamentally retains its value today.

Culture is everything that has been created, built, learned, conquered by man in the course of his entire history, in distinction from what nature has given, including the natural history of man himself as a species of animal. The science which studies man as a product of animal evolution is called anthropology. But from the moment that man separated himself from the animal kingdom — and this happened approximately when he first grasped primitive tools of stone and wood and armed the organs of his body with them — from that time there began the creation and accumulation of culture, that is, all kinds

Completed February 3, 1926, originally published in *Krasnaya Nov*, number 6, 1926, and reprinted in *Novy Mir*, number 1, 1927. The first English translation, by Brian Pearce, appeared in *Labour Review*, Autumn 1962.

of knowledge and skill in the struggle with nature and subjugation of nature.

When we speak of the culture accumulated by past generations we think first and foremost of its material achievements in the form of tools, machinery, buildings, monuments, and so on. Is this culture? Undoubtedly it is culture; the material forms in which culture is deposited — material culture. It creates, on the basis provided by nature, the fundamental setting of our lives, our everyday way of living, our creative work. But the most precious part of culture is its deposit in the consciousness of man himself — those methods, habits, skills, acquired abilities of ours which have developed out of the whole of pre-existing material culture and which, while drawing on this preexisting material culture, also improve upon it. We will, then, consider it as firmly established that culture has grown out of man's struggle with nature for existence, for the improvement of his conditions of life, for the enlargement of his power. But out of this same basis classes also have grown. In the process of adapting itself to nature, in conflict with the hostile forces of nature, human society has taken shape as a complex organization of classes. The class structure of society has determined to a decisive degree the content and form of human history, that is, its material relations and their ideological reflections. This means that historical culture has possessed a class character.

Slave-owning society, feudal serf-owning society, bourgeois society, each engendered a corresponding culture, different at different stages and with a multitude of transitional forms. Historical society has been an organization for the exploitation of man by man. Culture has served the class organization of society. Exploiters' society has given rise to an exploiters' culture. But does this mean that we are against all the culture of the past?

There exists, in fact, a profound contradiction here. Everything that has been conquered, created, built by man's efforts and which serves to enhance man's power is culture. But since it is not a matter of individual man but of social man, since culture is a social-historical phenomenon in its very essence, and since historical society has been and continues to be class society, culture is found to be the basic instrument of class oppression. Marx said: "The ruling ideas of an epoch are essentially the ideas of the ruling class of that epoch." This also applies to culture as a whole. And yet we say to the working class: master all the culture of the past, otherwise you will not build socialism. How is this to be understood?

Over this contradiction many people have stumbled, and they stumble so frequently because they approach the understanding of class society superficially, semi-idealistically, forgetting that fundamentally this is the organization of production. Every class society has been formed on the basis of definite modes of struggle with nature, and these modes have changed in accordance with the development of technique. What is the basis of bases — the class organization of society or its productive forces? Without doubt the productive forces. It is precisely upon them, at a certain level of their development, that classes are formed and re-formed. In the productive forces is expressed the materialized economic skill of mankind, his historical ability to ensure his existence. On this dynamic foundation there arise classes, which by their interrelations determine the character of culture.

And here, first and foremost, we have to ask ourselves regarding technique: is it *only* an instrument of class oppression? It is enough to put such a question for it to be answered at once: no, technique is the fundamental conquest of mankind; although it has also served, up to the present, as an instrument of exploitation, yet it is at the same time the fundamental condition for the emancipation of the exploited. The machine strangles the wage slave in its grip. But he can free himself only through the machine. Therein is the root of the entire question.

If we do not let ourselves forget that the driving force of the historical process is the growth of the productive forces, liberating man from the domination of nature, then we shall find that the proletariat needs to master the sum total of the knowledge and skill worked out by humanity in the course of its history, in order to raise itself up and rebuild life on principles of solidarity. . . .

2. The Heritage of Spiritual Culture

Spiritual culture is as contradictory as material culture.
And just as from the arsenals and storehouses of material
culture we take and put into circulation not bows and
arrows, not stone tools or the tools of the Bronze Age,
but the most improved tools available, of the most up-
to-date technique, in this way also must we approach spiritual culture as well. . . .

Dialectics and materialism are the basic elements in
the Marxist cognition of the world. But this does not mean
at all that they can be applied to any sphere of knowledge, like an ever-ready master key. Dialectics cannot
be imposed upon facts, it has to be deduced from facts,
from their nature and development. Only painstaking
work on a vast mass of material enabled Marx to advance the dialectical system of economics to the conception of value as social labor. Marx's historical works were
constructed in the same way, and even his newspaper articles likewise. Dialectical materialism can be applied to
new spheres of knowledge only by mastering them from
within. The purging of bourgeois science presupposes
a mastery of bourgeois science. You will get nowhere
with sweeping criticism or bald commands. Learning and
application here go hand in hand with critical reworking.
We have the method, but there is work enough for generations to do. . . .

Art is one of the ways in which man finds his bearings
in the world; in this sense the heritage of art is not distinguished from the heritage of science and technique — and
it is no less contradictory than they. Unlike science, however, art is a form of cognition of the world not as a
system of laws but as a group of images, and at the same
time it is a way of inspiring certain feelings and moods.
The art of past centuries has made man more complex
and flexible, has raised his mentality to a higher level,
has enriched him in an all-round way. This enrichment
is a precious achievement of culture. Mastery of the art
of the past is, therefore, a necessary precondition not
only for the creation of new art but also for the building

of the new society, for communism needs people with highly developed minds. Can, however, the art of the past enrich us with an artistic knowledge of the world? It can, precisely because it is able to give nourishment to our feelings and to educate them. If we were groundlessly to repudiate the art of the past, we should at once become poorer spiritually.

One notices nowadays a tendency here and there to put forward the idea that art has as its purpose only the inspiration of certain moods, and not at all the cognition of reality. The conclusion drawn from this is: with what sort of sentiments can the art of the nobility or of the bourgeoisie infect us? This is radically false. The significance of art as a means of cognition — including for the mass of the people, and in particular for them — is not at all less than its "sentimental" significance. The ancient epic, the fable, the song, the traditional saying, the folk rhyme provide knowledge in graphic form, they throw light on the past, they generalize experience, they widen the horizon, and only in connection with them and thanks to this connection is it possible to "tune it." This applies to all literature generally, not only to epic poetry but to lyric poetry as well. It applies to painting and to sculpture. The only exception, to a certain degree, is music, the effect of which is powerful but one-sided! Music too, of course, relies upon a particular knowledge of nature, its sounds and rhythms. But here the knowledge is so deeply hidden, the results of the inspiration of nature are to such an extent refracted through a person's nerves, that music acts as a self-sufficing "revelation." Attempts to approximate all forms of art to music, as to the art of "infection,"[1] have often been made and have always signified a depreciation in art of the role of the intelligence in favor of formless feeling, and in this sense they were and are reactionary. . . . Worst of all, of course, are those works of "art" which offer neither graphic knowledge nor artistic "infection" but instead advance exorbitant pretensions. In our country no few such works are printed, and, unfortunately, not in the students' books of art schools but in many thousands of copies. . . .

Culture is a social phenomenon. Just because of this,

language, as the organ of intercourse between men, is its most important instrument. The culture of language itself is the most important condition for the growth of all branches of culture, especially science and art. Just as technique is not satisfied with the old measuring apparatus but is creating new ones, micrometers, voltameters, and so on, striving for and attaining ever greater accuracy, so in the matter of language, of skill in choosing the appropriate words and combining them in the appropriate ways, constant, systematic, painstaking work is necessary in order to achieve the highest degree of accuracy, clarity and vividness. The foundation for this work must be the fight against illiteracy, semiliteracy and near-illiteracy. The next stage of this work is the mastering of Russian classical literature.

Yes, culture was the main instrument of class oppression. But it also, and only it, can become the instrument of socialist emancipation.

3. The Contradictions in Our Culture

What is special about our position is that we — at the point where the capitalist West and the colonial-peasant East meet — have been the first to make a socialist revolution. The regime of proletarian dictatorship has been established first in a country with a monstrous inheritance of backwardness and barbarism, so that among our people whole centuries of history separate a Siberian nomad from a Moscow or Leningrad worker. Our social forms are transitional to socialism and consequently are beyond comparison higher than capitalist forms. In this sense we rightly consider ourselves the most advanced country in the world. But technique, which lies at the basis of material and every other kind of culture, is extremely backward in our country in comparison with the advanced capitalist countries. This constitutes the fundamental contradiction of our present reality. The historical task which follows from this is to raise our technique to the height of our social formation. If we do not succeed in doing this, our social order will inevitably decline to the level of our technical backwardness. Yes, in order to appreciate the entire significance of technical progress for us it is necessary to tell ourselves frankly: if we do not succeed in filling the Soviet forms of our social order with the appropriate productive technique we shall shut off the possibility of our transition to socialism and we shall be turned back to capitalism — and to what sort of capitalism: semiserf, semicolonial capitalism. The struggle for technique is for us the struggle for socialism, with which the whole future of our culture is bound up.

Here is a fresh and very expressive example of our cultural contradictions. There recently appeared in the papers a report that our Leningrad Public Library holds first place for the number of books: it now possesses 4,250,000 books! Our first feeling is a legitimate feeling of Soviet pride: our library is the first in the world! To what are we indebted for this achievement? To the fact that we have expropriated private libraries. Through nationalizing private property we have created a richer cultural institution, accessible to everyone. The great advantages of the Soviet order are indisputably shown in this simple fact. But at the same time our cultural backwardness is expressed in the fact that in our country the percentage of illiterates is greater than in any other European country. The library is the biggest in the world, but as yet only a minority of the population reads books. And that is how things are in almost every respect. Nationalized industry, with gigantic and far from fantastic schemes for Dnieprostroi, the Volga-Don canal and so on — and the peasants do their threshing with chains and rollers. Our marriage laws are permeated with the spirit of socialism — and physical violence still plays no small part in our family life. These and similar contradictions result from the entire structure of our culture, at the meeting point of West and East. . . .

It is now, I think, clear to everybody that the creation of a new culture is not an independent task to be carried out separately from our economic work and our social and cultural construction as a whole. . . .

When Lenin spoke of the cultural revolution he saw its fundamental content as raising the cultural level of the masses. The metric system is a product of bourgeois science. But teaching this simple system of measurement to a hundred million peasants means carrying out a big revolutionary cultural task. It is almost certain that we shall not achieve it without the aid of tractors and electric power. At the foundation of culture lies technique. The decisive instrument in the cultural revolution must be a revolution in technique.

In relation to capitalism we say that the development of the productive forces is pressing against the social forms of the bourgeois state and bourgeois property. Having accomplished the proletarian revolution we say: the development of the social forms is pressing against the development of the productive forces, that is technique. The big link by seizing which we can carry through the cultural revolution is the link of industrialization, and not literature or philosophy at all. I hope that these words will not be understood in the sense of an unfriendly or disrespectful attitude to philosophy and poetry. Without generalizing thought and without art, man's life would be bare and beggarly. But that is just what the life of millions of people is to an enormous extent at the present time. The cultural revolution must consist in opening up to them the possibility of real access to culture and not only to its wretched fag ends. But this is impossible without creating very big material preconditions. That is why a machine which automatically manufactures bottles is at the present time a first-rate factor in the cultural revolution, while a heroic poem is only a tenth-rate factor.

Marx said once about philosophers that they had interpreted the world sufficiently, the task was to turn it upside down. There was no disesteem for philosophy in those words of his. Marx was himself one of the greatest philosophers of all time. These words meant only that the further development of philosophy, as of all culture in general, both material and spiritual, requires a revolution in social relations. And so Marx appealed from philosophy to the proletarian revolution, not against philosophy but on its behalf. In this same sense we can now say: it is good when poets sing of the revolution and the proletariat, but a powerful turbine sings even better. We have plenty of songs of middling quality, which have remained the property of small circles, but we have terribly few turbines. I don't wish to imply by this that mediocre verses hinder the appearance of turbines. No, that cannot be said at all. But a correct orientation of public opinion, that is, an understanding of the real relationship between phenomena, the how and why of things, is absolutely necessary.

The cultural revolution must not be understood in a superficially idealistic way or as something which is an affair for small study groups. It is a question of changing the conditions of life, the methods of work and the everyday habits of a great nation, of a whole family of nations. Only a mighty tractor system which for the first time in history will enable the peasant to straighten his back; only a glassblowing machine which produces hundreds of bottles and liberates the lungs of the old-time glassblower; only a turbine of dozens and hundreds of thousands horsepower; only an airplane available to everyone — only all these things together will ensure the cultural revolution, not for a minority but for all. And only such a cultural revolution will deserve the name. Only on that basis will a new philosophy and a new art come to flower. . . .

HISTORICAL OBJECTIVITY

AND ARTISTIC TRUTH

This is an excerpt from a reply by Trotsky to some of the critics of his History of the Russian Revolution.

Everyone digests his food and oxygenates his blood. But not everyone will dare write a thesis about digestion and blood circulation. Not so with the social sciences. Since every person lives under the influence of the market and of the historic process in general, it is considered sufficient to possess common sense in order to write exercises on economic and especially historic-philosophic themes. As a general rule only "objectivity" is demanded of a historical work. In point of fact whatever bears this high-sounding title in the language of common sense has nothing to do with scientific objectivity.

The philistine, especially if he is separated from the fighting arena by space and time, considers himself elevated above the fighting camps by the mere fact that he understands neither of them. He sincerely takes his blindness regarding the working of historical forces for the height of impartiality, just as he is used to considering

Written April 1, 1933, and published in *Bulletin of the Opposition*, number 35, July 1933, under the title "What is Historical Objectivity?" The first American translation, by Max Eastman, appeared in *The Militant*, July 15, 1933.

himself the normal measure of all things. Notwithstanding their documentary value, too many historical papers are being written according to this standard. A blunting of sharp edges, even distribution of light and shadow, a conciliatory moralizing, with a thorough disguising of the author's sympathies easily secures for a historical work the high reputation of "objectivity."

Insofar as the subject of investigation is a phenomenon as poorly reconcilable with common sense as revolution, this historical "objectivity" dictates in advance its immutable conclusions: the cause of the disturbances lies in the fact that the conservatives were much too conservative, the revolutionaries much too revolutionary: the historical excesses called civil war can in the future be avoided if the private owners will be more generous, and the hungry people more moderate. A book with such tendencies has a good effect on the nerves, especially during an epoch of world crisis.

The demand of science, and not a parlor-philistine "objectivity," really is that one should expose the social conditioning of historical events, no matter how unpleasant they may be for the nerves. History is not a dumping ground for documents and moral maxims. History is a science no less objective than physiology. It requires not a hypocritical "impartiality" but a scientific method. One can accept or reject the materialistic dialectic as the method of historical science, but one must reckon with it. Scientific objectivity can be and must be lodged in the very method itself. If the author did not manage its proper application, it must be pointed out exactly where. . . .

A literary work is "truthful" or artistic when the interrelations of the heroes develop, not according to the author's desires, but according to the latent forces of the characters and the setting. Scientific knowledge differs greatly from the artistic. But the two also have some traits in common, defined by the dependence of the description on the thing described. A historical work is scientific when facts combine into one whole process which, as in life, lives according to its own interior laws. . . .

CULTURE AND THE SOVIET
BUREAUCRACY

Trotsky attributed the rise and triumph of the Soviet bureaucracy to the Soviet Union being a backward country encircled by capitalist powers. With the development of industry, the extension of education and the increase of the specific weight of the world anticapitalist forces as a result of the postwar revolutions, a new intelligentsia, restive under the bureaucratic controls against which Trotsky inveighed has grown up. The "underground" literature circulating in manuscript among members of this intelligentsia is the expression of a thought and feeling inimical to the rule of the bureaucracy.

The official doctrine of culture changes in dependence upon economic zigzags and administrative expediencies. But with all its changes, it retains one trait—that of being absolutely categorical. Simultaneously with the theory of "socialism in one country," the previously frowned on theory of "proletarian culture" received official recognition. The opponents of this theory pointed out that the regime of proletarian dictatorship has a strictly transitional character, that in distinction from the bourgeoisie, the proletariat does not intend to dominate throughout a series of historical epochs, that the task of the present generation of the new ruling class reduces itself primarily to an assim-

Completed before the Moscow trials in 1936 and published as part of *The Revolution Betrayed* in 1937. The translation was by Max Eastman.

ilation of all that is valuable in bourgeois culture, that the longer the proletariat remains a proletariat — that is, bears the traces of its former oppression — the less is it capable of rising above the historic heritage of the past, and that the possibilities of new creation will really open themselves only to the extent that the proletariat dissolves itself in a socialist society. All this means, in other words, that the bourgeois culture should be replaced by a socialist, not a proletarian, culture.

In a polemic against the theory of a "proletarian art" produced by laboratory methods, the author of these lines wrote: "Culture feeds upon the juices of industry, and a material excess is necessary in order that culture should grow, refine and complicate itself." Even the most successful solution of elementary economic problems "would far from signify as yet a complete victory of the new historic principle of socialism. Only a forward movement of scientific thought on an all-national basis and the development of a new art would mean that the historic kernel had produced a blossom as well as a stalk. In this sense the development of art is the highest test of the viability and significance of every epoch." This point of view, which had prevailed up to that moment, was in an official declaration suddenly proclaimed to be "capitulatory," and dictated by a "disbelief" in the creative powers of the proletariat. There opened the period of Stalin and Bukharin, the latter of whom had long before appeared as an evangel of "proletarian culture," and the former never given a thought to these questions. They both considered, in any case, that the movement toward socialism would develop with a "tortoise stride," and that the proletariat would have at its disposal decades for the creation of its own culture. As to the character of this culture, the ideas of these theoreticians were as vague as they were uninspiring.

The stormy years of the first five-year plan upset the tortoise perspective. In 1931, on the eve of a dreadful famine, the country had already "entered into socialism." [1] Thus, before the officially patronized writers, artists and painters had managed to create a proletarian culture, or even the first significant models of it, the government announced that the proletariat had dissolved in the class-

less society. It remained for the artists to reconcile themselves with the fact that the proletariat did not possess the
most necessary condition for the creation of a proletarian
culture: time. Yesterday's conceptions were immediately
abandoned to oblivion. "Socialist culture" was placed in-
stantly upon the order of the day. We have already in
part become acquainted with its content.

Spiritual creativeness demands freedom. The very purpose of communism is to subject nature to technique and
technique to plan, and compel the raw material to give
unstintingly everything to man that he needs. Far more
than that, its highest goal is to free finally and once for
all the creative forces of mankind from all pressure, limitation and humiliating dependence. Personal relations,
science and art will not know any externally imposed
"plan," nor even any shadow of compulsion. To what
degree spiritual creativeness shall be individual or collective will depend entirely upon its creators.

A transitional regime is a different thing. The dictatorship reflects the past barbarism and not the future culture.
It necessarily lays down severe limitations upon all forms
of activity, including spiritual creation. The program of
the revolution from the very beginning regarded these
limitations as a temporary evil, and assumed the obligation, in proportion as the new regime was consolidated,
to remove one after the other all restrictions upon freedom.
In any case, and in the hottest years of the civil war, it
was clear to the leaders of the revolution that the government could, guided by political considerations, place limitations upon creative freedom, but in no case pretend to
the role of commander in the sphere of science, literature
and art. Although he had rather "conservative" personal
tastes in art, Lenin remained politically extremely cautious
in artistic questions, eagerly confessing his incompetence.
The patronizing of all kinds of modernism by Lunacharsky, the People's Commissar of Art and Education, was
often embarrassing to Lenin. But he confined himself to
ironical remarks in private conversations, and remained
remote from the idea of converting his literary tastes into
law. In 1924, on the threshold of the new period, the
author of this book thus formulated the relation of the

state to the various artistic groups and tendencies: "while holding over them all the categorical criterion, *for* the revolution or *against* the revolution, to give them complete freedom in the sphere of artistic self-determination."

While the dictatorship had a seething mass basis and a prospect of world revolution, it had no fear of experiments, searchings, the struggle of schools, for it understood that only in this way could a new cultural epoch be prepared. The popular masses were still quivering in every fiber, and were thinking aloud for the first time in a thousand years. All the best youthful forces of art were touched to the quick. During those first years, rich in hope and daring, there were created not only the most complete models of socialist legislation, but also the best productions of revolutionary literature. To the same times belong, it is worth remarking, the creation of those excellent Soviet films which, in spite of a poverty of technical means, caught the imagination of the whole world with the freshness and vigor of their approach to reality.

In the process of struggle against the party Opposition, the literary schools were strangled one after the other. It was not only a question of literature, either. The process of extermination took place in all ideological spheres, and it took place more decisively since it was more than half unconscious. The present ruling stratum considers itself called not only to control spiritual creation politically, but also to prescribe its roads of development. The method of command without appeal extends in like measure to the concentration camps, to scientific agriculture and to music. The central organ of the party prints anonymous directive editorials, having the character of military orders, in architecture, literature, dramatic art, the ballet, to say nothing of philosophy, natural science and history.

The bureaucracy superstitiously fears whatever does not serve it directly, as well as whatever it does not understand. When it demands some connection between natural science and production, this is on a large scale right; but when it commands that scientific investigators set themselves goals only of immediate practical importance, this threatens to seal up the most precious sources of invention, including practical discoveries, for these most often arise

on unforeseen roads. Taught by bitter experience, the
natural scientists, mathematicians, philologists, military
theoreticians, avoid all broad generalizations out of fear
lest some "red professor," usually an ignorant careerist,
threateningly pull up on them with some quotation dragged
in by the hair from Lenin, or even from Stalin. To defend
one's own thought in such circumstances, or one's scientific dignity, means in all probability to bring down re-
pressions upon one's head.

But it is infinitely worse in the sphere of the social sciences. Economists, historians, even statisticians, to say
nothing of journalists, are concerned above all things
not to fall, even obliquely, into contradiction with the mo-
mentary zigzag of the official course. About Soviet economy or domestic or foreign policy, one cannot write at
all except after covering his rear and flanks with banalities
from the speeches of the "leader," and having assumed in
advance the task of demonstrating that everything is going
exactly as it should go and even better. Although this
100 percent conformism frees one from everyday unpleas-
antnesses, it entails the heaviest of punishments: sterility.

In spite of the fact that Marxism is formally a state
doctrine in the Soviet Union, there has not appeared
during the last twelve years one Marxian investigation
— in economics, sociology, history or philosophy — which
deserves attention and translation into foreign languages.
The Marxian works do not transcend the limit of scholastic
compilations which say over the same old ideas, endorsed
in advance, and shuffle over the same old quotations according to the demands of the current administrative con-
juncture. Millions of copies are distributed through the state
channels of books and brochures that are of no use to
anybody, put together with the help of mucilage, flattery
and other sticky substances. Marxists who might say something valuable and independent are sitting in prison, or
forced into silence, and this in spite of the fact that the
evolution of social forms is raising gigantic scientific problems at every step!

Befouled and trampled underfoot is the one thing without
which theoretical work is impossible: scrupulousness. Even
the explanatory notes to the complete works of Lenin are

radically worked over in every new edition from the point of view of the personal interests of the ruling staff: the names of "leaders" magnified, those of opponents vilified; tracks covered up. The same is true of the textbooks on the history of the party and the revolution. Facts are distorted, documents concealed or fabricated, reputations created or destroyed. A simple comparison of the successive variants of one and the same book during the last twelve years permits us to trace infallibly the process of degeneration of the thought and conscience of the ruling stratum.

No less ruinous is the effect of the "totalitarian" regime upon artistic literature. The struggle of tendencies and schools has been replaced by interpretation of the will of the leaders. There has been created for all groups a general compulsory organization, a kind of concentration camp of artistic literature. Mediocre but "right-thinking" storytellers like Serafimovich or Gladkov are inaugurated as classics. Gifted writers who cannot do sufficient violence to themselves are pursued by a pack of instructors armed with shamelessness and dozens of quotations. The most eminent artists either commit suicide, or find their material in the remote past, or become silent. Honest and talented books appear as though accidentally, bursting out from somewhere under the counter, and have the character of artistic contraband.

The life of Soviet art is a kind of martyrology. After the editorial orders in *Pravda* against "formalism," there began an epidemic of humiliating recantations by writers, artists, stage directors and even opera singers. One after another, they renounced their own past sins, refraining, however — in case of further emergencies — from any clear-cut definition of the nature of this "formalism." In the long run, the authorities were compelled by a new order to put an end to a too copious flow of recantations. Literary estimates are transformed within a few weeks, textbooks made over, streets renamed, statues brought forward, as a result of a few eulogistic remarks of Stalin about the poet Mayakovsky. The impressions made by the new opera upon high-up auditors are immediately converted into a musical directive for composers. The secretary of the Communist Youth said at a conference of writers: "The suggestions of Comrade Stalin are a law for everybody," and the whole audience applauded, although some doubtless burned with shame. As though to complete the mockery of literature, Stalin, who does not know how to compose a Russian phrase correctly, is declared a classic in the matter of style. There is something deeply tragic in this Byzantinism and police rule, notwithstanding the involuntary comedy of certain of its manifestations.

The official formula reads: culture should be socialist in content, national in form. As to the content of a socialist culture, however, only certain more or less happy guesses are possible. Nobody can grow that culture upon an inadequate economic foundation. Art is far less capable than science of anticipating the future. In any case, such prescriptions as, "portray the construction of the future," "indicate the road to socialism," "make over mankind," give little more to the creative imagination than does the price list of a hardware store or a railroad timetable.

The national form of an art is identical with its universal accessibility. "What is not wanted by the people," *Pravda* dictates to the artists, "cannot have aesthetic significance." That old Narodnik formula, rejecting the task of artistically educating the masses, takes on a still more reactionary character when the right to decide what art the people want and what they don't want remains in the hands of the bureaucracy. It prints books according to its own choice. It sells them also by compulsion, offering no choice to the reader. In the last analysis the whole affair comes down in its eyes to taking care that art assimilates its interests, and finds such forms for them as will make the bureaucracy attractive to the popular masses.

In vain! No literature can fulfill that task. The leaders themselves are compelled to acknowledge that "neither the first nor the second five-year plan has yet given us a new literary wave which can rise above the first wave born in October." That is very mildly said. In reality, in spite of individual exceptions, the epoch of the Thermidor[2] will go into the history of artistic creation preeminently as an epoch of mediocrities, laureates and toadies.

THE FUTURE OF PARTISAN REVIEW: A LETTER TO DWIGHT MACDONALD

At the time Trotsky wrote this letter, the editors of Partisan Review *were shaking off the previous Stalinist influence over the magazine. Trotsky, however, had doubts about the strength of their convictions. Before too long these doubts proved justified: the editors' reaction against Stalinism, a distorted form of Marxism, became a reaction against Marxism itself, and* Partisan Review *became a "small cultural monastery." As one of its editors, Philip Rahv, put it in a symposium "Our Country and Our Culture," which appeared in the magazine in 1952: "If under present conditions we cannot stop the ruthless expansion of mass culture, the least we can do is to keep apart and refuse its favors."*

I shall speak with you very frankly inasmuch as reservations or insincere half-praises would signify a lack of respect for you and your undertaking.

It is my general impression that the editors of *Partisan Review* are capable, educated and intelligent people but *they have nothing to say.* They seek themes which are

Written on January 20, 1938, this letter was first published in *Fourth International* (New York) March-April 1950.

incapable of hurting anyone but which likewise are incapable of giving anybody a thing. I have never seen or heard of a group with such a mood gaining success, i.e., winning influence and leaving some sort of trace in the history of thought.

Note that I am not at all touching upon the *content* of your ideas (perhaps because I cannot discern them in your magazine). "Independence" and "freedom" are two empty notions. But I am ready to grant that "independence" and "freedom" as you understand them represent some kind of actual cultural value. Excellent! But then it is necessary to defend them with sword, or at least with whip, in hand. Every new artistic or literary tendency (naturalism, symbolism, futurism, cubism, expressionism and so forth and so on) has begun with a "scandal," breaking the old respected crockery, bruising many established authorities. This flowed not at all solely from publicity seeking (although there was no lack of this). No, these people — artists, as well as literary critics — had something to say. They had friends, they had enemies, they fought, and exactly through this they demonstrated their right to exist.

So far as your publication is concerned, it wishes, in the main instance, apparently to demonstrate its respectability. You defend yourselves from the Stalinists like well-behaved young ladies whom street rowdies insult. "Why are we attacked?" you complain, "we want only one thing: to live and let others live." Such a policy cannot gain success.

Of course, there are not a few disappointed "friends of the USSR" and generally dismal intellectuals who, having been burned once, fear more than anything else to become again engaged. These people will send you tepid, sympathetic letters but they will not guarantee the success of the magazine since serious success has never yet been based on political, cultural and aesthetic *disorientation*.

I wanted to hope that this was but a temporary condition and that the publishers of *Partisan Review* would cease to be afraid of themselves. I must say, however, that the symposium outlined by you is not at all capable of strengthening these hopes.[1] You phrase the question about Marxism as if you were beginning history from a clean page. The very symposium title itself sounds extremely pretentious and at the same time confused. The majority of the writers whom you have invited have shown by their whole past—alas!—a complete incapacity for theoretical thinking. Some of them are political corpses. How can a corpse be entrusted with deciding whether Marxism is a living force? No, I categorically refuse to participate in that kind of endeavor.

A world war is approaching. The inner political struggle in all countries tends to become transformed into civil war. Currents of the highest tension are active in all fields of culture and ideology. You evidently wish to create a small cultural monastery, guarding itself from the outside world by skepticism, agnosticism and respectability. Such an endeavor does not open up any kind of perspective.

It is entirely possible that the tone of this letter will appear to you as sharp, impermissible, and "sectarian." In my eyes this would constitute merely supplementary proof of the fact that you wish to publish a peaceful "little" magazine without participating actively in the cultural life of your epoch. If, on the contrary, you do not consider my "sectarian" tone a hindrance to a future exchange of opinion then I remain fully at your service.

ART AND POLITICS
IN OUR EPOCH

This letter to Partisan Review *was published when its editors were giving promise of belying Trotsky's doubts about them by becoming what the title of their magazine promised — avowed partisans of revolutionary socialism.*

You have been kind enough to invite me to express my views on the state of present-day arts and letters. I do this not without some hesitation. Since my book *Literature and Revolution* (1923), I have not once returned to the problem of artistic creation and only occasionally have I been able to follow the latest developments in this sphere. I am far from pretending to offer an exhaustive reply. The task of this letter is to correctly pose the question.

Generally speaking, art is an expression of man's need for a harmonious and complete life, that is to say, his need for those major benefits of which a society of classes has deprived him. That is why a protest against reality, either conscious or unconscious, active or passive, optimistic or pessimistic, always forms part of a really creative piece of work. Every new tendency in art has begun with rebellion.

Bourgeois society showed its strength throughout long

Written June 18, 1938, under the title "Art and Revolution," it was published in *Partisan Review,* August 1938, and in *Bulletin of the Opposition,* numbers 77-78, May-June 1939.

periods of history in the fact that, combining repression and encouragement, boycott and flattery, it was able to control and assimilate every "rebel" movement in art and raise it to the level of official "recognition." But each time this "recognition" betokened, when all is said and done, the approach of trouble. It was then that from the left wing of the academic school or below it—i.e., from the ranks of a new generation of bohemian artists—a fresher revolt would surge up to attain in its turn, after a decent interval, the steps of the academy. Through these stages passed classicism, romanticism, realism, naturalism, symbolism, impressionism, cubism, futurism. . . . Nevertheless, the union of art and the bourgeoisie remained stable, even if not happy, only so long as the bourgeoisie itself took the initiative and was capable of maintaining a regime both politically and morally "democratic." This was a question of not only giving free rein to artists and playing up to them in every possible way, but also of granting special privileges to the top layer of the working class, and of mastering and subduing the bureaucracy of the unions and workers' parties. All these phenomena exist in the same historical plane.

The decline of bourgeois society means an intolerable exacerbation of social contradictions, which are transformed inevitably into personal contradictions, calling forth an ever more burning need for a liberating art. Furthermore, a declining capitalism already finds itself completely incapable of offering the minimum conditions for the development of tendencies in art which correspond, however little, to our epoch. It fears superstitiously every new word, for it is no longer a matter of corrections and reforms for capitalism but of life and death. The oppressed masses live their own life. Bohemianism offers too limited a social base. Hence new tendencies take on a more and more violent character, alternating between hope and despair. The artistic schools of the last few decades—cubism, futurism, dadaism, surrealism—follow each other without reaching a complete development. Art, which is the most complex part of culture, the most sensitive and at the same time the least protected, suffers most from the decline and decay of bourgeois society.

To find a solution to this impasse through art itself is impossible. It is a crisis which concerns all culture, beginning at its economic base and ending in the highest spheres of ideology. Art can neither escape the crisis nor partition itself off. Art cannot save itself. It will rot away inevitably — as Grecian art rotted beneath the ruins of a culture founded on slavery — unless present-day society is able to rebuild itself. This task is essentially revolutionary in character. For these reasons the function of art in our epoch is determined by its relation to the revolution.

But precisely in this path, history has set a formidable snare for the artist. A whole generation of "leftist" intelligentsia has turned its eyes for the last ten or fifteen years to the East and has bound its lot, in varying degrees, to a victorious revolution, if not to a revolutionary proletariat. Now, this is by no means one and the same thing. In the victorious revolution there is not only the revolution, but there is also the new privileged stratum which raises itself on the shoulders of the revolution. In reality, the "leftist" intelligentsia has tried to change masters. What has it gained?

The October Revolution gave a magnificent impetus to all types of Soviet art. The bureaucratic reaction, on the contrary, has stifled artistic creation with a totalitarian hand. Nothing surprising here! Art is basically a function of the nerves and demands complete sincerity. Even the art of the court of absolute monarchies was based on idealization but not on falsification. The official art of the Soviet Union — and there is no other over there — resembles totalitarian justice, that is to say, it is based on lies and deceit. The goal of justice, as of art, is to exalt the "leader," to fabricate a heroic myth. Human history has never seen anything to equal this in scope and impudence. A few examples will not be superfluous.

The well-known Soviet writer Vsevolod Ivanov recently broke his silence to proclaim eagerly his solidarity with the justice of Vyshinsky.[1] The general extermination of the Old Bolsheviks, "those putrid emanations of capitalism," stimulates in the artists a "creative hatred" in Ivanov's words. Romantic, cautious by nature, lyrical, none too outspoken, Ivanov recalls Gorky, in many ways, but in miniature. Not a prostitute by nature, he preferred to remain quiet as long as possible but the time came when silence meant civil and perhaps physical annihilation. It is not a "creative hatred" that guides the pen of these writers but paralyzing fear.

Alexei Tolstoy, who has finally permitted the courtesan to master the artist, has written a novel expressly to glorify the military exploits of Stalin and Voroshilov at Tsaritsin.[2] In reality, as impartial documents bear witness, the army of Tsaritsin—one of the two dozen armies of the revolution—played a rather sorry role. The two "heroes" were relieved of their posts.[3] If the honest and simple Chapayev, one of the real heroes of the civil war is glorified in a Soviet film, it is only because he did not live until the "epoch of Stalin," who would have shot him as a fascist agent. The same Alexei Tolstoy is now writing a drama on the theme of the year 1919: *The Campaign of the Fourteen Powers*. The principal heroes of this piece, according to the words of the author, are Lenin, Stalin and Voroshilov. "Their images [of Stalin and Voroshilov!], haloed in glory and heroism, will pervade the whole drama." Thus, a talented writer, who bears the name of the greatest and most truthful Russian realist, has become a manufacturer of "myths" to order!

Very recently, the twenty-seventh of April of this year, the official government paper *Izvestia*, printed a reproduction of a new painting representing Stalin as the organizer of the Tiflis strike in March 1902. However, it appears from documents long known to the public that Stalin was in prison at that time and besides not in Tiflis but in Batum. This time the lie was too glaring! *Izvestia* was forced to excuse itself the next day for its deplorable blunder. No one knows what happened to the unfortunate picture, which was paid for from state funds.

Dozens, hundreds, thousands of books, films, canvases, sculptures immortalize and glorify such historic "episodes." Thus the numerous pictures devoted to the October Revolution do not fail to represent a revolutionary "center," with Stalin at its head, which never existed. It is necessary to say a few words concerning the gradual preparation of

this falsification. Leonid Serebriakov, shot after the Piata-
kov-Radek trial, drew my attention in 1924 to the publication in *Pravda,* without explanation, of extracts from the
minutes of the Central Committee of the latter part of
1917. An old secretary of the Central Committee, Serebriakov had numerous contacts behind the scenes with the
party apparatus, and he knew enough the object of this
unexpected publication: it was the first step, still a cautious one, towards the principal Stalinist myth, which now
occupies so great a place in Soviet art.

From a historical distance the October insurrection seems
much more planned and monolithic than what it proved
to be in reality. In fact, there were lacking neither vacilla-
tions, search for solutions, nor impulsive beginnings which
led nowhere. Thus, at the meeting of the Central Committee on the sixteenth of October, improvised in one night,
in the absence of the most active leaders of the Petrograd
Soviets, it was decided to round out the general staff of
the insurrection with an auxiliary "center" created by the
party and composed of Sverdlov, Stalin, Bubnov, Uritsky
and Dzerzhinsky. At the very same time at the meeting
of the Petrograd Soviet, a Revolutionary Military Committee was formed which from the moment of its appearance did so much work towards the preparation of the
insurrection that the "center," appointed the night before,
was forgotten by everybody, even by its own members.

There were more than a few of such improvisations in
the whirlwind of this period. [4] Stalin never belonged to the
Military Revolutionary Committee, did not appear at Smol-
ny, staff headquarters of the revolution, had nothing to
do with the practical preparation of the insurrection, but
was to be found editing *Pravda* and writing drab articles,
which were very little read. During the following years
nobody once mentioned the "practical center." In memoirs
of participants in the insurrection — and there is no short-
age of these — the name Stalin is not once mentioned. Stalin himself, in an article on the anniversary of the October insurrection, in *Pravda* of November 7, 1918, describing all the groups and individuals who took part
in the insurrection, does not say a word about the "practical center." Nevertheless, the old minutes, discovered

by chance in 1924 and falsely interpreted, have served as a base for the bureaucratic legend. In every compilation, bibliographical guide, even in recently edited school books, the revolutionary "center" has a prominent place with Stalin at its head. Furthermore, no one has tried, not even out of a sense of decency, to explain where and how this "center" established its headquarters, to whom it gave orders and what they were, and whether minutes were taken and where they are. We have here all the features of the Moscow trials.

With the docility which distinguishes it, Soviet art so-called has made this bureaucratic myth into one of its favorite subjects for artistic creation. Sverdlov, Dzerzhinsky, Uritsky and Bubnov are represented in oils or in tempera, seated or standing around Stalin and following his words with rapt attention. The building where the "center" has headquarters is intentionally depicted in a vague fashion, in order to avoid the embarrassing question of the address. What can one hope for or demand of artists who are forced to follow with their brushes the crude lines of what they themselves realize is a historical falsification?

The style of present-day official Soviet painting is called "socialist realism." The name itself has evidently been invented by some high functionary in the department of the arts. This "realism" consists in the imitation of provincial daguerreotypes of the third quarter of the last century; the "socialist" character apparently consists in representing, in the manner of pretentious photography, events which never took place. It is impossible to read Soviet verse and prose without physical disgust, mixed with horror, or to look at reproductions of paintings and sculpture in which functionaries armed with pens, brushes, and scissors, under the supervision of functionaries armed with Mausers, glorify the "great" and "brilliant" leaders, actually devoid of the least spark of genius or greatness. The art of the Stalinist period will remain as the frankest expression of the profound decline of the proletarian revolution.

This state of things is not confined, however, within the frontiers of the USSR. Under the guise of a belated recognition of the October Revolution, the "left" wing of the Western intelligentsia has fallen on its knees before the Soviet bureaucracy. As a rule, those artists with some character and talent have kept aloof. But the appearance in the first ranks of the failures, careerists and nobodies is all the more unfortunate. A rash of centers and committees of all sorts has broken out, of secretaries of both sexes, inevitable letters from Romain Rolland,[5] subsidized editions, banquets and congresses, in which it is difficult to trace the line of demarcation between art and the GPU. Despite this vast spread of activity, this militarized movement has not produced one single work that was able to outlive its author or its inspirers of the Kremlin.

In the field of painting, the October Revolution has found her greatest interpreter not in the USSR but in faraway Mexico, not among the official "friends," but in the person of a so-called enemy of the people whom the Fourth International is proud to number in its ranks. Nurtured in the artistic cultures of all peoples, all epochs, Diego Rivera has remained Mexican in the most profound fibres of his genius.[6] But that which inspired him in these magnificent frescoes, which lifted him up above the artistic tradition, above contemporary art in a certain sense, above himself, is the mighty blast of the proletarian revolution. Without October, his power of creative penetration into the epic of work, oppression and insurrection would never have attained such breadth and profundity. Do you wish to see with your own eyes the hidden springs of the social revolution? Look at the frescoes of Rivera. Do you wish to know what revolutionary art is like? Look at the frescoes of Rivera.

Come a little closer and you will see clearly enough, gashes and spots made by vandals: Catholics and other reactionaries, including, of course, Stalinists. These cuts and gashes give even greater life to the frescoes. You have before you, not simply a "painting," an object of passive aesthetic contemplation, but a living part of the class struggle. And it is at the same time a masterpiece!

Only the historical youth of a country which has not yet emerged from the stage of struggle for national independence has allowed Rivera's revolutionary brush to be used on the walls of the public buildings of Mexico. In the United States it was more difficult. Just as the monks in the Middle Ages, through ignorance, it is true, erased antique literary productions from parchments to cover them with their scholastic ravings, just so Rockefeller's lackeys, but this time maliciously, covered the frescoes of the talented Mexican with their decorative banalities.[7] This recent palimpsest will conclusively show future generations the fate of art degraded in a decaying bourgeois society.

The situation is no better, however, in the country of the October Revolution. Incredible as it seemed at first sight, there was no place for the art of Diego Rivera, either in Moscow, or in Leningrad, or in any other section of the USSR where the bureaucracy born of the revolution was erecting grandiose palaces and monuments to itself. And how could the Kremlin clique tolerate in its kingdom an artist who paints neither icons representing the "leader" nor life-size portraits of Voroshilov's horse? The closing of the Soviet doors to Rivera will brand forever with an ineffaceable shame the totalitarian dictatorship.

Will it go on much longer — this stifling, this trampling under foot and muddying of everything on which the future of humanity depends? Reliable indications say no. The shameful and pitiable collapse of the cowardly and reactionary politics of the Popular Fronts in Spain and France, on the one hand, and the judicial frame-ups of Moscow, on the other, portend the approach of a major turning point not only in the political sphere, but also in the broader sphere of revolutionary ideology. Even the unfortunate "friends" — but evidently not the intellectual and moral shallows of *The New Republic* and *Nation* — are beginning to tire of the yoke and whip.

Art, culture, politics need a new perspective. Without it humanity will not develop. But never before has the prospect been as menacing and catastrophic as now. That is the reason why panic is the dominant state of mind of the bewildered intelligentsia. Those who oppose an irresponsible skepticism to the yoke of Moscow do not weigh heavy in the balance of history. Skepticism is only another form, and not the best, of demoralization. Behind the act, so popular now, of impartially keeping aloof from the Stalinist bureaucracy as well as its revolutionary adver-

saries, is hidden nine times out of ten a wretched prostration before the difficulties and dangers of history. Nevertheless, verbal subterfuges and petty maneuvers will be
of no use. No one will be granted either pardon or respite.
In the face of the era of wars and revolutions which is
drawing near, everyone will have to give an answer: philosophers, poets, painters as well as simple mortals.

In the June issue of your magazine I found a curious
letter from an editor of a Chicago magazine, unknown
to me. Expressing (by mistake, I hope) his sympathy
for your publication, he writes: "I can see no hope however [?] from the Trotskyites or other anemic splinters
which have no mass base." These arrogant words tell
more about the author than he perhaps wanted to say.
They show above all that the laws of development of society have remained a seven times sealed book for him.
Not a single progressive idea has begun with a "mass
base," otherwise it would not have been a progressive idea.
It is only in its last stage that the idea finds its masses —
if, of course, it answers the needs of progress.

All great movements have begun as "splinters" of older
movements. In the beginning, Christianity was only a
"splinter" of Judaism; Protestantism a "splinter" of Cathol-
icism, that is to say, decayed Christianity. The group of
Marx and Engels came into existence as a "splinter" of the
Hegelian left. The Communist International germinated
during the war from the "splinters" of the Social Democratic International. If these pioneers found themselves
able to create a mass base, it was precisely because they
did not fear isolation. They knew beforehand that the
quality of their ideas would be transformed into quantity.
These "splinters" did not suffer from anemia; on the contrary, they carried within themselves the germs of the great
historical movements of tomorrow.

In very much the same way, to repeat, a progressive
movement occurs in art. When an artistic tendency has
exhausted its creative resources, creative "splinters" separate from it, which are able to look at the world with
new eyes. The more daring the pioneers show in their
ideas and actions, the more bitterly they oppose them-

selves to established authority which rests on a conservative "mass base," the more conventional souls, skeptics,
and snobs are inclined to see in the pioneers, impotent
eccentrics of "anemic splinters." But in the last analysis
it is the conventional souls, skeptics and snobs who are
wrong — and life passes them by.

The Thermidorian bureaucracy, to whom one cannot
deny either a certain animal sense of danger or a strong
instinct of self-preservation, is not at all inclined to estimate its revolutionary adversaries with such wholehearted
disdain, a disdain which is often coupled with lightness
and inconsistency. In the Moscow trials, Stalin, who is
not a venturesome player by nature, staked on the struggle against "Trotskyism" the fate of the Kremlin oligarchy
as well as his own personal destiny. How can one explain this fact? The furious international campaign against
"Trotskyism," for which a parallel in history will be difficult to find, would be absolutely inexplicable if the "splinters" were not endowed with an enormous vitality. He
who does not see this today will see it better tomorrow.

As if to complete his self-portrait with one brilliant
stroke, your Chicago correspondent vows — what bravery!
— to meet you in a future concentration camp — either
fascist or "communist." A fine program! To tremble at the
thought of a concentration camp is certainly not admi-
rable. But is it much better to foredoom oneself and one's
ideas to this grim hospitality? With the Bolshevik "amor-
alism" which is characteristic of us, we are ready to sug-
gest that gentlemen — by no means anemic — who capit-
ulate before the fight and without a fight really deserve
nothing better than the concentration camp.

It would be a different matter if your correspondent
simply said: in the sphere of literature and art we wish
no supervision on the part of "Trotskyists" any more
than from the Stalinists. This protest would be, in essence,
absolutely just. One can only retort that to aim it at those
who are termed "Trotskyists" would be to batter in an
open door. The ideological base of the conflict between
the Fourth and Third Internationals is the profound disagreement not only on the tasks of the party but in general on the entire material and spiritual life of mankind.

The real crisis of civilization is above all the crisis of revolutionary leadership. Stalinism is the greatest element of reaction in this crisis. Without a new flag and a new program it is impossible to create a *revolutionary* mass base; consequently it is impossible to rescue society from its dilemma. But a truly revolutionary party is neither able nor willing to take upon itself the task of "leading" and even less of commanding art, either before or after the conquest of power. Such a pretension could only enter the head of a bureaucracy — ignorant and impudent, intoxicated with its totalitarian power — which has become the antithesis of the proletarian revolution. Art, like science, not only does not seek orders, but by its very essence, cannot tolerate them. Artistic creation has its laws — even when it consciously serves a social movement. Truly intellectual creation is incompatible with lies, hypocrisy and the spirit of conformity. Art can become a strong ally of revolution only insofar as it remains faithful to itself. Poets, painters, sculptors and musicians will themselves find their own approach and methods, if the struggle for freedom of oppressed classes and peoples scatters the clouds of skepticism and of pessimism which cover the horizon of mankind. The first condition of this regeneration is the overthrow of the domination of the Kremlin bureaucracy.

May your magazine take its place in the victorious army of socialism and not in a concentration camp!

MANIFESTO:

TOWARDS A FREE

REVOLUTIONARY ART

This manifesto was published in the autumn 1938 Partisan Review *over the signatures of Diego Rivera and Andre Breton, the poet who was the leader of the French surrealist movement. In his* La Cle des Champs *Breton relates that this manifesto was the product of discussions with Trotsky and Rivera while he was visiting Trotsky in Mexico and asserts that Trotsky contributed most of it although he did not sign it. Indeed, the ideas expressed in it and the manner of their expression are recognizably those of the author of* Literature and Revolution, The Revolution Betrayed, *and "Art and Politics in Our Epoch."*

We can say without exaggeration that never has civilization been menaced so seriously as today. The Vandals, with instruments which were barbarous, and so comparatively ineffective, blotted out the culture of antiquity in one corner of Europe. But today we see world civilization, united in its historic destiny, reeling under the blows of reactionary forces armed with the entire arsenal of modern technology. We are by no means thinking only of the world war that draws near. Even in times of "peace" the position of art and science has become absolutely intolerable.

Completed July 25, 1938 and translated by Dwight Macdonald for *Partisan Review,* Fall 1938.

Diego Rivera finishing a painting at the New York Museum of Modern Art, 1931.

Andre Breton in his Paris apartment.

Insofar as it originates with an individual, insofar as it brings into play subjective talents to create something which brings about an objective enriching of culture, any philosophical, sociological, scientific or artistic discovery seems to be the fruit of a precious *chance*, that is to say, the manifestation, more or less spontaneous, of *necessity*. Such creations cannot be slighted, whether from the standpoint of general knowledge (which interprets the existing world), or of revolutionary knowledge (which, the better to change the world, requires an exact analysis of the laws which govern its movement). Specifically, we cannot remain indifferent to the intellectual conditions under which creative activity takes place, nor should we fail to pay all respect to those particular laws which govern intellectual creation.

In the contemporary world we must recognize the ever more widespread destruction of those conditions under which intellectual creation is possible. From this follows of necessity an increasingly manifest degradation not only of the work of art but also of the specifically "artistic" personality. The regime of Hitler, now that it has rid Germany of all those artists whose work expressed the slightest sympathy for liberty, however superficial, has reduced those who still consent to take up pen or brush to the status of domestic servants of the regime, whose task it is to glorify it on order, according to the worst possible aesthetic conventions. If reports may be believed, it is the same in the Soviet Union, where Thermidorian reaction is now reaching its climax.

It goes without saying that we do not identify ourselves with the currently fashionable catchword: "Neither fascism nor communism!" a shibboleth which suits the temperament of the philistine, conservative and frightened, clinging to the tattered remnants of the "democratic" past. True art, which is not content to play variations on ready-made models but rather insists on expressing the inner needs of man and of mankind in its time — true art is unable *not* to be revolutionary, *not* to aspire to a complete and radical reconstruction of society. This it must do, were it only to deliver intellectual creation from the chains which bind it, and to allow all mankind to raise itself to

those heights which only isolated geniuses have achieved
in the past. We recognize that only the social revolution
can sweep clean the path for a new culture. If, however,
we reject all solidarity with the bureaucracy now in control
of the Soviet Union, it is precisely because, in our eyes,
it represents, not communism, but its most treacherous and
dangerous enemy.

The totalitarian regime of the USSR, working through
the so-called cultural organizations it controls in other
countries, has spread over the entire world a deep twilight
hostile to every sort of spiritual value. A twilight of filth
and blood in which, disguised as intellectuals and artists,
those men steep themselves who have made of servility a
career, of lying for pay a custom, and of the palliation
of crime a source of pleasure. The official art of Stalinism
mirrors with a blatancy unexampled in history their efforts
to put a good face on their mercenary profession.

The repugnance which this shameful negation of principles of art inspires in the artistic world — a negation
which even slave states have never dared to carry so far
— should give rise to an active, uncompromising condemnation. The *opposition* of writers and artists is one
of the forces which can usefully contribute to the discredit-
ing and overthrow of regimes which are destroying, along
with the right of the proletarian to aspire to a better world,
every sentiment of nobility and even of human dignity.

The communist revolution is not afraid of art. It realizes
that the role of the artist in a decadent capitalist society
is determined by the conflict between the individual and
various social forms which are hostile to him. This fact
alone, insofar as he is conscious of it, makes the artist
the natural ally of revolution. The process of *sublimation*,
which here comes into play and which psychoanalysis has
analyzed, tries to restore the broken equilibrium between
the integral "ego" and the outside elements it rejects. This
restoration works to the advantage of the "ideal of self,"
which marshals against the unbearable present reality
all those powers of the interior world, of the "self,"
which are *common to all men* and which are constantly
flowering and developing. The need for emancipation felt
by the individual spirit has only to follow its natural

course to be led to mingle its stream with this primeval necessity — the need for the emancipation of man.

The conception of the writer's function which the young Marx worked out is worth recalling. "The writer," he declared, "naturally must make money in order to live and write, but he should not under any circumstances live and write in order to make money. . . . The writer by no means looks on his work as a *means*. It is *an end in itself* and so little a means in the eyes of himself and of others that if necessary he sacrifices his existence to the existence of his work. . . . *The first condition of the freedom of the press is that it is not a business activity."* It is more than ever fitting to use this statement against those who would regiment intellectual activity in the direction of ends foreign to itself, and prescribe, in the guise of so-called reasons of state, the themes of art. The free choice of these themes and the absence of all restrictions on the range of his exploitations — these are possessions which the artist has a right to claim as inalienable. In the realm of artistic creation, the imagination must escape from all constraint and must under no pretext allow itself to be placed under bonds. To those who urge us, whether for today or for tomorrow, to consent that art should submit to a discipline which we hold to be radically incompatible with its nature, we give a flat refusal and we repeat our deliberate intention of standing by the formula *complete freedom for art.*

We recognize, of course, that the revolutionary state has the right to defend itself against the counterattack of the bourgeoisie, even when this drapes itself in the flag of science or art. But there is an abyss between these enforced and temporary measures of revolutionary self-defense and the pretension to lay commands on intellectual creation. If, for the better development of the forces of material production, the revolution must build a *socialist* regime with centralized control, to develop intellectual creation an *anarchist* regime of individual liberty should from the first be established. No authority, no dictation, not the least trace of orders from above! Only on a base of friendly cooperation, without constraint from outside, will it be possible for scholars and artists to carry out

their tasks, which will be more far-reaching than ever
before in history.

It should be clear by now that in defending freedom
of thought we have no intention of justifying political
indifference, and that it is far from our wish to revive
a so-called pure art which generally serves the extremely
impure ends of reaction. No, our conception of the role
of art is too high to refuse it an influence on the fate of
society. We believe that the supreme task of art in our
epoch is to take part actively and consciously in the preparation of the revolution. But the artist cannot serve the
struggle for freedom unless he subjectively assimilates its
social content, unless he feels in his very nerves its meaning and drama and freely seeks to give his own inner
world incarnation in his art.

In the present period of the death agony of capitalism,
democratic as well as fascist, the artist sees himself threatened with the loss of his right to live and continue working. He sees all avenues of communication choked with
the debris of capitalist collapse. Only naturally, he turns
to the Stalinist organizations which hold out the possibility
of escaping from his isolation. But if he is to avoid complete demoralization, he cannot remain there, because of
the impossibility of delivering his own message and the
degrading servility which these organizations exact from
him in exchange for certain material advantages. He
must understand that his place is elsewhere, not among
those who betray the cause of the revolution and mankind,
but among those who with unshaken fidelity bear witness
to the revolution, among those who, for this reason, are
alone able to bring it to fruition, and along with it the
ultimate free expression of all forms of human genius.

The aim of this appeal is to find a common ground
on which may be reunited all revolutionary writers and
artists, the better to serve the revolution by their art and
to defend the liberty of that art itself against the usurpers
of the revolution. We believe that aesthetic, philosophical
and political tendencies of the most varied sort can find
here a common ground. Marxists can march here hand
in hand with anarchists, provided both parties uncompro-
misingly reject the reactionary police patrol spirit repre-

sented by Joseph Stalin and by his henchman Garcia Oliver.[1]

We know very well that thousands on thousands of isolated thinkers and artists are today scattered throughout the world, their voices drowned out by the loud choruses of well-disciplined liars. Hundreds of small local magazines are trying to gather youthful forces about them, seeking new paths and not subsidies. Every progressive tendency in art is destroyed by fascism as "degenerate." Every free creation is called "fascist" by the Stalinists. Independent revolutionary art must now gather its forces for the struggle against reactionary persecution. It must proclaim aloud the right to exist. Such a union of forces is the aim of the *International Federation of Independent Revolutionary Art* which we believe it is now necessary to form.

We by no means insist on every idea put forth in this manifesto, which we ourselves consider only a first step in the new direction. We urge every friend and defender of art, who cannot but realize the necessity for this appeal, to make himself heard at once. We address the same appeal to all those publications of the left wing which are ready to participate in the creation of the International Federation and to consider its task and its methods of action.

When a preliminary international contact has been established through the press and by correspondence, we will proceed to the organization of local and national congresses on a modest scale. The final step will be the assembly of a world congress which will officially mark the foundation of the International Federation.

Our aims:

The independence of art — for the revolution.

The revolution — for the complete liberation of art!

THE INDEPENDENCE
OF THE ARTIST:
A LETTER TO ANDRE BRETON

Like Louis Aragon and other French surrealist leaders, Breton joined the Communist Party in the 1920s. He always insisted on the need of artists to be free of political controls, and in 1935 he broke with the party while remaining a Marxist. His former associate, Louis Aragon, having become one of the leaders of the party, continued to follow the Stalinist line through thick and thin.

The International Federation of Independent Revolutionary Art, which Trotsky regarded with such hope, was unsuccessful in rallying independent revolutionary artists on a world scale, for the coming of the war, foreseen in the manifesto proclaiming the federation, drowned out its call. Following the war, the temporary stabilization of the Western capitalist countries caused the ardor of their writers for the Stalinist bureaucracy to cool.

My Dear Breton:

With all my heart I congratulate Diego Rivera and yourself on the creation of the FIARI — an international federation of truly revolutionary and truly independent artists. And why not add — of *true* artists? It is time, it is high time! The entire globe is becoming a dirty and reeking imperialist barracks. The heroes of democracy,

Written December 22, 1938 and published in *Bulletin of the Opposition*, number 74, February 1939 and *Partisan Review*, Winter 1939.

with the inimitable Daladier at their head, make every effort to ape the heroes of fascism (which will not prevent them from landing in a fascist concentration camp). [1] The duller and more ignorant the dictator, the more he feels called upon to prescribe the development of science, philosophy and art. The sheep-like servility of the intelligentsia is, in turn, a not unimportant sign of the rottenness of contemporary society. France is no exception.

Why speak of the Aragons, the Ehrenburgs [2] and other *petites canailles?* Why name those gentlemen (death has not absolved them) who compose, with equal enthusiasm, biographies of Christ and Stalin. [3] Let us also pass over the pitiful, not to say ignoble, decline of Romain Rolland. . . . But one feels too strongly to ignore the case of Malraux. I followed his first literary steps with much interest. At that time there was already a strong element of pose and affectation in him. His pretentiously cold studies of heroism in other lands often made one uneasy. But it was impossible to deny him talent. With undeniable power he aimed at the very peak of human emotion—of heroic struggle, self-sacrifice, extreme anguish. One might expect —and I, for one, earnestly hoped—that the sense of revolutionary heroism would enter more profoundly into his being, would purify him of pose and make him the major poet of an epoch of disasters. But what in fact happened? The artist became a reporter for the GPU, a purveyor of bureaucratic heroism in prudently proportioned slices, just so long and so wide. (They have no third dimension.)

During the civil war I was obliged to fight stubbornly against the vague or lying military reports submitted by officers who tried to hide their errors, failures and defeats in a torrent of generalities. The present productions of Malraux are just such lying reports from the fields of battle (Germany, Spain, etc.). However, the lie is more repugnant dressed up in artistic form. The fate of Malraux is symbolic for a whole stratum of writers, almost for a whole generation. It is the generation of those who lie from pretended "friendship" for the October Revolution.

The unhappy Soviet press, evidently on orders from above, complains bitterly in these latter days of the "impoverishment" of scientific and artistic production in the

USSR and reproaches Soviet artists and writers with lack
of sincerity, courage and vitality. One can't believe one's
eyes: the boa constrictor delivers to the rabbit a homily
on independence and personal dignity. Hideous and ignoble picture, but how worthy of our time!

The struggle for revolutionary ideas in art must begin
once again with the struggle for artistic *truth*, not in terms
of any single school, but in terms of *the immutable faith
of the artist in his own inner self.* Without this there is
no art. "You shall not lie!"—that is the formula of salvation.

Properly understood, the FIARI is not an aesthetic or
political school and cannot become one. But FIARI can
oxidize the atmosphere in which artists breathe and create.
In our epoch of convulsive reaction, of cultural decline
and return to savagery, truly independent creation cannot
but be revolutionary by its very nature, for it cannot but
seek an outlet from intolerable social suffocation. But art
as a whole, and each artist in particular, seeks this outlet
in ways proper to himself—not relying upon orders from
outside, but rejecting such orders and heaping scorn upon
all who submit to them. To encourage such attitudes
among the best circles of artists—this is the task of the
FIARI. I firmly believe that its name will enter history.

PART II
Essays in Literary Criticism

TOLSTOY:

POET AND REBEL

*"Tolstoy: Poet and Rebel" is an appreciation written on
the eightieth birthday of the great Russian artist, two years
before his death. Trotsky was then living in Vienna, in
his second exile, after having been sentenced to deporta-
tion for life for his role as leader of the Petrograd Soviet
during the Russian Revolution of 1905. The essay was
originally written in German and printed in* Neue Zeit,
the journal edited by Karl Kautsky.

I

Tolstoy has passed his eightieth birthday and now stands
before us like an enormous jagged cliff, moss-covered and
from a different historical world.

A remarkable thing! Not alone Karl Marx but, to cite
a name from a field closer to Tolstoy's, Heinrich Heine
as well appear to be contemporaries of ours. But from
our great contemporary of Yasnaya Polyana we are already separated by the irreversible flow of time which
differentiates all things.

This man was thirty-three years old when serfdom was
abolished in Russia. As the descendant of "ten generations

Published in *Neue Zeit*, September 15, 1908 and in Russian in 1926.
The first American translation by John G. Wright appeared in *Fourth
International* (New York) May-June 1951.

untouched by labor," he matured and was shaped in an atmosphere of the old nobility, among inherited acres, in a spacious manorial home and in the shade of linden-tree alleys, so tranquil and patrician.

The traditions of landlord rule, its romanticism, its poetry, its whole style of living were irresistibly imbibed by Tolstoy and became an organic part of his spiritual makeup. From the first years of his consciousness he was, as he remains to this very day, an *aristocrat* in the deepest and most secret recesses of his creativeness; and this, despite all his subsequent spiritual crises.

In the ancestral home of the Princes Volkonsky, inherited by the Tolstoy family, the author of *War and Peace* occupies a simple, plainly furnished room in which there hangs a handsaw, stands a scythe and lies an ax. But on the upper floor of this same dwelling, like stony guardians of its traditions, the illustrious ancestors of a whole number of generations keep watch from the walls. In this there is a symbol. We find both of these floors also in the heart of the master of the house, only inverted in order. If on the summits of consciousness a nest has been spun for itself by the philosophy of the simple life and of self-submergence in the people, then from below, whence well up the emotions, the passions and the will, there look down upon us a long gallery of ancestors.

In the wrath of repentance Tolstoy renounced the false and worldly-vain art of the ruling classes which glorifies their artificially cultivated tastes and envelops their caste prejudices in the flattery of false beauty. But what happened? In his latest major work *Resurrection*, Tolstoy still places in the center of his artistic attention the one and the same wealthy and wellborn Russian landlord, surrounding him just as solicitously with the golden cobweb of aristocratic connections, habits and remembrances as if outside this "worldly-vain" and "false" universe there were nothing of importance or of beauty.

From the landlord's manor there runs a short and narrow path straight to the hut of the peasant. Tolstoy, the poet, was accustomed to make this passage often and lovingly even before Tolstoy, the moralist, turned it into a road of salvation. Even after the abolition of serfdom, he continues to regard the peasant as "his"—an inalienable part of his material and spiritual inventory. From behind Tolstoy's unquestionable "physical love for the genuine toiling people" about which he himself tells us, there looks down upon us just as unquestionably his collective aristocratic ancestor—only illumined by an artist's genius.

Landlord and moujik—these are in the last analysis the only people whom Tolstoy has wholly accepted into his creative sanctuary. But neither before nor after his spiritual crisis was he ever able to or did he strive to free himself from the purely patrician contempt for all those figures who stand between the landlord and the peasant, or those who occupy positions beyond the sacred poles of this ancient order—the German superintendent, the merchant, the French tutor, the physician, the "intellectual" and, finally, the factory worker with his watch and chain. Tolstoy never feels a need to understand these types, to peer into their souls, or question them about their faith. And they pass before his artist's eye like so many insignificant and largely comical silhouettes. When he does create images of revolutionists of the seventies or eighties, as for example in *Resurrection*, he simply adapts his old landlord and peasant types to a new milieu or offers us purely external and humorously painted sketches.

At the beginning of the sixties when a flood of new European ideas and, what is more important, of new *social relations* swept over Russia, Tolstoy, as I said, had already left a third of a century behind him: psychologically he was already molded.

Needless to recall, Tolstoy did not become an apologist for serfdom as did his intimate friend Fet (Shenshin), landlord and subtle lyric poet, in whose heart a tender receptivity to nature and to love was coupled with adoring prostration before the salutary whiplash of feudalism. But imbued in Tolstoy was a deep hatred for the new social relations, coming in the place of the old. "Personally I fail to see any amelioration of morals," he wrote in 1861, "nor do I propose to take anyone's word for it. I do not find, for instance, that the relation between the factory owner and the worker is more humane than that between the landlord and the serf."

Everywhere and in everything there came hurly-burly and turmoil, there came the decomposition of the old nobility, the disintegration of the peasantry, universal chaos, the rubbish and litter of demolition, the hum and ding-dong of city life, the tavern and cigarette in the village, the factory limerick in place of the folksong — and all this repelled Tolstoy, both as an aristocrat and as an artist. Psychologically he turned his back on this titanic process and forever refused it artistic recognition. He felt no inner urge to defend feudal slavery, but he did remain wholeheartedly on the side of those ties in which he saw wise simplicity and which he was able to unfold into artistically perfected forms.

His whole heart was fixed there where life is reproduced changelessly from one generation to the next, century after century. There where sacred necessity rules over everything; where every single step hinges on the sun, the rain, the wind and the green grass growing. Where nothing comes from one's own reason or from an individual's rebellious volition and, therefore, no personal responsibility exists, either. Everything is predetermined, everything justified in advance, sanctified. Responsible for nothing, thinking nothing, man lives only by *hearing and obeying,* says Uspensky, the remarkable poet of "The Dominion of the Land." And this perpetual hearing and obeying, converted into perpetual toil, is precisely what shapes the *life* which outwardly leads to no results whatever but which has its result in its very self . . . And lo, a miracle! This convict-labor dependence — without reflection or choice, without errors or pangs of repentance — is what gives rise to the great moral *"ease"* of existence under the harsh guardianship of "the ears of rye." Mikula Selyanovich, peasant hero of the folk epic, says of himself: "I am the *beloved* of raw mother earth."

Such is the religious myth of Russian populism which ruled for decades over the minds of the Russian intellectuals. Stone deaf to its radical tendencies, Tolstoy always remained personally, and represented in the populist movement, its aristocratic conservative wing.

Tolstoy was repelled by the new and in order to create artistically Russian life as he knew, understood and loved it, he was compelled to withdraw into the past, back to the very beginnings of the nineteenth century. *War and Peace* (written in 1867-69) is his best and unsurpassed work.

The anonymous massiveness of life and its sacred irresponsibility were incarnated by Tolstoy in his character Karatayev, a type least comprehensible to a European reader; at all events, furthest removed from him.

"Karatayev's life, as he himself saw it, had no meaning as an individual life. It had meaning only as a small particle of the great whole, which Karatayev constantly felt. Of attachments, of friendship, and love as Pierre understood them, Karatayev had none. He loved and lovingly lived with everything that life brought him into contact with, and particularly with human beings. . . . Pierre felt that Karatayev, despite all his affectionate tenderness toward him, would not grieve for a moment over their parting."

It is that stage when the spirit, as Hegel put it, has not yet attained inner self-consciousness and therefore manifests itself only as spirit indwelling in nature. Despite his rather rare appearances, Karatayev is the philosophical, if not the artistic, axis of *War and Peace;* and Kutuzov whom Tolstoy turns into a national hero is this very same Karatayev, only in the post of commander-in-chief.

In contrast to Napoleon, Kutuzov has no personal plans, no personal ambition. In his semiconscious tactics, he is not guided by reason but by that which rises above reason—by a dim instinct for physical conditions and by the promptings of the people's spirit. Czar Alexander, in his more lucid moments, as well as the least of Kutuzov's soldiers all stand equally under the dominion of the land. . . . In this moral unity is the pathos of Tolstoy's book.

How miserable, in reality, is this Old Russia with its nobility disinherited by history, without any elegant past of hierarchical estates, without the Crusades, without knightly love or tournaments of knighthood, without even romantic highway robberies. How poverty-stricken so far as inner beauty is concerned; what a ruthless plunder

of the peasant masses amid the general semi-animal existence!

But what a miracle of reincarnation is a genius capable
of! From the raw material of this drab and colorless
life he extracts its secret multicolored beauty. With Homeric
calm and with Homer's love of children, he endows everything and everybody with his attention. Kutuzov, the
manorial household servants, the cavalry horse, the adoles-
cent countess, the moujik, the czar, a louse on a soldier,
the freemason — he gives preference to none among them,
deprives none of his due share. Step by step, stroke by
stroke, he creates a limitless panorama whose parts are
all inseparably bound together by an internal bond. In
his work Tolstoy is as unhurried as the life he pictures.
It is a terrifying thing to say, but he rewrote his colossal
book *seven times*. . . . Perhaps what is most astounding
in this titan creativeness is that the artist permits neither
himself nor the reader to become attached to any individual character.

He never puts his heroes on display, as does Turgenev
whom Tolstoy disliked, amid bursts of firecrackers and
the glare of magnesium flares. He does not seek out sit-
uations for them that would set them off to advantage;
he hides nothing, suppresses nothing. The restless seeker
of truth, Pierre Bezukhov, he shows us at the end as a
smug head of a family and a happy landlord; Natasha
Rostov, so touching in her semichildlike sensitiveness, he
turns, with godlike mercilessness, into a shallow breeding
female, untidy diapers in hand. But from behind this
seemingly indifferent attentiveness to individual parts there
rises a mighty apotheosis of the whole, where everything
breathes the spirit of inner necessity and harmony. It
might perhaps be correct to say that this creative effort
is permeated with *aesthetic pantheism* for which there
is neither beauty nor ugliness, neither the great nor the
small, because it holds as the great and beautiful only
the whole of life itself, in the perpetual circuit of its manifestations. This is an *agricultural aesthetic,* mercilessly
conservative by nature. And it is this that lends to the
epics of Tolstoy kinship with the Pentateuch and the Iliad.

Tolstoy's two recent attempts to find some room for

psychologic images and "beautiful types" to which he feels closest affinity within the framework of a more recent historical past—in the days of Peter the First and of the Decembrists of 1825—have been shattered against the artist's hostility to foreign influences which color both of these periods so sharply. But even where Tolstoy approaches most closely to our own times as in *Anna Karenina* (1873), he remains inwardly alien to the reigning hurly-burly and inflexibly stubborn in his artistic conservatism, scaling down the sweep of his own horizons and singling out of the whole of Russian life only the surviving oases of gentility, with the old ancestral home, ancestral portraits and luxurious linden alleys in whose shade, from one generation to the next, the cycle of birth, love and death, changeless in its forms, is repeated.

And Tolstoy delineates the spiritual life of his heroes in accord with the day-to-day life of their motherland: calmly, without haste and with vision unclouded. He never runs ahead of the inner play of emotions, thoughts or the dialogue. He is in no hurry to go anywhere nor is he ever late. His hands hold the strands tying together a host of lives, but he never loses his head. Like the master of an enormous enterprise who keeps an ever-wakeful eye on all its many parts, he mentally keeps an errorless balance sheet. All he does, seemingly, is to keep watch while nature itself carries out all the work. He casts a seed upon the soil and like a good husbandman calmly permits it to put out its stalk naturally, and grow full of ears. Why, this is the genial Karatayev with his silent worship of the laws of nature!

He will never seek to touch a bud in order forcibly to unfold its petals, but permits them silently to open in the warmth of the sun. He is both alien and deeply hostile to the aesthetic of the big-city culture which, in its self-devouring voracity, violates and torments nature, demanding from it only extracts and essences; and which with convulsively clutching fingers searches on the palette for colors nonexistent in a sunray's spectrum.

Tolstoy's style is identical with all of his genius: calm, unhurried, frugal, without being miserly or ascetic; it is muscular, on occasion awkward, and rough. It is so simple and always incomparable in its results. (He is just as far removed from Turgenev who is lyrical, flirtatious, scintillating and aware of the beauty of his style as he is from Dostoyevsky's language, so sharp, so choked-up and so uneven.)

In one of his novels Dostoyevsky — the city dweller without rank or title and the genius with an incurably pincered soul — this voluptuous poet of cruelty and commiseration, counterposes himself profoundly and pointedly, as the artist of the new and "accidental Russian families," to Count Tolstoy, the singer of the perfected forms of the landlord past.

"If I were a Russian novelist and a talented one," says Dostoyevsky, speaking through the lips of one of his characters, "I would unfailingly take my heroes from the well-born Russian nobility, because this is the only type of Russian capable of at least a semblance of beautiful order and beautiful sensations. . . . Saying this, I am not at all joking, although I am not at all a noble myself, which besides, you yourself know. . . . Believe me, it is here that we have everything truly beautiful among us up till now. At any rate, here is everything among us that is in the least perfected. I do not say it because I unreservedly agree with either the correctness or the truth of this beauty; but here, for example, we have already perfected forms of honor and duty which apart from the nobility are not to be found anywhere in Russia let alone perfected but even started. . . . The position of our novelist," continues Dostoyevsky without naming Tolstoy but unquestionably having him in mind, "in such a case would be quite definitive. He would not be able to write in any other way except historically, for the beautiful type no longer exists in our own day, and if there are remnants abroad, then, according to the prevailing consensus of opinion, they have not retained any beauties for themselves."

When the "beautiful type" disappeared, there came tumbling down not only the immediate object of artistic creativeness but also the foundations of Tolstoyan moral fatalism and his aesthetic pantheism. The sanctified Karatayevism of the Tolstoyan soul was perishing. Everything that had been previously taken for granted as part of an unchallenged whole now became chipped into a sliver and by this token into a problem. What was rational had become the irrational. And, as always happens, precisely at the moment when being had lost its *old* meaning, Tolstoy started asking himself about the meaning of being in general. In the life not of a youth but of a man fifty years of age there ensued a great spiritual crisis (toward the latter part of the seventies). Tolstoy returns to God, accepts the teachings of Christ, rejects division of labor and, along with it, culture and the state; he becomes the preacher of agricultural labor, of the simple life and of nonresistance to evil by force.

The deeper was the internal crisis — and by his own admission the fifty-year-old artist for a long time contemplated suicide — all the more surprising must it seem that Tolstoy returned, as the end result, to what is essentially his starting point. *Agricultural labor* — isn't this, after all, the basis on which the epopee of *War and Peace* unfolds? *The simple life,* self-submergence in the elementary people — isn't that where Kutuzov's strength lies? *Nonresistance to evil by force* — isn't the whole of Karatayev contained in fatalistic resignation?

But if that is so, then of what does the *crisis* of Tolstoy consist? Of this, that what had previously been secret and subterranean breaks through the crust and passes over into the sphere of consciousness. Inasmuch as the spirituality indwelling in nature disappeared along with that "nature" which incarnated it, the spirit begins striving toward inner self-consciousness. That automatic harmony against which the automatism of life itself had risen must henceforth be preserved by the conscious power of the idea. In this conservative struggle for moral and aesthetic self-preservation, the artist summons to his aid the philosopher-moralist.

II

It would not be easy to determine which of these two Tolstoys — the poet or the moralist — has won greater popularity in Europe. In any case, it is unquestionable that behind the condescending smirk of the bourgeois public at the genius innocence of the Yasnaya Polyana elder, there lurks a peculiar sort of moral satisfaction: a famous poet, a millionaire, one of "our own circle," and an aristocrat to boot, wears out of moral conviction a peasant shirt, walks in bast shoes, chops wood. It is as if here was a certain redemption of the sins of a whole class, of a whole culture. This does not, of course, prevent every bourgeois ninny from looking down his nose on Tolstoy and even lightly casting doubts about his complete sanity. A case in point is the not unknown Max Nordau, one of the brotherhood who take the philosophy of old and honest Samuel Smiles, spiced with cynicism, and dress it up in a clown's costume for columns on Sunday. With his reference text from Lombroso in hand, Nordau discovers in Tolstoy all the symptoms of degeneration.[1] For all these petty shopkeepers, insanity begins at the point where profit ceases.

But whether his bourgeois devotees regard Tolstoy suspiciously, ironically or with favor, he remains for all of them a psychological enigma. Aside from a couple of his worthless disciples and propagandists — one of them, Menshikov, is now playing the role of a Russian Hammerstein — one would have to say that for the last thirty years of his life, Tolstoy, the moralist, has stood completely alone.[2]

Truly his was the tragic position of a prophet crying in the wilderness. Completely under the dominion of his conservative agricultural sympathies, Tolstoy has unceasingly, tirelessly and triumphantly defended his spiritual world against the dangers threatening it from all sides. He has dug, once and for all, a deep moat between himself and every variety of bourgeois liberalism, and, in the first instance, has cast aside "the superstition of progress universally prevalent in our times."

"It's all very well," he cries, "to have electricity, telephones, exhibitions and all the gardens of Arcadia with their concerts and performances, along with all the cigars and match boxes, suspenders and motors; but I wish them all at the bottom of the sea. And not only them but also the railroads and all the manufactured cotton and wool cloth in the world. Because to produce them ninety-nine out of every hundred people must be in slavery and perish by the thousands in factories where these items are manufactured."

Aren't our lives adorned and enriched by division of labor? But division of labor maims the living human soul. Let division of labor rot! Art? But *genuine* art must unite all the people in the idea of God and not disunite them. Our art serves only the elite, it sunders people apart and therefore it is a lie. Tolstoy courageously rejects as "false" the art of — Shakespeare, Goethe, himself, Wagner, Boecklin. [3]

He divests himself of all material cares connected with business and enrichment and dons peasant clothing as if performing a symbolic rite, renouncing culture. But what lurks behind this symbolic act? What does it oppose to the "lie," that is, to the historic process.

After doing some violence to himself, Tolstoy's social philosophy may be summed up, on the basis of his writings, in the following "programmatic theses":

1. It is not some kind of iron sociologic laws that produce the enslavement of peoples, but legal codes.

2. Modern slavery rests on three statutes: those on land, taxes and property.

3. Not alone the Russian state but every state is an institution for committing, by violence and with impunity the most horrible crimes.

4. *Genuine social progress is attained only through the religious and moral self-perfection of individuals.*

5. "To get rid of states it is not necessary to fight against them with external means. All that is needed is not to take part in them and not to support them." That is to say: (a) not to assume the calling of either *soldier* or *field marshal,* either *minister* or *village head,* either *juryman* or *member of parliament;* (b) not to pay taxes, direct or indirect, to the state voluntarily; (c) not to utilize state institutions nor government funds whether for *salaries* or *pensions;* and (d) not to safeguard one's property by measures of state violence.

If from this schema we were to remove the fourth point — which clearly stands by itself and which concerns religious and moral self-perfection — then we would get a

rather rounded anarchist program. First, there is a purely mechanical conception of society as the product of
evil legislation. Next, a formal denial of the state and
politics generally. And finally, as the method of struggle —
a passive general strike and universal boycott. But by
removing the religious-moral thesis, we actually remove
the single nerve which connects this whole rationalistic
structure with its architect: the soul of Lev Tolstoy. For
him, owing to all the conditions of his evolution and position, the task does not at all consist in establishing
"communist" anarchy in place of the capitalist order. The
task is to safeguard the communal-agricultural order
against destructive influences "from without."

As in his populism, so, too, in his "anarchism," Tolstoy
represents conservative agricultural interests. Like the early freemasons who sought by ideological means to restore
and strengthen in society the caste-guild morality of mutual
aid which was falling apart naturally under the blows
of economic development, Tolstoy seeks to revive by dint
of a religious-moral idea the life under a purely natural
economy.

Along this road he becomes a conservative anarchist,
because what he requires, first and foremost, is that the
state with its whips of militarism and its scorpions of
the federal treasury let live in peace the all-saving Karatayev commune. Tolstoy has no inkling whatever of the
globe-encompassing struggle between the two worlds —
that of the bourgeoisie and that of socialism — on the out-
come of which hinges the destiny of mankind. In his eyes
socialism always remained a variety of liberalism, of
little interest to him. In his eyes Karl Marx as well as
Frederic Bastiat were representatives of one and the
same "false principle" of capitalist culture, of landless workers, of state coercion. [4] In general, once mankind has ven-
tured onto a false road, it really matters little how near
or how far this road has been traveled. Salvation can
come only by turning back.

Tolstoy is at a loss for words contemptuous enough to
hurl against that science which maintains that while we
shall continue for a very long time to live badly "in accordance with the historic, sociologic and other laws of

progress," our life shall nevertheless "become very good by itself ultimately."

It is necessary to put an end to evil right now; and for this it is enough to understand that evil is evil. All the moral feelings which have historically held the people together and all the moral-religious fictions arising from these ties are reduced by Tolstoy to the most abstract commandments of love, of temperance and of passive resistance. And since these commandments lack any historical content, and are therefore without any content whatever, they seem to him to be applicable at all times and to all peoples.

To history Tolstoy grants no recognition; and this provides the basis for all his thinking. Upon this rests the freedom of his metaphysical negations as well as the practical impotence of all his preachings. The human life which he accepts — the former life of Ural-Cossack farmers in the sparsely populated steppes of Samara province — took place *outside* of history; it constantly reproduced itself like the life of a beehive or ant heap. What people call history is the product of senselessness, delusions and cruelties which deformed the true soul of humanity. Fearlessly consistent, Tolstoy throws property out of the window, along with history.

Newspapers and magazines are abhorrent to him as documents of current history. With his breast he would beat back all the waves of the global ocean. His historical blindness renders him childishly helpless when it comes to the world of social problems. Tolstoy's philosophy resembles Chinese painting. Ideas of entirely different epochs are not located in perspective but arranged on one and the same plane. Against war he launches arguments of pure logic and to reinforce them adduces the opinions of Epictetus as well as those of Molinari (nineteenth century Belgian economist of the Manchester school); of Lao Tse (Chinese philosopher of the pre-Confucian era) as well as Friedrich II; of the prophet Isaiah as well as the columnist Hardouin, oracle of the Parisian grocers. In his eyes writers, philosophers and prophets represent not their own epochs but rather eternal moral categories.

With him, Confucius strolls shoulder to shoulder with

Harpagus (a minister of the Median King Astyages, sixth century BC); and Schopenhauer finds himself keeping company not alone with Jesus but also Moses. In his tragic single-combat against the dialectic of history to which he opposes his *yes-yes* or *no-no,* Tolstoy falls at every step into hopeless self-contradictions. And from this he draws a conclusion wholly worthy of the stubbornness of this genius. "The incongruity between man's position and man's moral activity," he says, "is the *surest sign* of truth." But this idealistic pride bears within it its own punishment. It would be hard to mention another writer whom history has used so cruelly as she has Tolstoy, against his own will.

Moralist and mystic, foe of politics and revolution, he nourishes with his criticism the confused revolutionary consciousness of many populist sects.

Denier of all capitalist culture, he meets with benevolent acceptance by the European and American bourgeoisie, who find in his preachments a delineation of their own purposeless humanism along with a psychologic shield against the philosophy of the revolutionary overturn.

Conservative anarchist, mortal enemy of liberalism, Tolstoy finds himself on his eightieth birthday a banner and a vehicle for the noisy and tendentious political manifestation of Russian liberalism.

History has gained a victory over him, but failed to break him. Even now, in his declining years, he has preserved intact his priceless talent for moral indignation.

In the heat of the vilest and most criminal counterrevolution on record[5] which seeks with its hempen web of gallows to eclipse forever our country's sun; amid the stifling atmosphere of degraded and cowardly official public opinion, this last apostle of Christian all-forgiving, in whom kindles the wrath of Biblical prophets, has flung his pamphlet *I Cannot Keep Silent* as a curse upon the heads of those who serve as hangmen and a condemnation upon those who stand by in silence.

And though he refuses a sympathetic hearing to our revolutionary objectives, we know it is because history has refused him personally an understanding of her revolutionary pathways. We shall not condemn him. And we shall always value in him not alone his great genius, which shall never die so long as human art lives on, but also his unbending moral courage which did not permit him tranquilly to remain in the ranks of *their* hypocritical church, *their* society and *their* state but doomed him to remain a solitary among his countless admirers.

Leo Tolstoy and Maxim Gorky at Yasnaya Polyana in 1900.

ON TOLSTOY'S DEATH

This article was written in Vienna shortly after Tolstoy's death on November 8, 1910. In some respects this obituary piece might have been written for our own time. Martin Luther King, although he lacked the creative genius of Tolstoy and did not engage in such thoroughgoing criticism of orthodox religion and society as Tolstoy did, was a respected apostle of nonviolence whose death by assassination caused liberals to shed plentiful tears and the masses of blacks to give vent to their fury at the oppressive system which had produced King's assassin. The "student light cavalry," arrayed against the war, racism and repression, has received its "baptism of fire" at Kent State University and Jackson State University. The "heavy reserves of the proletariat" are just beginning to assemble.

For several weeks now the thoughts and feelings of literate and thinking people throughout the world have been concentrated, first, on the name and image of Tol-

First printed in *Pravda,* no. 17, November 20, 1910. This was a Russian-language journal published by Trotsky in Vienna and smuggled into Russia. Translated into English for this volume by Frank Manning and George Saunders.

stoy and, afterwards, on his grave and ashes. His de-
cision — in the face of imminent death — to break with his
family and the conditions into which he had been born
and in which he had matured and grown old; his flight
from his ancient home — to disappear among the people,
among the gray, anonymous millions; his death in the
view of the whole world — all this gave rise not only to
a powerful surge of sympathy, love, and respect for the
great old man in every unreconciled heart; it also aroused
an intangible anxiety in the ironclad consciousness of
those who are the maintainers of today's social structure.
Something is wrong, it seems, with their sacrosanct property, their state authority, their church, and their family
structure if the eighty-three-year-old Tolstoy could stand
it no longer and, in his final days, became a fugitive
from all this illustrious "culture."

More than thirty years ago, when he was already a
man of fifty, Tolstoy, in the torments of conscience, broke
with the faith and traditions of his fathers and created
his own, Tolstoyan, faith. He then propagated it in mor-
al-philosophical works, in his voluminous correspondence,
and in the literary works of his last period (e.g., *Resurrection*).

Tolstoy's teaching is not our teaching. He proclaimed
nonresistance to evil. He saw the chief motive power not
in social conditions but in the soul of man. He believed
that it was possible to eradicate evil by moral example,
to disarm despotism by arguments of love. He wrote
remonstrative letters to Alexander III and Nicholas II
— as though the root of violence lay in the conscience of
the oppressor, and not in the social conditions that give
rise to it and nurture it. Organically, the proletariat cannot accept this teaching. For with every surge toward the
ideal of moral rebirth — toward knowledge, toward the
light, toward "resurrection" — the worker feels the cast-
iron shackles of social slavery on his hands and feet,
and he cannot be delivered from these shackles by inner
striving; he must smash them and cast them off. In contrast to Tolstoy, we say and teach: the organized violence of the minority can be destroyed only through the
organized revolt and insurrection of the majority.

Tolstoy's faith is not our faith.

After he had discarded the ritualistic side of Orthodoxy
—baptism, anointing with oil, the swallowing of bread
and wine, prayerful incantations, all this crude sorcery
of churchly worship—Tolstoy stayed the knife of his criticism before the idea of God as the inspirer of love, father
of all people, and creator and master of the world. We
go further than Tolstoy. As the basis of the universe
and of life we know and acknowledge only primeval
matter, obedient to its own internal laws; in human society, as well as in the individual human being, we see
only a particle of the universe, subject to general laws.
And just as we do not want any kind of crowned sovereign over our bodies, we do not recognize any kind
of divine master over our souls.

Nevertheless—despite this profound distinction—there
is a deep moral affinity between the beliefs of Tolstoy
and the teachings of socialism: in the honesty and fear-
lessness of their renunciation of oppression and slavery
and in their indomitable striving for the brotherhood
of man.

Tolstoy did not consider himself a revolutionary and
was not one. But he passionately sought the truth and,
having found it, was not afraid to proclaim it. Truth
in and of itself possesses a terrible, explosive power: once
proclaimed, it irresistibly gives rise to revolutionary conclusions in the consciousness of the masses. Everything
that Tolstoy stated publicly: about the senselessness of
rule by the czar, about the criminality of military service,
about the dishonesty of landed property, about the lies
of the church—in thousands of ways all this seeped into
the minds of the laboring masses, agitated millions in
the populist sects. And the word became deed. Although
not a revolutionary, Tolstoy nurtured the revolutionary
element with his words of genius. In the book about the
great storm of 1905 an honorable chapter will be dedicated to Tolstoy.

Tolstoy did not consider himself a socialist and was
not one. But in the search for truth in the relations between man and man, he did not hesitate to reject the
idols of autocracy and orthodoxy—he went further and,

to the great perturbation of the propertied classes, he pronounced an anathema on those social relations which doom one man to carry off the dung of another.

Those of property, especially the liberals, slavishly flocked around him, praised him to the skies, hushed up what was said against him — tried to flatter his spirit, to drown his thought in glory. But he did not yield. And no matter how sincere are the tears that liberal society sheds on the grave of Tolstoy, we have the indisputable right to say: liberalism does not answer Tolstoy's questions; liberalism cannot absorb Tolstoy; it is helpless before him. "Culture? Progress? Industry?" says Tolstoy to the liberals. "The devil take your progress and your industry if my sisters must sell their bodies on the sidewalks of your cities!"

Tolstoy did not know or show the way out of the hell of bourgeois culture. But with irresistible force he posed the question that only scientific socialism can answer. And in this vein one might say that everything in Tolstoy's teaching that is lasting and permanent flows into socialism as naturally as a river into the ocean.

Because Tolstoy served the cause of human emancipation with his life, his death resounded throughout the country like a reminder of the revolutionary legacy — a reminder and a summons. And this summons met with an unexpectedly rousing response.

In Petersburg, Moscow, Kiev, Kharkov, and Tomsk, student funeral observances for Tolstoy took on the character of political rallies, and the rallies spilled out onto the streets as stormy demonstrations under the slogans "Down with capital punishment!" and "Down with the priests!" And as in the good old days, the doleful figures of liberal professors and deputies emerged from the gateways before the aroused student body, and they timidly waved their hands at the students and summoned them to "tranquillity." And as in the good old days, the sensible-conciliatory liberal was shoved aside; the newly revolutionary student began to disturb the peace of the Stolypin cemetery;[1] the constitutional Cossacks displayed their prowess on the heads and backs of students; and scenes in the spirit of 1901 were played out on the streets of both capitals.

But on the horizon the shape of another, incomparably more menacing figure appeared. The workers' ranks in the plants, factories, and printshops of Petersburg, Moscow, and other cities immediately sent telegrams of sympathy, initiated a "Tolstoy Fund," passed resolutions, went out on strike in memory of Tolstoy, demanded initiation by the Social-Democratic fraction in the Duma of legislation abolishing capital punishment, and even took to the streets with this slogan. In the workers' districts there was an air of tension and alarm that was not to be smoothed over quickly.

Such is the interconnection of ideas and events, which Tolstoy, evidently, did not foresee on his deathbed. Hardly had the man who had cast the unforgettable "I cannot be silent!" in the teeth of triumphant counterrevolution closed his eyes forever than revolutionary democracy awoke from slumber: the student light cavalry has already had its baptism of fire—and the heavy reserves of the proletariat, which goes into action more slowly, is getting ready, on the morrow, to dissolve the protest against capital punishment in the midst of banners with the glorious slogans of the revolution, invincible, like truth.

A DRAMA OF THE FRENCH WORKING CLASS: MARCEL MARTINET'S *LA NUIT*

"A Drama of the French Working Class" is an introduction to a play about World War I, La Nuit *by Marcel Martinet (Paris, 1922). Trotsky himself had lived in France during the war, from 1914 until he was expelled from the country in 1916 for his antiwar activity. He closely collaborated with the antiwar tendency grouped around the syndicalist journal* La Vie Ouvriere, *with which Martinet too was associated.*

The French poet Marcel Martinet has written a play which fully deserves to be called a drama of the French working class. This alone assures it the right to our attention. Martinet is a Communist who has passed through the syndicalist school of *La Vie Ouvriere*—that is to say, a good school. As an artist, Martinet studied in the worthy school of Romain Rolland; consequently one need neither expect nor fear from him purely propagandist productivity —for politics are only rarely to be found in a dramatic setting or poetic nature. Martinet is deeply psychological. All the problems of our great epoch pass through his individual consciousness and emerge fired with the light

Written May 15, 1922 as a preface to Martinet's play in *Izvestia*, May 16, 1922. It first appeared in English in *Labour Monthly*, August 1922.

of his own personality, or, more correctly, he finds his
way to the general and universal only through the medium
of his own personal individuality. It is this that makes him
an artist. Martinet is a product of the school of Rolland,
but spiritually he has outgrown it. It is this that makes
it possible for him to be a Communist.

During the war, Rolland, having raised himself "above
the battle," inspired loyal respect for his personal courage
in a period when mass heroism was covering the plains
and villages of Europe with corpses, but when personal
courage even in a modest measure was very scarce, especially amongst the "spiritual aristocracy." Rolland, refusing
to "howl with the wolves" of his own country, lifted himself
"above the battle," or, to be more precise, stepped aside
from it and entrenched himself in a neutral country.

He continued during the thunder of war (true this was
but faintly heard in Switzerland) to prize German science
and German art, and to propagate cooperation between
both countries. This program of activity was not, after
all, so courageous; but in that period of raging chauvinism to carry it out needed at least a modicum of personal
independence. And this he had. However, even then the
limitations of his philosophy were clearly discernible as
also, if one may term it so, the egoistic character of his
humanitarianism.

Rolland entrenched himself in neutral Switzerland, but
what of the others? The people could not be "above the
battle," because they themselves were its cannon fodder.
The French proletariat could not go to Switzerland, and
Rolland did not give it any plan of action. Rolland's
banner was designed exclusively for his personal use—
it was the banner of a great artist brought up on French
and German literature, above military age, and assured
of the necessary means for passing from one country to
another. The limitations of the Rolland type of humanitarianism were plainly revealed later, when the problems
of war, peace, and cultural cooperation became the problem of revolution.

Here also Rolland decided to be "above the battle." He
recognizes neither dictatorship nor violence, whether from
the right or from the left. It is true that historical events

do not depend upon recognition or nonrecognition, and
that he as a great poet retains the right to give his moral
and aesthetic criticism. For him, a humanitarian egoist,
this was sufficient. But what of the masses? As long as
the people slavishly suffer the dictatorship of capital, Rolland poetically and aesthetically condemns the bourgeoisie,
but should the working class endeavor to burst the yoke
of their exploiters by the only means in their power, by
the force of revolution, they in their turn encounter the
ethical and aesthetic condemnation of Rolland. After all,
the history of mankind is only material upon which to
base artistic production or moral valuations! Rolland, the
pretentious individualist, belongs to the past.

Martinet, in his relation to human history, is much
broader, more realistic, and more human. He does not
place himself "above the battle," but attacks the problems
of war and peace, the liberation of human culture and
cooperation between nations, not as a problem of personal
values, but as problems of mass activity. He has drama-
tized the revolutionary activity of the oppressed in his last
production, called *La Nuit* [The Night]. It is written in
blank verse. It is written so finely that the verse is not a
constraint on language, but a means of raising it above
the ordinary, endowing it with a significance of form
corresponding with the deeply historical significance of
events. And so, at least on reading, one feels its necessity.

Is the drama realistic? Yes, fundamentally as a whole
it is, as is also each individual figure in particular. The
characters are alive. But through their personal existence
in every stage of the drama is delineated the life of their
class, their country, and of our present-day humanity.
Above their heads flock unseen social forces, thus giving
a symbolic meaning to the play.

The central figure is old Mariette, a peasant woman
seventy years old. Round her are grouped peasants, men
and women, from the northern parts of the country which
have been devastated by artillery. With her wise courage,
with her tender kindness, Mariette governs her little world
completely. This is a French mother! This is a mother

of the French people! She has ingrained peasant ideas, but she has already lived through an age of new history, through a series of revolutions, known many hopes and disappointments, and much suffering for her children. However, despair she did not know, and even now, in the years of the Great War, she does not want to know it. Her heart remains an inexhaustible source of tireless kindness.

Mariette's eldest son is at the front. With her remains her little, silent, heroic daughter-in-law, Anna Maria, whom the old woman in a tragic moment of tender confidence calls "a quiet little grey kitten." With them is the grandson, Louison, twelve years old, whose soul has become awakened and strong beyond his years in the awful strain of war.

All the neighbors meet in the only remaining hut—that of Mariette. Homeless people, old men who have lost their sons, mothers whom the artillery of their own or a strange country has robbed of their children, flock there. They are surrounded by cold, snow, devastation, war. People who for four years have lived under the fire and thunder of war, tired of hoping, tired even of despairing, huddle to their common mother, Mariette, who, though with greater wisdom and greater goodness, lives and suffers just as they do.

But something has happened! The sound of the artillery has ceased. The people are enveloped in a sudden hush. What does this portend?

The astounding rumor that the war has ended pierces the cold and the storm. The enemy's soldiers have refused to fight! They have said: "We do not want to fight any more." They have arrested their officers, even—is it believable?—their emperor. He is in their hands, and the soldiers opposing them, after communication with the others, have also ceased fighting. Why *should* they fight? This is the cause of the sudden silence.

More and more soldiers, half drunk with fatigue, hope, and anxiety, appear at the hut and corroborate the news. It was the end.

Now begins something that has never happened before. The enemy soldiers have seized their emperor, and actually wish to hand him over to the opposing armies "for safe-keeping." Isn't it wonderful, eh? But the chief thing is that *it* has stopped. At last the end.

But now comes the Generalissimo Bourbousse. He is an old soldier with a natural, but partly affected, roughness, and with an affected, though perhaps partly natural, good naturedness. He is an insignificant figure, but in his very insignificance dangerous. Bourbousse intends temporarily to install himself and his staff in Mariette's little abode, and he asks his hosts to leave their house. But where should they go to? Around them is a plowed-up desert, covered with debris, with still unburied corpses, and steeped in cold and snow. Mariette protests, "for the war has ended," she cries. Bourbousse explains that it is from here that he intends to complete the victory, but finally he gives Mariette and her family permission to remain in the attic.

The vanquished emperor suddenly appears on the scene. Some enemy soldiers have accompanied him here. Bourbousse welcomes the monarch, who has been beaten in more senses than one, for his body is covered with bruises. Having entered the enemies' headquarters, the emperor immediately regains courage. He is no more among his own soldiers. He explains to Bourbousse that his, the emperor's, downfall deprives Bourbousse of the fruits of victory. With whom can the victor treat now? "Who," he asks, "will sign the treaty?" Surely not the revolution! Bourbousse becomes anxious, and rightly so. Thus they discover common interests. Will not, for instance, the example of the revolution be followed by the victors? "In any case," continues Bourbousse, "his Highness can . . . hm . . . hm . . . make himself quite at home."

Mariette's hut is given over to his highness, and the Generalissimo and staff climb to the attic. The old woman, her daughter-in-law, and grandson are thrust out of the house — out into the darkness, the cold, and the snow.

But the infection is already beginning to spread. There is unrest among the soldiery of Bourbousse. They seem to be waiting for something. They talk excitedly, and apparently, by accident, hundreds of them forgather under the roof of a partly demolished cafe. They want to understand what has happened. They shout for reasons, ideas, slogans, leaders. They nominate those who gained their confidence in the trenches. There is the honest old peasant Goutodiet; the openhearted, well-spoken Favrol; there is the young Ledru, with the eagle's glance, but without power. And this is where the real drama of the beginning of the rising of the suppressed class is unfolded — without banners, without proper organization, under inexperienced and untried leadership.

Goutodiet was, with all his soul, for the solidarity of the working people, for the end of the war, for coming to terms with the enemy. He was an honest narrow pacifist, and the speech of this aged peasant in soldier's uniform was much better and more agreeable than the conglomeration of pacifist jokes delivered by Victor Meric. The mass welcomes Goutodiet, but is not satisfied, because the goal is not defined and the methods are not clear. Pacifism is passive; the substance of it is patience; it has hopes and fears, but no definite plan of action. It is the latter which is at present of most importance, because the masses have risen.

Favrol steps forward. His emptiness, his noisy irresponsibility are hidden under definite suggestions. He tries immediately to formulate a suggestion which he must have discussed more than once with the frequenters of the anarchist cafe, viz., to kill the officers, including Bourbousse, and *then* to think of what else to do. The soldiers become attentive; some agree, but the majority are frightened. The split causes the majority to lose their heads, and that leads to a demoralizing feeling of weakness.

Then young Ledru steps forward. He is not afraid of revolutionary force. He recognizes that it is unavoidable, but the country would not at once understand the summary execution of the officers. Extreme measures which are not at first prepared for by evolutionary methods, which have no psychological motive, would cause a split among the soldiers. Premature use of revolutionary terrorism would isolate the people who took part in it. Ledru suggests that a representative organ of the revolutionary army be created first, that every hundred soldiers send a representative to the Soviet, and . . . here the curtain falls.

The revolution spreads in the army and the country. Everywhere soviets are being formed. In the capital a temporary government has already been set up of active men from the extreme left reserve of the bourgeoisie. Their task is to break up and paralyze the revolution—to control it themselves. For this they utilize the customary methods of democracy, the weighty authority of official statesmanship, the artistic web of lies, the distrust of the masses in themselves, the wait-and-see pacifism of Goutodiet, and the bloody adventurism of Favrol. Ordinary people, not geniuses, sit in the temporary government. Their task, however, is not to create anything new, but to preserve the old order of things. They have the experience and help of the ruling class to back them up. In this lies their power. Their first problem was to keep their feet when the first wave of the revolution passed over them, and to discover its weak, unguarded points — to plunder, weaken, and exploit the revolution, and to destroy the faith and morale of the masses before the second, more deadly, wave could arise.

The critical moment!

In the army, in the workers' districts, the movement is spreading; soviets have been chosen, local conflicts with the authorities are going in favor of the revolutionaries, but the real enemy, the ruling class, is not done away with. The latter maneuver expectantly. It has a comfortable intelligence department in the capital; it has a well-known centralized mechanism; it has a very rich experience in deceit; and it is convinced of its right to victory.

After the partial success of the first attack against the old regime, it is necessary to place the movement on a higher level — to give it more of a national character — in order to assure an internal agreement, a common aim, and a common method of realizing that aim. Otherwise, of course, disaster is inevitable.

The local leaders, men brought out by circumstance — improvised revolutionaries, who have never before thought of the problems of mass movement — are buffeted like small pieces of wood on the waves of that movement, hoping against hope that circumstances according to their own logic would assure success for them in the future as in the past. For the solution of every difficulty, the dilettantes of the revolution can only put forward clichés instead of ideas. "The people who have risen are invincible"; "You cannot stop conscience with bayonets!" and so on. But the revolution demands not general phrases, but regulations corresponding to internal necessities and to the various stages of the movement. This is lacking. A fatal delay occurs in the development of events. Ledru, with political instinct, comprehends the logic of the revolution. Quite recently he resisted the empty boasting of Favrol, rejecting his proposal to shoot the officers. In the past they have limited themselves to the arrest of Bourbousse. Today Ledru feels that a fateful crisis is approaching. The masses do not realize that the chief difficulties are still to come. The enemy seizes, without a struggle, any unfortified position, and immediately afterwards pushes its tentacles further forward. Tomorrow the "good-natured" Bourbousse will again be leader of the armed forces of reaction and will crush the movement in its infancy. Ledru comes to the conclusion that there is needed a cry of danger, thunderous warnings, encouragement to ruthlessness. Now he is for decisive measures, the shooting of Bourbousse, but the logic of the revolution, which the young leader, with his finger on the troubled pulse of the masses, has already mastered, finds only a belated reflection in the minds of its semileaders.

At the head of the mass there is no organization which can reason collectively, which can consider in common the relation of events to one another, and thus to intervene at the right moment. There is no revolutionary party. Unanimity only occurs in a movement as long as it meets no obstacles. As soon as the position becomes complicated, improvised leaders without experience, without a program, always begin to fight amongst themselves. Each one has his own course, his own method. There is neither discipline of thought nor of action. Difficulties, inadequacies, deficiencies — the consequences of war and of the revolution itself — stand out more sharply. Hesitation appears. Then follows loss of morale. Those who before kept their doubts secret now shout at the tops of their voices. There is nothing easier than to oppose the present difficulties with the problems of tomorrow. Those who have not lost faith endeavor to shout above the skeptics — but each in his own way. The masses grope about amid the growing difficulties and try to follow their leaders, but the dissension frightens and weakens them.

Here there appears on the scene a member of the temporary government, Bordiet Dupatois. An experienced demagogue, with a political knowledge not of a very high calibre, but with a practically flawless instinct for the division and demoralization of the mass and the corruption of its leaders. All the art of the French Revolution is at the disposal of Dupatois, who is fat, who pretends to be simple and a humorist, and who wears a coachman's cape inside out. He makes his way slowly through the crowd of soldiers, spies, and listens, chatters, flatters the revolutionaries, praises the leaders, makes promises, reproaches in a friendly fashion, and shakes hands with everybody. From the moment when he appears at the entrance of the revolutionary headquarters of Ledru, large numbers of soldiers, tired of waiting and uncertainty, already put their hopes in him, as if he were a harbor of safety. The uninvited guest Dupatois welcomes them to the revolutionary headquarters in the tone of a benevolent host, and praises Ledru in such a sly fashion as must inevitably shatter the young leader's authority. Favrol is already on the side of the temporary government. The honest Goutodiet is not heard of because events have become too complicated for him. He has become muddled and has melted into the "muddled crowd." Ledru understands the trend of events, but he now stands before the crowd, not as a leader of the revolution, but as a hero of tragedy. With him and around him there is no organization but a few of his hardened followers who are used to thinking and fighting together. There is no revolutionary party. The energy of the masses, which has been wrongly directed, has become an irritant poison directed against the parent growth itself, gradually weakening it. Dupatois is already firmly established. He transforms doubts, uneasiness, worry, fatigue, uncertainty, into political flattery. Amongst the crowd he has his paid and voluntary agents. They interrupt Ledru, protest, grumble, curse, thus creating the necessary atmosphere for Dupatois.

In the chaos of the stormy meeting a sudden shot is heard and Ledru falls dead.

The greatest moment for Dupatois approaches. He says a few complimentary words over the grave of his fallen "young friend," in which, admitting the latter's faults and foolhardiness, he pays compliment to the altruism of ideals destined to bear no fruit.

With this secretly insincere eulogy he succeeds in winning over even the most revolutionary of his opponents. The revolution is broken. The power of the provisional government is assured. Is not this a historical drama of the French proletariat?

The same peasants forgather at old Mariette's. With all her heart she was on the side of the revolutionaries. How could it be otherwise? Mariette — a mother of the French people — is France itself. She is a peasant, with mind and memory loaded and enriched by age after age of struggle and suffering. She remembers her sons fallen in the battles of the great revolution, which ended with a Caesarist dictatorship. She has witnessed the return of the Bourbons, the new revolution, new treacheries, internal strife amidst the working class itself, the hopes and disappointments of the Commune, its terrible downfall, the monstrous, cowardly, and crafty militarism of the Third Republic, the Great War, in which the best of their generation had been wiped out and the very existence of the French people threatened. . . . All this has old Mariette, a mother of the French people, lived through, felt, and thought over in her own way. She was a common peasant, who, by her experience and mother's instinct, had raised herself to the level of the working class, its hopes and struggles.

Absolutely on the side of the revolutionaries, Mariette gave them a mother's blessing, awaited their victory, and hoped for the return of her eldest son from the trenches. But the revolution was shattered, and all the sacrifices had been in vain. Bourbousse is again head of the army. The delusion of brotherhood with those who deposed their emperor is dispersed like smoke.

The enemy is retreating, and the enemy must pay in full for the devastation he has caused!

Forward! To arms!! Bourbousse is in command, and after a considerable lapse in the development of events, after the internal strife, this persecution of the retreating enemy, this "forward" movement, seems to the people who are being hoodwinked like a way of surmounting the crisis — a way out of the *cul-de-sac*. The peasants, both men and women, turn from Mariette, though she had upheld their spirits during the blackest months of the war. She had raised their hopes in the revolutionary days to an unaccustomed degree, and so doing had deceived them, and they revenge themselves mercilessly upon her for their shattered dreams. One after another leaves the house of the old peasant woman with words of bitter reproach upon his lips.

Mariette is alone. Her grandson, Louison, is sleeping restlessly upon his bed. Her daughter-in-law, Anna Maria, breaks her heroic silence to tell old Mariette that she (Anna Maria) is on her side. She has been with her during the war, during the times when revolutionary hopes ran high, and she is with her now in the bitter days of defeat and isolation. Mariette clasps her quiet, grey kitten to her heart. Anna Maria goes up the steps to her room, and Mariette sits near the bed where her grandson, the future France, lies under the oppression of a nightmare — the new France, which is growing under the thunder and lightning of this most terrible epoch.

And there, on the floor above, is Anna Maria — the new French mother who will relieve the old, tired Mariette.

A knock on the door is heard. Three men enter carrying a fourth — the corpse of the first-born son. He had perished during the strife of the last few days, during the persecution of the revolutionary army of the enemy, after the destruction of his own revolution.

The last shred of hope is shattered about the poor old head. The three men who have just entered place that which had once been her son by the side of the bed where the grandson lies asleep. But no — the grandson is not asleep. On the contrary, he has heard all. Beautiful is the tragic dialogue between himself and his grandmother.

They both (the past and the future) bow at the bedside where the "present" lies dead.

Louison again lies dreaming.

Mariette feels that she has no more strength to bear her sufferings. She has nothing to expect — nothing to live for; and she feels that it is now time to quit the old life and to go forward into the night which lies brooding outside her window. But in that inexhaustible bourn of hope and kindness, the mother's heart, the old woman again finds herself. She has a daughter-in-law and a grandson, and a new life is built up upon the ruins of the old. It *must* be, it *shall* be, better than the past life is the watchword.

The night passes. . . .

The old woman climbs heavily up the stairs to her daughter-in-law and calls: "Anna Maria, it is time to get up — it is already dawn!"

With this the play ends. It is a veritable drama of revolution; a political tragedy of the working class; a tragedy of all its past and a warning for the future. No other proletariat but the French is so rich in historical memories, for no other but the French has had such a dramatic destiny. But this very past weighs down upon it like a terrible threat for the future. The dead are like a chain fettering the living. Each stage has left behind it not only its experiences, but also its prejudices, its formulas deprived of content, and its sects who refuse to die.

Goutodiet? We have all met him. He is a worker with the instincts of the petty bourgeois, or a petty bourgeois attracted to the workers' cause — the democrat, the pacifist, always for half measures, always for going half the way. He is Bourderon, the father of the people, whose honest limitations have in the past proved more than once a brake on the revolution.

And we all know Favrol, knight of the phrase, who today preaches a bloody settlement in order tomorrow to show himself in the camp of the victorious bourgeoisie. Favrol is the most widespread, the most multifarious, and in all its variety the most uniform type in the French working-class movement. He is Herve, the shouter, the

vulgar reviler, the antimilitarist, "without a fatherland,"
the preacher of sabotage and direct action — and then the
patriotic oracle of the concierges, the journalistic tool of
the drunken chauvinism of a petty bourgeois clique. He
is Sebastian Faure, the libertine, the pedagogue, the Mal-
thusian, the smooth-tongued orator, the antimilitarist,
always furnished with a program full of promises freeing
him from the necessity of undertaking any practical step,
and always ready for a shameful deal with the "prefect,"
if the latter only knows how to flatter him.

Verbal radicalism, a policy of irreconcilable formulas
which in no way lead to action, and consequently sanction
inaction under the cloak of extremism, have been and
remain the most corrosive element in the French working-
class movement. Orators who begin their first phrase
and do not know what they are going to say next; adept
bureaucrats of journalism whose writings bear no relation
to actual events: "leaders" who never reflect on the consequences of their own actions; individualists who, under the
banner of "autonomy" — whether of provinces, towns, trade
unions, organizations, newspapers, or what not — guard
inviolate their own petty bourgeois individualism from
control, responsibility, and discipline; syndicalists who
not only have no sense of what is needed, but who are
instinctively afraid to say what exists, to call a mistake
a mistake, and to demand from themselves and from
others a definite answer to any question, and who mask
their helplessness under the accustomed wrappings of revolutionary ritual; great-souled poets who wish to deluge
the working class with their reservoirs of magnanimity
and confusion of ideas; stage artists and improvisors who
are too lazy to think, and who feel hurt that people exist
in the world who are able and accustomed to think; chat-
terers, players with words, village oracles, petty revolutionary priests of churches struggling one against the
other — it is here that is to be found the terrible poison in
the French working-class movement; here is the menace,
here the danger!

Martinet's drama speaks out on this in bold language,
making the highest truth of life, *historical truth*, correspond with artistic truth. Speaking through the medium

of artistic creation, the drama is a call to the proletarian vanguard for internal purification, increased unity, and discipline.

The last act takes place in an atmosphere heavy with tragedy; the play as a whole is called *La Nuit*. Superficially it may appear to be imbued with pessimism — almost with despair. It is in fact inspired by a deep uneasiness, by a natural anxiety. France has been drained of blood. The best of her generation lie buried. Mariette's first-born son did not return from the war to set up the new order. But there is the grandson, twelve years old at the end of the war and now, therefore, sixteen.

In such a time months appear as years. Louison personifies the future. About his young head, waking with feverish energy, is breaking the dawn of tomorrow, and it is this that is meant by that last exclamation of Mariette's, bespeaking peace and hope. But it is essential that Louison should not repeat the history of Ledru. Remember this, you, the best workers of France! Martinet's drama is not a gloomy prophecy, but a stern forewarning.

TO THE MEMORY

OF SERGEI ESSENIN

Sergei Essenin, one of the outstanding Russian poets in the early years of the Soviet Union, founded the imagist group in 1919. He committed suicide on December 27, 1925, at the age of 30.

We have lost Essenin, that fine poet, so genuine and of so lovely a freshness. He has gone, of his own will, saying farewell, in his own blood, to an unknown friend — perhaps to us all.

His last lines are striking in their tenderness and gentleness; he left life without crying out that he had been offended, without a "pose" of protest, without slamming doors, but closing them quietly with a hand from which blood was flowing. Because of this gesture, an unforgettable aura of farewell illumines the image of Essenin as a man and as a poet.

Essenin composed the harsh *Songs of a Guttersnipe*, and gave the coarse choruses of the Moscow taverns that melodiousness that was all his own and that cannot be imitated.

He very often liked to boast of a vulgar gesture, of trivial words, but underneath there throbbed the tenderness of a defenseless soul. By means of this half-feigned coarseness, Essenin was seeking refuge from the harsh

Published in *Pravda*, January 19, 1926. The first American publication was in *New Masses*, June 1926.

period into which he had been born — and born, further-more, in vain, for, beaten by life, on December 27, with-out provocation and without complaint, the poet said: "I cannot go on."

It is necessary to emphasize his "mask" of vulgarity, for this was not merely a form chosen by Essenin, but the imprint made on him by the conditions of our period, which is neither gentle nor tender. Protecting himself from life by this mask of insolence, paying to this "attitude" a tribute that was deep and not incidental, Essenin, it seems, never "felt himself to be of this world" — I say this neither to honor him nor to censure him; indeed, it is by that nonadaptation of Essenin to the world that the poet was lost to us; furthermore, can we cast blame on this great lyric poet whom we did not know how to save for our-selves?

Bitter times, these, perhaps among the bitterest in the history of so-called civilized humanity. A revolutionary, born for these decades, is obsessed by a wild "patriotism" for his period, which is his fatherland-in-time. Essenin was not a revolutionary.

The author of *Pugachev* and the *Ballads of the Twenty-Six* was an inner lyricist. But our period is not lyric: that is the essential reason why Sergei Essenin, of his own will, and so soon, went far away from us and from his times.

Essenin's roots are deeply popular, and like everything about him, his background of "the people" is not artificial: the proof of this lies, not in his poems on rioting, but, once more, in his lyricism:

In the bay thickets, near the hillside slopes, it is soft
Autumn . . . a russet mare tosses her mane.

This image of autumn, as well as many others, sur-prised at first; they were considered unjustifiably daring; but, forced by the poet to feel the peasant origin of his images, we felt them penetrate deeply into us.

Obviously Fet would not have written so, and Tiuchev even less.

Essenin passed the inspiration coming to him from his peasant origins through the prism of his creative gift and thus made it finer; solidly rooted in him, this peasant background's very solidity was what explains the poet's special weakness: he was uprooted from the past, and had not been able to sink his roots into the new times. His trips abroad, to Europe and across the ocean, had not been able to "pull him up again." He assimilated Teheran much more deeply than New York, and the wholly inner lyricism of this child of Riazan found in Persia far more points in common with his peasant origins than he could find in the civilized capitals of Europe and America.

Essenin was no enemy of the revolution, and it was never even alien to him; on the contrary, he turned constantly toward it, writing in 1918:

O my country. Bolshevik, yes, I am.

He still was saying, in his last years:

And now, in the land of the soviets,
Here am I, one of your most ardent traveling companions.

Violently the revolution broke into the structure of his verses and his images, which, at first confused, later grew clearer. In the collapse of the past, Essenin lost nothing, missed nothing. Alien to the revolution? No indeed; but it and he were not of the same nature: Essenin was an inward being, tender and lyrical; the revolution was "public," epic, full of disasters; and so it was a disaster that snapped off the poet's brief life.

It has been said that every being bears within him the spring of his destiny, unwound to the end by life. In this case, that is only partially true. The creative spring of Essenin was unwinding when the period, with its sharp angles, knocked against it — the spring was broken.

There are, however, with Essenin, many priceless strophes, wholly suffused by his times, yet Essenin "was not of this world"; he was not the poet of the revolution.

I accept everything; everything, as it is, I accept.
I am ready to walk in paths already traced.
I will give my whole soul for our October, our May,
But I will not give my lyre, my beloved lyre.

His lyric spring could have unwound to the end only

under conditions where life was harmonious, happy, full of songs, a period when there ruled as master, not rough combat, but friendship, love, and tenderness. This time will come; in our own there are still many implacable and salutary combats of men against men; but after it, there will come other times which the present struggles are preparing; then the individual can blossom into genuine flower, just as then the poetry of each being will bloom. *The revolution, above all, will in lofty struggle win for every individual the right not only to bread but to poetry.*

In his last hour, to whom was Essenin writing his letter in blood? Perchance he was calling from afar to a friend who is not yet born, to the man of the future, whom some are preparing by their struggles and Essenin by his songs? The poet is dead, because he was not of the same nature as the revolution, but, in the name of the future, the revolution will adopt him forever.

From the very first years of his poetic work, Essenin, realizing his inherent inability to defend himself, had a tendency toward death. In one of his last songs, he said farewell to the flowers:

Well then, my friends, well, well . . .
I have seen you, and I have seen the earth . . .
And your funereal trembling
I shall take as a last caress.

Those who scarcely knew Essenin, those who did not know him at all, can *only now,* after December 27, understand completely the intimate sincerity of his poetry, almost every verse of which was written in blood from a wounded vein; our bitterness is all the harsher.

Without emerging from his inner domain, Essenin found in the premonition of his coming end a melancholy and moving consolation:

. . . listening to a song in silence,
my beloved, with another friend,
will perhaps be reminded of me,
as a flower — never to be repeated . . .

In our consciences, one thought softens the acute and still fresh pain: this great, this inimitable poet did, accord-

ing to his temperament, reflect his period and enriched it
with his songs, telling, in a new way, of love, of the blue
sky fallen in the river, of the moon which, like a lamb,
pastures in the sky, and of the never-to-be-repeated flower
— himself.

Let there be nothing, in this memory we bring to the
poet, that may beat us down or make us lose courage.
Our period has a spring stronger than that of each of us,
and the spiral of history will unwind till the end; let us
not oppose it, but help it, by our conscious efforts of
thought and will. Let us prepare the future, let us win
for every being the right to bread and song.

The poet is dead, long live poetry!

Defenseless, a child of man has rolled into the abyss.
But long live the creative life where, till his last moment,
Sergei Essenin braided the priceless threads of his poetry!

CHURCHILL

AS BIOGRAPHER

AND HISTORIAN

Trotsky had just been exiled to Turkey when Winston Churchill published The Aftermath, *a book on post-World War I developments in which Lenin was bitterly attacked. Trotsky immediately answered the attack with this article, which appeared in* John O'London's Weekly.

In 1918-19 Mr. Churchill attempted to overthrow Lenin by force of arms. In 1929 he attempts a psychological and political portraiture of him in his book, *The Aftermath*. Perhaps he was hoping thereby to secure some sort of literary revenge for his unsuccessful appeal to the sword. But his methods are no less inadequate in the second mode of attack than they were in the first.

"His [Lenin's] sympathies, cold and wide as the Arctic Ocean; his hatreds, tight as the hangman's noose," writes Mr. Churchill. Verily, he juggles with antithesis as an athlete with dumbbells. But the observant eye soon notices that the dumbbells are painted cardboard and the bulging biceps are eked out with padding.

The true Lenin was instinct with moral force—a force whose main characteristic was its absolute simplicity. To try to assess him in terms of stage athletics was bound to spell failure.

Written March 23, 1929 and published in *John O'London's Weekly*, April 20, 1929.

Mr. Churchill's facts are miserably inaccurate. Consider his dates, for instance. He repeats a sentence, which he has read somewhere or other, referring to the morbid influence exercised on Lenin's evolution by the execution of his elder brother. He refers the fact to the year 1894. But actually the attempt against Alexander III's life was organized by Alexander Ulianov (Lenin's brother) on March 1, 1887. Mr. Churchill avers that in 1894 Lenin was sixteen years of age. In point of fact, he was then twenty-four, and in charge of the secret organization at Petersburg. At the time of the October Revolution he was not thirty-nine, as Mr. Churchill would have it, but forty-seven years old. Mr. Churchill's errors in chronology show how confusedly he visualizes the period and people of which he writes.

But when from the point of view of chronology and fisticuffs, we turn to that of the philosophy of history, what we see is even more lamentable.

Mr. Churchill tells us that discipline in the Russian army was destroyed, after the February Revolution, by the order abolishing the salute to officers. This was the point of view of discontented old generals and ambitious young subalterns; otherwise, it is merely absurd. The old army stood for the supremacy of the old classes and was destroyed by the revolution. When peasants had taken away the landowner's property the peasants' sons could hardly continue to serve under officers who were sons of landowners. The army is no mere technical organization, associated only with marching and promotion, but a moral organization, founded on a definite scheme of mutual relations between individuals and classes. When a scheme of this kind is upset by a revolution, the army unavoidably collapses. It was always thus. . . .

Mr. Churchill grants that Lenin had a powerful mind and will. According to Lord Birkenhead, Lenin was purely and simply nonexistent: what really exists is a Lenin myth (see his letter in *The Times*, February 26, 1929). The real Lenin was a nonentity upon which the colleagues of Arnold Bennett's Lord Raingo could look down contemptuously.[1] But despite this one difference in their appraisal of Lenin, both Tories are exactly alike in their

utter incapacity to understand Lenin's writings on economy, on politics, and on philosophy — writings that fill
over twenty volumes.

I suspect that Mr. Churchill did not even deign to take
the trouble carefully to read the article on Lenin which I
wrote for the *Encyclopedia Britannica* in 1926. If he had,
he would not have committed those crude, glaring errors
of dates which throw everything out of perspective.

One thing Lenin could not tolerate was muddled thought.
He had lived in all European countries, mastered many
languages, had read and studied and listened and observed and compared and generalized. When he became
the head of a revolutionary country, he did not fail to
avail himself of this opportunity to learn conscientiously
and carefully. He did not cease to follow the life of all
other countries. He could read and speak fluently English,
German and French. He could read Italian and a number
of Slavic languages. During the last years of his life,
though overburdened with work, he devoted every spare
minute to studying the grammar of the Czech language
in order to have access, without intermediaries, to the inner life of Czechoslovakia.

What can Mr. Churchill and Lord Birkenhead know of
the workings of this forceful, piercing, tireless mind of his,
with its capacity to translate everything that was superficial, accidental, external, into terms of the general and
fundamental? Lord Birkenhead in blissful ignorance imag-
ines that Lenin never had thought of the password: "Power
to the Soviets," before the Revolution of February 1917.
But the problem of the Soviets and of their possible functions was the very central theme of the work of Lenin and
of his companions from 1905 onwards, and even earlier.

By way of completing and correcting Mr. Churchill, Lord
Birkenhead avers that if Kerensky had been gifted with
a single ounce of intelligence and courage, the Soviets
would never have come into power. Here is, indeed, a
philosophy of history that is conducive to comfort! The
army falls to pieces in consequence of the soldiers having
decided not to salute the officers whom they meet. The
contents of the cranium of a radical barrister happens to
have been one ounce short, and this deficiency is enough

to lead to the destruction of a pious and civilized community! But what indeed can a civilization be worth which
at the time of dire need is unable to supply the needful
ounce of brain?

Besides, Kerensky did not stand alone. Around him was
a whole circle of Entente officials. Why were they unable
to instruct and inspire him, or, if need was, replace him?
To this query Mr. Churchill can find but this reply: "The
statesmen of the Allied nations affected to believe that all
was for the best, and that the revolution constituted a
notable advantage for the common cause"— which means
that the officials in question were utterly incapable of
understanding the Russian Revolution— or, in other words,
did not substantially differ from Kerensky himself.

Today, Lord Birkenhead is incapable of seeing that
Lenin, in signing the Brest-Litovsk peace, had shown any
particular foresight. (I do not insist upon the fact that
Lord Birkenhead represents me as in favor of war with
Germany in 1918. The honorable Conservative, on this
point, follows far too docilely the utterances of historians
of the Stalin school.)[2] He considers, today, that the peace
was then inevitable. In his own words, "only hysterical
fools" could have imagined that the Bolsheviks were capable of fighting Germany: a very remarkable, though
tardy, acknowledgment!

The British government of 1918 and, indeed, all the
Entente governments of that time, categorically insisted
on our fighting Germany, and when we refused to do so
replied by blockade of, and intervention in, our country.
We may well ask, in the energetic language of the Conservative politician himself: Who were, at that moment,
the hysterical fools? Was it not they who decided the fate
of Europe? Lord Birkenhead's view would have been
very farseeing in 1917; but I must confess that I, for
one, have little use for foresight which asserts itself twelve
years after the time when it could have been of use.

Mr. Churchill brings up against Lenin— and it is the
very keystone of his article— statistics of the casualties of
the civil war. These statistics are quite fantastic. This,
however, is not the main point. The victims were many
on either side. Mr. Churchill expressly specifies that he in-

cludes neither the deaths from starvation nor the deaths from epidemics. In his would-be athletic language he describes that neither Tamerlane nor Genghis Khan were as reckless as Lenin in expenditure of human lives. Judging by the order he adopts, one would think Churchill holds Tamerlane more reckless than Genghis Khan. In this he is wrong; statistical and chronological figures are certainly not the strong point of this finance minister. But this is by the way.

In order to find examples of mass expenditure of human life, Mr. Churchill must needs go to the history of Asia in the thirteenth and fourteenth centuries. The great European war of 1914-18, in which ten million men were killed and twenty million crippled, appears to have entirely escaped his memory. The campaigns of Genghis Khan and Tamerlane were child's play in comparison with the doings of civilized nations from 1914 to 1918. But it is in a tone of lofty moral indignation that Mr. Churchill speaks of the victims of civil war in Russia — forgetting Ireland, and India, and other countries.

In short, the question is not so much the victims as it is the duties and the objects for which war was waged. Mr. Churchill wishes to make clear that all sacrifices, in all parts of the world, are permissible and right so long as the object is the power and sovereignty of the British Empire — that is, of its governing classes. But the incomparably lesser sacrifices are wrong which result from the struggle of peoples attempting to alter the conditions under which they exist — as occurred in England in the seventeenth century, in France at the end of the eighteenth, in the United States twice (eighteenth and nineteenth centuries), in Russia in the twentieth century, and as will occur more than once in the future.

It is in vain that Mr. Churchill seeks assistance in the evocation of the two Asiatic warrior chiefs, who both fought in the interests of nomadic aristocracies, but yet aristocracies coveting new territories and more slaves — in which respect their dealings were in accordance with Mr. Churchill's principles, but certainly not with Lenin's. Indeed, we may recall that Anatole France, the last of the great humanists, often expressed the idea that of all kinds

of the bloodthirsty insanity called war, the least insane
was civil war, because at least the people who waged it
did so of their own accord and not by order.

Mr. Churchill has committed yet another mistake, a
very important one, and, indeed, from his own point of
view, a fatal one. He forgot that in civil wars, as in all
wars, there are two sides; and that in this particular case
if he had not come in on the side of a very small minority, the number of the victims would have been considerably
less. In October, we conquered power almost without a
fight. Kerensky's attempt to reconquer it evaporated as a
dewdrop falling on a red-hot stone. So mighty was the
driving power of the masses that the older classes hardly
dared attempt to resist.

When did the civil war, with its companion, the Red Terror, really start? Mr. Churchill being weak in the matter
of chronology, let us help him. The turning point was the
middle of 1918. Led by the Entente diplomatists and officers, the Czechoslovakians got hold of the railway line
leading to the east. The French ambassador Noulens organized the resistance at Yaroslavl. Another foreign representative organized deeds of terror and an attempt to cut
off the water supply of Petersburg. Mr. Churchill encour-
ages and finances Savinkov; he is behind Yudenich. He
determines the exact dates on which Petersburg and Moscow are to fall. He supports Denikin and Wrangel. The
monitors of the British fleet bombard our coast. Mr.
Churchill proclaims the coming of "fourteen nations." He
is the inspirer, the organizer, the financial backer, the
prophet of civil war; a generous backer, a mediocre organizer, and a very bad prophet.

He had been better advised not to recall the memories
of those times. The number of the victims would have
been, not ten times, but a hundred or a thousand times
smaller but for British guineas, British monitors, British
tanks, British officers, and British food supplies.

Mr. Churchill understands neither Lenin nor the duties
that lay before him. His lack of comprehension is at its
worst when he attempts to deal with the inception of the
New Economic Policy. For him, Lenin thereby gave himself the lie. Lord Birkenhead adds that in ten years the very

principles of the October Revolution were bankrupt. Yes: he who in ten years failed to do away with the miners' unemployment, or to palliate it, expects that in ten years we Russians can build up a new community without committing one mistake, without one flaw, without one setback; a wonderful expectation which gives us the measure of the primitive and purely theoretical quality of the honorable Conservative's outlook. We cannot foretell how many errors, how many setbacks, will mark the course of history; but to see, amid the obstacles and deviations and setbacks of all kinds, the straight line of historical evolution was the achievement of Lenin's genius. And had the Restoration been successful at the time, the need for radical changes in the organization of the community would have remained as great.

THE SUICIDE OF

VLADIMIR MAYAKOVSKY

Vladimir Mayakovsky, a great poet who reached ar-
tistic maturity before the 1917 Revolution, sought to ad-
just himself to and express the new society being built in
the Soviet Union. He lived through the heroic period of
the revolution, and into the first stages following the tri-
umph of the Stalin faction of the Bolshevik Party, com-
mitting suicide in 1930.

Even Blok[1] recognized in Mayakovsky an "enormous
talent." Without exaggeration it can be said that Mayakovsky had the spark of genius. But his was not a harmonious talent. After all, where could artistic harmony come
from in these decades of catastrophe, across the unsealed
chasm between two epochs? In Mayakovsky's work the
summits stand side by side with abysmal lapses. Strokes
of genius are marred by trivial stanzas, even by loud
vulgarity.

It is not true that Mayakovsky was first of all a revolutionary and after that a poet, although he sincerely
wished it were so. In fact Mayakovsky was first of all

Published in *Bulletin of the Opposition*, number 11, May 1930. The
first American translation by George Saunders appeared in *Interna-*
tional Socialist Review, January-February 1970.

a *poet,* an artist, who rejected the old world without breaking with it. Only after the revolution did he seek to find
support for himself in the revolution, and to a significant
degree he succeeded in doing so; but he did not merge
with it totally, for he did not come to it during his years
of inner formation, in his youth. To view the question in
its broadest dimensions, Mayakovsky was not only the
"singer," but also the victim, of the epoch of transformation, which while creating elements of the new culture with
unparalleled force, still did so much more slowly and
contradictorily than necessary for the harmonious development of an individual poet or a generation of poets
devoted to the revolution. The absence of inner harmony
flowed from this very source and expressed itself in the
poet's style, in the lack of sufficient verbal discipline and
measured imagery. There is a hot lava of pathos side
by side with an inappropriate palsy-walsy attitude toward
the epoch and the class, or an outright tasteless joking
which the poet seems to erect as a barrier against being
hurt by the external world. Sometimes this seemed to be
not only artistically but even psychologically false. But
no, even the presuicide letters are in the same tone. That
is the import of the phrase, "the incident is closed," with
which the poet sums himself up. We would say the following: that which, in the latterday Romantic poet Heinrich
Heine, was lyricism and irony (irony against lyricism
but at the same time in defense of it), is in the latterday
"futurist" Vladimir Mayakovsky a mixture of pathos and
vulgarity (vulgarity against pathos but also as protection
for it).

The official report on the suicide hastens to declare, in
the language of judicial protocol as edited in the "Secre-
tariat," that the suicide of Mayakovsky "has nothing in
common with the public and literary activity of the poet."
That is to say, that the willful death of Mayakovsky was
in no way connected with his life or that his life had
nothing in common with his revolutionary-poetic work.
In a word, this turns his death into an adventure out of
the police records. This is untrue, unnecessary, and stupid.
"The ship was smashed up on everyday life," says Mayakovsky in his presuicide poems about his intimate per-

sonal life. This means that "public and literary activity" *ceased to carry him high enough over the shoals of everyday life*—not enough to save him from unendurable personal shocks. How can they say "has nothing in common with"!

The current official ideology of "proletarian literature" is based—we see the same thing in the artistic sphere as in the economic—on a total lack of understanding of the *rhythms and periods of time* necessary for cultural maturation. The struggle for "proletarian culture" —something on the order of the "total collectivization" of all humanity's gains within the span of a single five-year plan—had at the beginning of the October Revolution the character of utopian idealism, and it was precisely on this basis that it was rejected by Lenin and the author of these lines. In recent years it has become simply a system of bureaucratic command over art and a way of impoverishing it. The incompetents of bourgeois literature, such as Serafimovich, Gladkov, and others, have been declared the classical masters of this pseudoproletarian literature. Facile nonentities like Averbach are christened the Belinskys of . . . "proletarian" (!) literature.[2] The top leadership in the sphere of creative writing is put in the hands of Molotov, who is a living negation of everything creative in human nature. Molotov's chief helper—going from bad to worse—is none other than Gusev, an adept in various fields but not in art. This selection of personnel is totally in keeping with the bureaucratic degeneration in the official spheres of the revolution. Molotov and Gusev have raised up over literature a collective Malashkin, the pornographic literariness of a sycophant "revolutionary" with sunken nose.[3]

The best representatives of the proletarian youth who were summoned to assemble the *basic elements* of a new literature and culture have been placed under the command of people who convert their personal lack of culture into the measure of all things.

Yes, Mayakovsky was braver and more heroic than any other of the last generation of old Russian literature, yet was unable to win the acceptance of that literature and sought ties with the revolution. And yes, he achieved those ties much more fully than any other. But a profound inner split remained with him. To the general contradictions of revolution—always difficult for art, which seeks perfected forms—was added the decline of the last few years, presided over by the epigones. Ready to serve the "epoch" in the dirty work of everyday life, Mayakovsky could not help being repelled by the pseudorevolutionary officialdom, even though he was not able to understand it theoretically and therefore could not find the way to overcome it. The poet rightfully speaks of himself as "one who is not for hire." For a long time he furiously opposed entering Averbach's administrative collective of so-called proletarian literature. From this came his repeated attempts to create, under the banner of LEF, an order of frenzied crusaders for proletarian revolution who would serve it out of conscience rather than fear. But LEF was of course unable to impose its rhythms upon "the 150 million." The dynamics of the ebbing and flowing currents of the revolution is far too profound and weighty for that.

In January of this year Mayakovsky, defeated by the logic of the situation, committed violence against himself and finally entered VAPP (the All-Union Association of Proletarian Writers). That was two or three months before his suicide. But this added nothing and probably detracted something. When the poet liquidated his accounts with the contradictions of "everyday life," both private and public, sending his "ship" to the bottom, the representatives of bureaucratic literature, those who are for hire, declared it was "inconceivable, incomprehensible," showing not only that the great poet Mayakovsky remained "incomprehensible" for them, but also the contradictions of the epoch "inconceivable."

The compulsory, official Association of Proletarian Writers, barren ideologically, was erected upon a series of preliminary pogroms against vital and genuinely revolutionary literary groupings. Obviously it has provided no moral cement. If at the passing of the greatest poet of Soviet Russia there comes from this corner only officialdom's perplexed response—"there is no connection, nothing in common"—this is much too little, much, much too little, for the building of a new culture "in the shortest possible time."

Mayakovsky was not and could not become a direct progenitor of "proletarian literature" for the same reason that it is impossible to build socialism in one country. But in the battles of the transitional epoch he was a most courageous fighter of the word and became an undoubted precursor of the literature of the new society.

THE STRANGLED REVOLUTION:

ANDRE MALRAUX'S

THE CONQUERORS

Trotsky here, after his opening observations about the artistic merits of Malraux's novel, regards it as a social document to be analyzed for political lessons. Malraux replied, and Trotsky wrote another article in answer. Since that article, "A Strangled Revolution and Its Stranglers," is more concerned with Malraux's politics, as revealed in his reply, than with his novel, it is not included here. It should be noted, however, that Trotsky charges in it that Malraux confuses the "functionary-adventurer," the adventurer acting as agent of the Comintern, and the genuine revolutionist, who works with the proletariat, serving its needs and aims, rather than imposing a policy formulated from above. Fascination with adventurers and "supermen" standing above the masses was to make Malraux succumb first to Stalinism and then to Gaullism.

Trotsky's sharp political disagreement with Malraux did not prevent him from urging his own publisher to bring out an American edition of Man's Fate, *the novel that was to make such an impact on American intellectuals in the 1930s.*

The book by Andre Malraux, *Les Conquerants* [*The Conquerors*], has been sent to me from various parts and I think in four copies, but to my regret I read it after

Written February 9, 1931 and published in *Bulletin of the Opposition*, number 21-22, May-June 1931. The first American translation by

a delay of a year and a half or two. The book is devoted to the Chinese Revolution, that is, to the greatest
subject of the last five years. A fine and well-knit style,
the discriminating eye of an artist, original and daring
observation—all confer upon the novel an exceptional
importance. If we write about it here it is not because the
book is a work of talent, although this is not a negligible
fact, but because it offers a source of political lessons of
the highest value. Do they come from Malraux? No, they
flow from the recital itself, unknown to the author, and
they go against him. This does honor to the author as
an observer and an artist, but not as a revolutionist. However, we have the right to evaluate Malraux too from this
point of view; in his own name and above all in the name
of Garine, his other self, the author does not hesitate
with his judgments on the revolution.

This book is called a novel. As a matter of fact, we
have before us a romanticized chronicle of the Chinese
Revolution, from its first period to the period of Canton.
The chronicle is not complete. Social vigor is sometimes
lacking from the picture. But for that there pass before
the reader not only luminous episodes of the revolution
but also clear-cut silhouettes which are graven in the
memory like social symbols.

By little colored touches, following the method of *poin-
tillisme*, Malraux gives an unforgettable picture of the
general strike, not, to be sure, as it is below, not as it
is carried out, but as it is observed from above: the Euro-
peans do not get their breakfast, they swelter in the heat,
the Chinese have ceased to work in the kitchens and to
operate the ventilators. This is not a reproach to the
author: the foreign artist could undoubtedly not have
dealt with his theme otherwise. But there is a reproach
to be made, and not a small one: the book is lacking
in a congenital affinity between the writer, in spite of all
he knows, understands and can do, and his heroine, the
revolution.

The active sympathies of the author for insurgent China

Max Shachtman appeared in *The Militant,* June 15, 1931. It was
reprinted in Trotsky's *Problems of the Chinese Revolution,* along
with "A Strangled Revolution and Its Stranglers" mentioned above.

are unmistakable. But chance bursts upon these sympathies. They are corroded by the excesses of individualism and by aesthetic caprice. In reading the book with
sustained attention one sometimes experiences a feeling of
vexation when in the tone of the persuasive recital one
perceives a note of protective irony towards the barbarians
capable of enthusiasm. That China is backward, that
many of its political manifestations bear a primitive character — nobody asks that this be passed over in silence.
But a correct perspective is needed which puts every object
in its place. The Chinese events, on the basis of which
Malraux's "novel" unfolds itself, are incomparably more
important for the future destiny of human culture than the
vain and pitiful clamor of European parliaments and the
mountain of literary products of stagnant civilization.
Malraux seems to feel a certain fear to take this into
account.

In the novel, there are pages, splendid in their intensity,
which show how revolutionary hatred is born of the yoke
of ignorance, of slavery, and is tempered like steel. These
pages might have entered into the Anthology of the Revolution if Malraux had approached the masses with greater
freedom and intrepidity, if he had not introduced into his
observations a small note of blasé superiority, seeming to
excuse himself for his transient contact with the insurrection
of the Chinese people, as much perhaps before himself as
before the academic mandarins in France and the traf-
fickers in spiritual opium.

Borodin represents the Comintern in the post of "high
counsellor" in the Canton government. [1] Garine, the favorite of the author, is in charge of propaganda. All the
work is done within the framework of the Kuomintang.
Borodin, Garine, the Russian "General" Galen, the Frenchman Gerard, the German Klein and others, constitute an
original bureaucracy of the revolution raising itself above
the insurgent people and conducting its own "revolutionary" policy instead of the policy of the revolution.

The local organizations of the Kuomintang are defined
as follows: "groups of fanatics — brave . . . of a few pluto-
crats out for notoriety or for security — and crowds of

students and coolies." Not only do bourgeoisie enter into
every organization but they completely lead the party. The
Communists are subordinate to the Kuomintang. The
workers and the peasants are persuaded to take no action
that might rebuff the devoted friends of the bourgeoisie.
"Such are the societies that we control (more or less, do
not fool yourself on this score)." An edifying avowal!
The bureaucracy of the Comintern tried to "control" the
class struggle in China, like the international bankocracy
controls the economic life of the backward countries. But
a revolution cannot be controlled. One can only give a
political expression to its internal forces. One must know
to which of these forces to link his destiny.

"Today coolies are beginning to discover that they exist,
simply that they exist." That's well aimed. But to feel that
they exist, the coolies, the industrial workers and the
peasants must overthrow those who prevent them from
existing. Foreign domination is indissolubly bound up
with the domestic yoke. The coolies must not only drive
out Baldwin or MacDonald but also overthrow the ruling
classes. [2] One cannot be accomplished without the other.
Thus, the awakening of the human personality in the
masses of China, who exceed ten times the population
of France, is immediately transformed into the lava of
the social revolution. A magnificent spectacle!

But here Borodin appears on the scene and declares:
"In the revolution the workers must do the coolie work
for the bourgeoisie" (see the letter of Chen Tu-hsiu in *Bulletin of the Opposition*, no. 15-16, p. 21). The social
enslavement from which they want to liberate themselves,
the workers find transposed into the sphere of politics.
To whom do they owe this perfidious operation? To the
bureaucracy of the Comintern. In trying to "control" the
Kuomintang, it actually aids the bourgeoisie which seeks
"notoriety and security" in enslaving the coolies who want
to exist.

Borodin, who remains in the background all the time,
is characterized in the novel as a "man of action," as a
"professional revolutionist," as a living incarnation of
Bolshevism on the soil of China. Nothing is further from
the truth! Here is the political biography of Borodin: in

1903, at the age of nineteen, he emigrated to America; in 1918, he returned to Moscow where, thanks to his knowledge of English, he "insured contact with the foreign parties"; he was arrested in Glasgow in 1922; then he was delegated to China as representative of the Comintern. Having quit Russia *before* the first revolution and having returned *after* the third, Borodin appeared as the consummate representative of that state and party bureaucracy which recognized the revolution only after its victory. When it is a question of young people, it is sometimes nothing more than a matter of chronology. With people of forty or fifty, it is already a political characterization. If Borodin rallied successfully to the victorious revolution in Russia, it does not in the least signify that he was called upon to assure the victory of the revolution in China. People of this type assimilate without difficulty the gestures and intonations of "professional revolutionists." Many of them, by their protective coloration, not only deceive others but also themselves. The audacious inflexibility of the Bolshevik is most usually metamorphosed with them into that cynicism of the functionary ready for anything. Ah! to have a mandate from the Central Committee! This sacrosanct safeguard Borodin always had in his pocket.

Garine is not a functionary, he is more original than Borodin and perhaps even closer to the revolutionary type. But he is devoid of the indispensable formation; dilettante and theatrical, he gets hopelessly entangled in the great events and he reveals it at every step. With regard to the slogans of the Chinese Revolution, he expresses himself thus: ". . . democratic chatter — 'the rights of the proletariat,' etc." This has a radical ring but it is a false radicalism. The slogans of democracy are execrable chatter in the mouth of Poincare, Herriot, Leon Blum, sleight-of-hand artists of France and jailors of Indochina, Algeria and Morocco. [3] But when the Chinese rebel in the name of the "rights of the proletariat," this has as little to do with chatter as the slogans of the French Revolution in the eighteenth century. At Hong Kong, the British birds of prey threatened, during the strike, to reestablish corporal punishment. "The rights of man and of the citizen" meant at Hong Kong the right of the Chinese not to

be flogged by the British whip. To unmask the democratic rottenness of the imperialist is to serve the revolution: to call the slogans of the insurrection of the oppressed
"chatter" is to aid involuntarily the imperialist.

   A good inoculation of Marxism would have preserved
the author from fatal contempt of this sort. But Garine
in general considers that revolutionary doctrine is "doc-
trinary rubbish" *(le fatras doctrinal)*. He is, you see, one
of those to whom the revolution is only a definite "state
of affairs." Isn't this astonishing? But it is just because
the revolution is a "state of affairs," that is, a stage in the
development of society conditioned by objective causes and
subjected to definite laws, that a scientific mind can foresee
the general direction of processes. Only the study of the
anatomy of society and of its physiology permits one to
react to the course of events by basing oneself upon scientific foresight and not upon a dilettante's conjectures. The
revolutionist who "despises" revolutionary doctrine is not
a bit better than the healer who despises medical doctrine
which he does not know, or than the engineer who rejects
technology. People who without the aid of science try to
rectify the "state of affairs," which is called a disease, are
called sorcerers or charlatans and are prosecuted by law.
Had there existed a tribunal to judge the sorcerers of the
revolution, it is probable that Borodin, like his Muscovite
inspirers, would have been severely condemned. I am
afraid Garine himself would not have come out of it un-
scathed.

   Two figures are contrasted to each other in the novel,
like the two poles of the national revolution; old Chen-
dai, the spiritual authority of the right wing of the Kuomintang, the prophet and saint of the bourgeoisie, and
Hong, the young leader of the terrorists. Both are depicted with great force. Chen-dai embodies the old Chinese
culture translated into the language of European breeding;
with this exquisite garment, he "ennobles" the interests of
all the ruling classes of China. To be sure, Chen-dai wants
national liberation, but he dreads the masses more than
the imperialists; he hates the revolution more than the
yoke placed upon the nation. If he marches towards it,
it is only to pacify it, to subdue it, to exhaust it. He con-

ducts a policy of passive resistance on two fronts, against imperialism and against the revolution, the policy of Gandhi in India, the policy which, in definite periods and in one form or another, the bourgeoisie has conducted at every longitude and latitude. Passive resistance flows from the tendency of the bourgeoisie to canalize the movement of the masses and to make off with it.

When Garine says that Chen-dai's influence rises above politics, one can only shrug his shoulders. The masked policy of the "upright man" in China as in India expresses in the most sublime and abstractly moralizing form the conservative interests of the possessors. The personal disinterestedness of Chen-dai is in no sense in opposition to his political function: the exploiters need "upright men" like the corrupted ecclesiastical hierarchy needs saints.

Who gravitates around Chen-dai? The novel replies with meritorious precision: a world of "aged mandarins, smugglers of opium and of obscene photographs, of scholars turned bicycle dealers, of Parisian barristers, of intellectuals of every kind." Behind them stands a more solid bourgeoisie bound up with England, which arms General Tang against the revolution. In the expectation of victory, Tang prepares to make Chen-dai the head of the government. Both of them, Chen-dai and Tang, nevertheless continue to be members of the Kuomintang which Borodin and Garine serve.

When Tang has a village attacked by his armies, and when he prepares to butcher the revolutionists, beginning with Borodin and Garine, his party comrades, the latter with the aid of Hong, mobilize and arm the unemployed. But after the victory won over Tang, the leaders do not seek to change a thing that existed before. They cannot break the ambiguous bloc with Chen-dai because they have no confidence in the workers, the coolies, the revolutionary masses, they are themselves contaminated with the prejudices of Chen-dai whose qualified arm they are.

In order "not to rebuff" the bourgeoisie they are forced to enter into struggle with Hong. Who is he and where does he come from? "The lowest dregs." He is one of those who are making the revolution and not those who rally to it when it is victorious. Having come to the idea of

killing the English governor of Hong Kong, Hong is
concerned with only one thing: "When I have been sentenced to capital punishment, you must tell the young to
follow my example." To Hong a clear program must be
given: to arouse the workers, to assemble them, to arm
them and to oppose them to Chen-dai as to an enemy.
But the bureaucracy of the Comintern seeks Chen-dai's
friendship, repulses Hong and exasperates him. Hong
exterminates bankers and merchants one after another,
the very ones who "support" the Kuomintang, Hong kills
missionaries: "those who teach people to support misery
must be punished, Christian priests or others. . . ." If
Hong does not find the right road, it is the fault of Borodin and Garine who have placed the revolution in the
hands of the bankers and the merchants. Hong reflects
the mass which is already rising but which has not yet
rubbed its eyes or softened its hands. He tries by the revol-
ver and the knife to act *for* the masses whom the agents
of the Comintern are paralyzing. Such is the unvarnished
truth about the Chinese Revolution.

Meanwhile, the Canton government is "oscillating, in
its attempt to stay straight, between Garine and Borodin,
who control the police and the trade unions, on the one
hand, and Chen-dai, who controls nothing, but who exists
all the same, on the other." We have an almost perfect
picture of the duality of power. The representatives of the
Comintern have in their hands the trade unions of Canton, the police, the cadet school of Whampoa, the sympathy of the masses, the aid of the Soviet Union. Chen-
dai has a "moral authority," that is, the prestige of the
mortally distracted possessors. The friends of Chen-dai
sit in a powerless government willingly supported by the
conciliators. But isn't this the regime of the February
Revolution, the Kerenskyist system, with the sole difference that the role of the Mensheviks is played by the
pseudo-Bolsheviks? Borodin has no doubt of it even
though he is made up as a Bolshevik and takes his makeup seriously.

The central idea of Garine and Borodin is to prohibit
Chinese and foreign boats, cruising towards the port of

Canton, from putting in at Hong Kong. By the commercial boycott these people, who consider themselves revolutionary realists, hope to shatter English domination in southern China. They never deem it necessary first of all to overthrow the government of the Canton bourgeoisie, which only waits for the moment to surrender the revolution to England. No, Borodin and Garine knock every day at the door of the "government," and hat in hand, beg that the saving decree be promulgated. One of them reminds Garine that at bottom the government is a phantom. Garine is not disconcerted. Phantom or not, he replies, let it go ahead while we need it. That is the way the priest needs relics which he himself fabricates with wax and cotton. What is concealed behind this policy which weakens and debases the revolution? The respect of a petty bourgeois revolutionist for a solid conservative bourgeois. It is thus that the reddest of the French radicals is always ready to fall on his knees before Poincare.

But perhaps the masses of Canton are not yet mature enough to overthrow the power of the bourgeoisie? From this whole atmosphere, the conviction arises that without the opposition of the Comintern, the phantom government would long before have been overthrown under the pressure of the masses. But let us admit that the Cantonese workers were still too weak to establish their own power. What, generally speaking, is the weak spot of the masses? Their inclination to follow the exploiters. In this case, the first duty of revolutionists is to help the workers liberate themselves from servile confidence. Nevertheless, the work done by the bureaucracy of the Comintern was diametrically opposed to this. It inculcated in the masses the notion of the necessity to submit to the bourgeoisie and it declared that the enemies of the bourgeoisie were their own enemies.

Do not rebuff Chen-dai! But if Chen-dai withdraws in spite of this, which is inevitable, it would not mean that Garine and Borodin will be delivered of their voluntary vassaldom towards the bourgeoisie. They will only choose as the new focus of their activity, Chiang Kai-shek, son of the same class and younger brother of Chen-dai. Head of the military school of Whampoa, founded by the Bol-

sheviks, Chiang Kai-shek does not confine himself to passive resistance; he is ready to resort to bloody force, not
in the plebeian form, the form of the masses, but in the
military form and only within limits that will permit the
bourgeoisie to retain an unlimited power over the army.
Borodin and Garine, by arming their enemies, disarm
and repulse their friends. This is the way they prepare the
catastrophe.

But are we not overestimating the influence of the revolutionary bureaucracy upon the events? No, it showed
itself stronger than it might have thought, if not for good
then at least for evil. The coolies who are only beginning
to exist politically require a courageous leadership. Hong
requires a bold program. The revolution requires the energies of millions of rising men. But Borodin and his bureaucrats require Chen-dai and Chiang Kai-shek. They
strangle Hong and prevent the worker from raising his
head. In a few months, they will stifle the agrarian insurrection of the peasantry so as not to repulse the bourgeois
army command. Their strength is that they represent the
Russian October, Bolshevism, the Communist International. Having usurped authority, the banner and the material resources of the greatest of revolutions, the bureaucracy bars the road to another revolution which also had
all chances of being great.

The dialogue between Borodin and Hong is the most
terrific indictment of Borodin and his Moscow inspirers.
Hong, as always, is after decisive action. He demands the
punishment of the most prominent bourgeois. Borodin
finds this sole objection: those who are "paying" must not
be touched. "Revolution is not so simple," says Garine for
his part. "Revolution involves paying an army," adds
Borodin. These aphorisms contain all the elements of the
noose in which the Chinese Revolution was strangled.
Borodin protected the bourgeoisie which, in recompense,
made contributions to the "revolution," the money going to
the army of Chiang Kai-shek. The army of Chiang Kai-
shek exterminated the proletariat and liquidated the revolution. Was it really impossible to foresee this? And wasn't
it really foreseen? The bourgeoisie pays willingly only for
the army which serves it against the people. The army of

the revolution does not wait for donations: it makes them
pay. This is called the revolutionary dictatorship. Hong
comes forward successfully at workers' meetings and thunders against the "Russians," the bearers of ruin for the
revolution. The way of Hong himself does not lead to the
goal but he is right as against Borodin. "Had the Tai
Ping leaders Russian advisers? Had the Boxers?" Had the
Chinese Revolution of 1924-1927 been left to itself it would
perhaps not have come to victory immediately but it would
not have resorted to the methods of hara-kiri, it would not
have known shameful capitulations and it would have
trained revolutionary cadres. Between the dual power of
Canton and that of Petrograd there is the tragic difference
that in China there was no Bolshevism in evidence; under
the name of Trotskyism, it was declared a counterrevolutionary doctrine and was persecuted by every method of
calumny and repression. Where Kerensky did not succeed
during the July days, Stalin succeeded ten years later in
China.

Borodin and "all the Bolsheviks of his generation," Garine assures us, were distinguished by their struggle against
the anarchists. This remark was needed by the author
so as to prepare the reader for the struggle of Borodin
against Hong's group. Historically it is false. Anarchism
was unable to raise its head in Russia not because the
Bolsheviks fought successfully against it but because they
had first dug up the ground under its feet. Anarchism, if
it does not live within the four walls of intellectuals' cafes
and editorial offices, but has penetrated more deeply,
translates the psychology of despair in the masses and
signifies the political punishment for the deceptions of
democracy and the treachery of opportunism. The boldness of Bolshevism in posing the revolutionary problems
and in teaching their solution left no room for the development of anarchism in Russia. But if the historical investigation of Malraux is not exact, his recital shows admirably
how the opportunist policy of Stalin-Borodin prepared the
ground for anarchist terrorism in China.

Driven by the logic of this policy, Borodin consents to
adopt a decree against the terrorists. The firm revolutionists, driven onto the road of adventurism by the crimes

of the Moscow leaders, are declared outlaws by the bourgeoisie of Canton, with the benediction of the Comintern. They reply with acts of terrorism against the pseudorevolutionary bureaucrats who protect the moneyed bourgeoisie. Borodin and Garine seize the terrorists and destroy them, no longer defending the bourgeois alone but also their own heads. It is thus that the policy of conciliation inexorably slips down to the lowest degree of treachery.

The book is called *Les Conquerants*. The author applies this ambiguous title, which depicts the revolution in the colors of imperialism, to the Russian Bolsheviks, or more exactly, to a certain part of them. The conquerors? The Chinese masses rose for a revolutionary insurrection, with the influence of the October upheaval as their example and with Bolshevism as their banner. But the "conquerors" conquered nothing. On the contrary, they surrendered everything to the enemy. If the Russian Revolution called forth the Chinese Revolution, the Russian epigones strangled it. Malraux does not make these deductions. He does not even suspect their existence. All the more clearly do they emerge upon the background of his remarkable book.

CELINE AND POINCARE:
NOVELIST AND POLITICIAN

This essay, begun in Turkey and completed in France, was written in a time when Trotsky was absorbed in French politics and literature.

Louis-Ferdinand Celine walked into great literature as other men walk into their own homes. A mature man, with a colossal stock of observations as physician and artist, with a sovereign indifference toward academism, with an extraordinary instinct for intonations of life and language, Celine has written a book which will survive, independently of whether he writes other books, and whether they attain the level of his first. *Journey to the End of the Night* is a novel of pessimism, a book dictated by terror in the face of life, and weariness of it, rather than by indignation. Active indignation is linked up with hope. In Celine's book there is no hope.

A Parisian student, who comes from a family of little men, a rationalist, an antipatriot, and a semianarchist— the cafes of the Latin quarter swarm with such types—

A first draft of this essay was completed May 10, 1933, and was modified the following year in France. It was printed in *Atlantic Monthly,* October 1935.

enlists, to his own astonishment, at the very first trumpet
call, as a volunteer in the army; he is sent to the front,
and in the mechanized slaughter finds himself envying
the horses who perish as men do, but without mouthing
false phrases; after being wounded and bemedaled, he wanders through the hospitals where successful doctors exhort
him to speed his return to the "flaming cemetery of battles";
as an invalid, he is discharged from the army; he de-
parts for an African colony and there pines away from
human baseness, from the heat and the malaria of the
tropics; he makes his way illegally into the United States,
and finds employment in Ford's plant; he finds a true mate
in a prostitute (these are the genuinely tender pages in the
book); he returns to France, becomes a physician to the
poor, and, soul-sick, wanders through the night of life
among the sick and the hearty, all equally pathetic, depraved, and miserable.

Celine does not at all set himself the goal of exposing
social conditions in France. True, in passing, he spares
neither priests nor generals nor ministers, nor the president of the republic. But all the while the warp of his tale
extends considerably below the level of the ruling classes,
cutting across the milieu of little men, functionaries, students, traders, artisans, and concierges; and in addition,
on two occasions, it transports itself beyond the bound-
aries of France. The present social system is as rotten
as every other, whether past or future. Celine, in general,
is dissatisfied with men and their affairs.

The novel is conceived and executed as a panorama of
life's meaninglessness, with its cruelties, conflicts, and lies,
with no issue, and no light flickering. A noncommissioned
officer torturing the soldiers just before he perishes together with them; an American coupon clipper airing
her emptiness in European hotels; French colonial functionaries brutalized by greed and failure; New York, with
its automatic unconcern for the man without a checkbook, technically perfected to suck the marrow from human bones; then Paris again; the petty and envious little
universe of scholars; the protracted and docile death of
a seven-year-old boy; the rape of a little girl; the little
virtuous rentiers who murder their mother in order to

economize; the priest in Paris and the priest in darkest Africa, both equally alert to sell a man for a few hundred francs, the one an accomplice of civilized rentiers, the other in cahoots with cannibals . . . from chapter to chapter, from one page to the next, the slivers of life compose themselves into a mud-caked, bloody nightmare of meaninglessness. Receptivity which is passive, with its nerves sliced open, without the will straining toward the future—that is the psychological base of despair, sincere in the convulsions of its cynicism.

Celine the moralist follows the footsteps of the artist, and step by step he rips away the halo from all those social values which have become highly acclaimed through custom, from patriotism and personal ties down to love. Is the fatherland in danger? "No great loss, when the landlord's house burns down. . . . There will be rent to pay just the same." He has no use for historical criteria. Danton's war is not superior to Poincare's: in both instances the "patriotic function" was paid in the coin of blood. [1] Love is poisoned by selfishness and vanity. All forms of idealism are merely "petty instincts draped in highfaluting phrases." Even the image of the mother is not spared: on meeting her wounded son "she squealed like a bitch whose pup had been restored. But she was beneath a bitch because she had faith in those syllables she was told in order to deprive her of her son."

Celine's style is subordinated to his receptivity of the objective world. In his seemingly careless, ungrammatical, passionately condensed language there lives, beats, and vibrates the genuine wealth of French culture, the entire emotional and mental experience of a great nation, in its living content, in its keenest tints.

And, concurrently, Celine writes like a man who has stumbled across human language for the first time. The artist has newly threshed the dictionary of French literature. Pat expressions fly off like chaff. And, instead, words that have been excluded from circulation by academic aesthetics and morality become irreplaceable to give expression to life in its crudeness and abjectness. Erotic terms serve Celine only to rip the glamour from eroticism. He operates with them in the same manner in which he

utilizes the names of other physiological functions which
do not meet with recognition on the part of art.

On the very first page of the novel the reader unexpectedly runs across the name of Poincare, the president
of the republic, who, as the latest issue of *Le Temps* reports, hies himself in the morning to open a lap-dog show.

This detail is not a piece of fiction. Evidently this is
one of the duties of the president of the republic, and
personally we see no ground for objecting to it. But the
mischievous newspaper quotation obviously is not intended to serve the ends of glorifying the head of the
state.

Yet, ex-President Poincare, the most prosaic of all outstanding personalities of the republic, happens to be its
most authoritative political figure. Since his illness he has
become an icon. Not only the Rights, but the Radicals
deem it impossible to mention his name without pronounc-
ing a few words in pathetic avowal of love. Poincare is,
incontestably, the purest distillate of a bourgeois culture
such as the French nation is — the most bourgeois of all
nations, pickled in the consciousness of its bourgeoisdom,
and proud of it as the mainspring of its providential
role toward the rest of mankind.

The national conceit of the French bourgeoisie, cloaked
in exquisite forms, is the crystallized precipitate of the
ages. The past, the time when their forefathers had a great
historic mission to perform, has left the descendants a rich
wardrobe which serves as a cloak for the most hidebound
conservatism. The entire political and cultural life of
France is staged in the costumes of the past.

Just as in countries whose currency is fixed, so in French
life fictitious values have a compulsory circulation. The
formulas of liberationist messianism, which have long
since gone off the parity of objective reality, still preserve
their high compulsory rate. Conventionalities seem to have
taken on flesh and blood, attaining an independent existence. Powder and rouge might still be considered fraudu-
lent; but a mask ceases to be a forgery: it is simply a
technical instrument. It exists apart from the flesh, and
it subordinates gestures and intonations to its own self.

Poincare is almost a social symbol. His supreme repre-
sentativeness molds his individuality. He has no other.
Just as in the youthful verses of this man — he did have
a youth — so in his senile memoirs there is not to be found
a single original note. The interests of the bourgeoisie
form his genuine moral shell, the source of his icy pathos.
The conventional values of French politics have entered
into his marrow and blood. "I am a bourgeois, and nothing bourgeois is alien to me." The political mask has
fused with the face. Hypocrisy, attaining the character of
the absolute, becomes a sincerity of its own sort.

So peaceloving is the French government, according to
Poincare, that it is incapable even of presupposing any
mental reservations on the part of the enemy. "Beautiful
is the trust of the people always endowing others with its
own virtues." This is not hypocrisy any longer, not subjective falsehood, but a compulsory element in a ritual, like
a postscript vowing eternal faithfulness appended to a
perfidious letter.

Emil Ludwig put a question to Poincare, at the time of
the occupation of the Ruhr: [2] "In your opinion, is it that
we don't want to pay, or that we are unable to pay?"
And Poincare replied: "No one likes to pay of his own
accord."

In July, 1931, Bruening [3] asked Poincare by telegraph
for cooperation, and he received for an answer, "Learn
to suffer."

But just as personal egoism, when it transcends a certain
limit, begins to devour itself, so too does the egoism of a
conservative class. Poincare wished to crucify Germany
so as to free France from anxiety once and for all. Meantime, the chauvinistic distillations of the Versailles peace,
criminally mild in the eyes of Poincare, condensed in Germany into the ominous visage of Hitler. Without the Ruhr
occupation, the Nazis would not have come to power so
easily. And Hitler in power opens up the prospect of new
wars.

The national French ideology is built upon the cult of
lucidity — that is, logic. It is not the logic of the eighteenth
century, wined by an audacity that overthrew the entire
world, but the niggardly, cautious, and ready-for-any-

compromise logic of the Third Republic. With the condescending sense of superiority with which an old master explains the precepts of his craft, Poincare speaks in his memoirs of "these difficult operations of the mind: selection, classification, coordination." Unquestionably, difficult operations. But Poincare himself performs them not within the three-dimensional space of the historical process, but in the two-dimensional plane of documents. To him truth is merely the product of law proceedings, the rational interpretation of treaties and laws. The conservative rationalism of ruling France bears the same relation to Descartes as does, say, medieval scholasticism to Aristotle.

The much-trumpeted "sense of proportion" has become the sense of *petty* proportions. It endows the mind with a tendency toward mosaics. With what loving care does Poincare depict the most insignificant episodes of statecraft! He copies the order of the White Elephant, bestowed upon him by the Danish king, as if it were a priceless miniature: its dimensions, shape, pattern, and the coloring of the stupid fingle-fangle — nothing is left out in his memoirs.

Words serve him either to define the size of the reparations or to figure as rhetorical decorations. He compares his sojourn in the Elysee palace with the incarceration of Silvio Pellico in the dungeons of the Austrian monarchy! [4] "In these salons of gilded banality nothing struck a responsive chord in my imagination." Gilded banality, however, is the official style of the Third Republic. And Poincare's imagination is the sublimation of this style.

On the very eve of the impending war, Poincare was making a maritime journey between Petersburg and France: he does not miss the opportunity to insert an oil landscape into the anxious chronicle of his journey: "the pale, almost deserted sea, indifferent to human conflicts." Word for word, precisely what he had written in his matriculating examination at the Lycee! When he dilates upon his patriotic worries, he lists, in passing, every kind of flower that decorated his summer retreat: between a code telegram and a telephone conversation — a scrupulous catalogue of a florist shop! At the most critical moments, the Siamese cat also intrudes, as the symbol of family intimacy. It is impossible to read without a feeling of suffocation this autobiographic protocol, lacking a single living image, lacking human feeling even, but replete instead with "indifferent" seas, ferns, garlands, hyacinths, doves, and the all-pervading odor of a Siamese cat.

There are two spheres in life: the one public and official, which is passed off for the whole of life, the other secret and most important. This dualism cuts across personal relationships, as well as social: across the intimate family circle, the school, the courtroom, parliament, and the diplomatic service. It is lodged in the conditions of the contradictory development of human society, and it is peculiar to all civilized countries and peoples. But the forms, the scope, and the masks of this dualism are luminously tinted with national colorations.

In Anglo-Saxon countries religion enters as an important element into the system of moral dualism. Official France has deprived itself of this important resource. While the British masonry is incapable of comprehending a universe without God, and, similarily, a parliament without a king, or property without the proprietor, the French masons have deleted "the Great Architect of the universe" from their statutes. In political deals the wider the couches are, the better the service: to sacrifice earthly interests for the sake of heavenly problematics would imply going headlong against Latin lucidity. Politicians, however, like Archimedes, require a fulcrum; the will of the Great Architect had to be supplanted by values on this side of the great divide. The first of these is — France.

Nowhere is the "religion of patriotism" spoken of so readily as in the secular republic. All the attributes with which human imagination has endowed the Father, the Son, and the Holy Ghost have been transferred to his own nation by the free-thinking French bourgeois. And since France is an image female in gender, she has had conferred upon her the traits of the Virgin Mary as well. The politician steps forward as the lay priest of a secular divinity. The liturgy of patriotism worked out in elaborate detail forms a necessary part of the political ritual. Words and expressions obtain which automatically engender their echo of applause in parliament, just as certain church words are cued to call forth kneeling or tears on the part of the believers.

However, there is a difference. By its very nature the sphere of true religion is removed from daily practice; given the necessary delimitation of jurisdiction, collisions are as little likely as the crash between an automobile and an airplane. The secular religion of patriotism, on the contrary, impinges directly upon day-to-day politics. Personal appetite and class interests rise up in hostility at every step against the formulas of pure patriotism. Fortunately the antagonists are so well educated, and above all so bound by mutual pledges, that they turn their eyes aside on all ticklish occasions. The governmental majority and the responsible opposition adhere voluntarily to the rules of the political game. The chief of these reads: "Just as the movement of physical bodies is subject to the laws of gravity, so the actions of politicians are subject to the love of the fatherland."

Yet even the sun of patriotism has its spots. A surfeit of mutual indulgence is inconvenient in that it engenders the feeling of impunity and erases the boundary between what is laudable and what is reprehensible. Thus political gases accumulate which explode from time to time and poison the atmosphere. The Union-General crash, Panama, the Dreyfus case, the Rochette case, the Stavisky crash — these are landmarks on the road of the Third Republic familiar to all.[5] Clemenceau was nicked by Panama. Poincare personally always remained on the side lines. But his politics fed from the very same sources. Not without cause does he proclaim his teacher in morality to be Marcus Aurelius, whose Stoic virtues managed to abide quite well with the morals of the imperial throne in decaying Rome.

In his memoirs Poincare laments that "during the first six months of 1914 . . . the abject spectacle of parliamentary intrigues and financial scandals passed before my eyes." But war, of course, with a single swoop swept away all selfish motives. *Union sacree* cleansed the souls. This is to say: the intrigues and the rascalities swung inward behind the patriotic scenes, there to assume unheard-of proportions. As Celine relates, the more drawn out the crit-ical resolution at the front, the more depraved the rear became. The picture of Paris in wartime is depicted in the novel by the hand of a merciless master. There is almost no politics. But there is something more: the living sub-stratum out of which it takes form.

In all court, parliamentary, and financial scandals of France, what hits one between the eyes is their organic character. From the industry and thriftiness of the pea-sant and the artisan, from the wariness of the merchant and the industrialist, from the blind greed of the rentier, the courtesy of the parliamentarian, and the patriotism of the press, the numberless threads lead to the ganglia which bear the generic name of Panama. In the web of connections, favors, mediations, masked semibribes, there are thousands of transitional forms between civic virtue and capital crime. No sooner does an unfortunate incident shrivel the irreproachable veils, exposing to view the anat-omy of politics — at any time, in any place — than it be-comes immediately necessary to appoint a parliamentary or judicial committee of investigation.

But precisely here arises the difficulty: what to begin with, and where to end?

Only because Stavisky went bankrupt at an inopportune moment was it revealed that this Argonaut among small saloonkeepers had, as his errand boys, deputies and jour-nalists, ex-ministers and ambassadors, some denoted by initials, others by their full names; that papers profitable to the banker passed through the ministries like lightning, while the harmful ones were held up until rendered harm-less. Using the resources of his fancy, salon ties, and print-ing paper, the financial magus created wealth, played with the lives of thousands of people, bribed — what a coarse and an impermissibly precise word! — rewarded, support-ed, and encouraged the press, the officials, and the par-liamentarians. And almost always in a nonincriminating manner!

As the scope of the work of the investigation committee grew wider, the more obviously hopeless the investigation became. Where one was prepared to unearth crime, one revealed only the usual reciprocity between politics and finance. Where the source of the disease was sought, the normal tissue of the organism was found.

As attorney, X was the guardian of the interests of Stavisky's enterprises; as journalist, he supported the tariff system which happened to coincide with Stavisky's interests; as people's representative, he specialized in revamping tariff duties. And as minister? The committee was endlessly occupied with the question whether X, while holding the post of minister, continued to receive his attorney's fee, or whether in the interval between two ministerial crises his conscience had remained as clear as crystal.

What a load of moral pedantry is there injected into hypocrisy! Raoul Peret, former chairman of the Chamber of Deputies, candidate for president of the republic, turned out to be a candidate for capital criminal.[6] Yet, according to his profound conviction, he had acted "like everybody else," perhaps only a trifle less carefully — at any rate, not so fortunately.

Against the background of the "abject spectacle of parliamentary intrigues and financial scandals" — to use Poincare's expression — Celine's novel attains a twofold significance. Not without cause did the well-meaning press, which in its own time was wroth with the public investigation, immediately damn Celine for calumniating the "nation." The parliamentary committee had, at any rate, carried on its investigation in the courteous language of the initiated, from which neither the accusers nor the accused departed. But Celine is not bound by convention. He rudely discards the gratuitous colors of the political palette. He has his own colors. These he has ripped from life, with the artist's privilege.

True, he takes life not in its parliamentary cross section, not on the ruling heights, but in its most prosaic manifestations. But this does not ease matters any. He bares the roots. From underneath the veils of decorum he exposes the mud and blood. In his ominous panorama, murder for the sake of trifling gain loses its extraordinariness: it is just as inseparable from the day-to-day me-

chanics of life, propelled by greed and self-seeking, as the
Stavisky affair is inseparable from the much higher me-
chanics of modern finance. Celine shows what is. For this
reason he appears as a revolutionist.

But Celine is no revolutionist, and does not aim to be
one. He does not occupy himself with the goal of reconstructing society, which is chimerical in his eyes. He only
wants to tear away the prestige from everything that frightens and oppresses him. To ease his conscience from terror
in the face of life, this physician to the poor had to resort
to new modes of imagery. He turned out to be the revolutionist of the novel. Generally speaking, that is the law
governing the movement of art: it moves through the
reciprocal repulsion of tendencies.

Decay hits not only parties in power, but schools of
art as well. The creative methods become hollow and
cease to react upon human sensibilities — an infallible sign
that the school has become ripe enough for the cemetery
of exhausted possibilities — that is to say, for the Academy.
Living creativeness cannot march ahead without repulsion away from official tradition, canonized ideas and
feelings, images and expressions covered by the lacquer
of use and wont. Each new tendency seeks for the most
direct and honest contact between words and emotions.
The struggle against pretense in art always grows to a
lesser or greater measure into the struggle against the
injustice of human relations. The connection is self-evident:
art which loses the sense of the social lie inevitably defeats
itself by affectation, turning into mannerism.

The richer and more solid is national cultural tradition,
the more abrupt is the repulsion from it. Celine's power
lies in that through supreme effort he divests himself of
all canons, transgresses all conventions. He not only
undresses life's model, but rips her skin off. Hence flows
the indictment of calumny.

But it is precisely in his impetuous radicalism of negat-
ing the national tradition that Celine is deeply nationalistic.
Just as the French antimilitarists prior to the war were
most often desperate patriots, so is Celine a Frenchman
to the marrow of his bones, a Frenchman who has torn
himself loose from the official masks of the Third Republic.

Celinism is moral and artistic anti-Poincareism. In that is Celine's strength, but, too, his limitation.

When Poincare compares himself to Silvio Pellico, he is apt to give one the chills by this combination of smugness and bad taste. But does not the real Pellico, who was incarcerated not in a palace, as head of the government, but in the dungeons of Santa Margherita and Spielberg as a patriot—does he not reveal another and a much higher side of human nature? Instead of this Italian Catholic believer, who was besides a victim rather than a fighter, Celine might have reminded the eminent captive of the Elysee palace of another prisoner who spent four decades of his life in the prisons of France, prior to the time when the sons and grandsons of his jailers named one of the Parisian boulevards after him—namely, Auguste Blanqui. [7] Is that not evidence that there is something lodged in man which is capable of raising him above himself?

Only because there are numerous and well-paid priests serving the altars of false altruism does Celine turn away from greatness of mind and heroism, from great projects and hopes, from everything that leads humanity out from the dark night of the circumscribed I. It seems almost as if the moralist who is so ruthless to himself had been repelled by his own image in the mirror, and smashed the glass, cutting his hands. Such a struggle may enervate, but it does not break out toward the light's glimmer. Hopelessness ever leads to docility. Conciliation opens the doors to the Academy. There has been more than one previous occasion when those who have blasted the literary foundations ended underneath the dome of immortality.

In the music of this book there is a dissonance pregnant with much meaning. By rejecting not only the present but also what must take its place, the artist gives his support to what is. To that extent Celine, willy-nilly, is the ally of Poincare. But, exposing the lie, he instills the want for a more harmonious future. Though he himself may consider that nothing good can generally come from man, the very intensity of his pessimism bears within it a dose of the antidote.

Celine, as he is, stems from French reality and the French novel. He does not have to be ashamed of his ancestry. The French genius has found its unsurpassed expression in the novel. Beginning with Rabelais, likewise a physician, there has branched, in the course of four centuries, a splendid genealogy of the masters of epic prose: from life-loving belly laughter down to hopelessness and despair, from the brilliant break of day to the depths of the night.

Celine will not write a second book with such an aversion for the lie and such a disbelief in the truth. The dissonance must resolve itself. Either the artist will make his peace with the darkness or he will perceive the dawn.

Louis-Ferdinand Celine

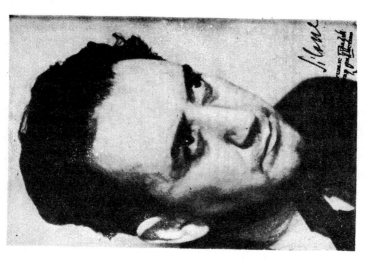

Ignazio Silone

SILONE'S *FONTAMARA*

This short, enthusiastic notice was written on the steamer which was taking Trotsky from Turkey to France, his new place of exile. It was dashed off while he was busy hammering out his ideas about the Fourth International.

A remarkable book! From the first line to the last it is directed against the fascist regime in Italy, against its lies, its violence, a book of passionate political propaganda. But revolutionary passion is raised here to such heights that it creates a truly artistic work. Fontamara is only a poor godforsaken village in the south of Italy. In the space of the book's two hundred pages, this name becomes a symbol of the whole Italian countryside, its poverty, its despair, but also its indignation.

Silone knows the Italian peasantry remarkably well; the first twenty years of the author's life, according to his own words, were spent in Fontamara. Embellishment and sentimentality are foreign to him. He knows how to see life as it is, to generalize what he sees by means of the Marxist method and then to embody its generalizations in artistic images. The story is told by the peasants, cafoni, paupers themselves. Despite the exceptional diffi-

Written July 19, 1933, this article appeared in *Bulletin of the Opposition*, numbers 36-37, October 1933 and in *The Militant*, August 26, 1933.

culties of this style, the author executes like a real master. Some chapters have a stupendous force!

Has this book appeared in the Soviet Union? Has it drawn the attention of the publishing houses of the Comintern? The book deserves a circulation of millions of copies. But no matter what the attitude of the official bureaucracy may be towards works of truly revolutionary literature, *Fontamara* — we are convinced — will make its way. To assist the circulation of this book is the duty of every revolutionist.

CRITICAL JOTTINGS

These are excerpts from Trotsky's Diary in Exile, 1935 *which was written in France and Norway. Trotsky in his first entry states that he is planning to keep a "political diary" as "ersatz journalism," a substitute for genuine journalism during a time when the conditions of his exile cut him off from such activity. Later he comments on the fact that he has been keeping a literary diary as well as a political one: "And could it actually be otherwise? For politics and literature constitute in essence the content of my personal life." The literary portion, however, is larger than it would otherwise have been because, although he devoted most of his tremendous energy to the political work he was able to carry on, that energy was frequently vitiated by a recurring fever. At such times Trotsky turned to the reading of novels.*

Aleksei Tolstoy's novel, *Peter I,* is a work remarkable for the immediacy of its feeling for the remote Russian past. Of course this is not "proletarian literature": as a writer A. Tolstoy has his roots in old Russian literature — and world literature as well, naturally. But undoubtedly

it was the Revolution—by the law of contrast—that gave
him (and not him alone) an especially keen feeling for
the peculiar nature of Russian antiquity—immobile, wild
and unwashed. It taught him something more: to look
beneath the ideological conceptions, fantasies and super-
stitions for the simple vital interests of the various social
groups and of the individuals belonging to them. With
great artistic penetration A. Tolstoy lays bare the hidden
material underpinnings of the ideological conflicts in
Peter's Russia. In this way individual psychological realism is elevated to social realism. This is undoubtedly an
achievement of the Revolution as an immediate experience
and of Marxism as a general doctrine.

Mauriac, a French novelist whom I do not know,[1] an
Academician (which is a poor recommendation), wrote
or said recently: we shall recognize the USSR when it
produces a new novel of the calibre of Tolstoy or Dostoev-
sky. Mauriac was apparently making a distinction between
this artistic, idealistic criterion and a Marxist, materialistic
one, based on relations of production. Actually, there is
no contradiction here. In the preface to my book *Literature
and Revolution* I wrote about twelve years ago:

"But even a successful solution of the elementary problems of food, clothing, shelter, and even of literacy, would
in no way signify a complete victory of the new historic
principle, that is, of Socialism. Only a movement of scientific thought on a national scale and the development of
a new art would signify that the historic seed has not only
grown into a plant, but has even flowered. In this sense,
the development of Art is the highest test of the vitality
and significance of each epoch."

However, it is impossible in any sense to represent the
novel of A. Tolstoy as a "flower" of the new epoch. It
has already been stated why this is true. And the novels
which are officially regarded as "proletarian art" (in a
period of complete liquidation of classes!) are as yet totally
lacking in artistic significance. Of course, there is nothing
"alarming" in this. It takes some time for a complete overturn of social foundations, customs and assumptions to
produce an artistic crystallization along new axes. How
much time? One cannot say offhand, but a long time.

Art is always carried in the baggage train of a new epoch, and great art — the novel — is an especially heavy load. That there has been no great new art so far is quite natural and, as I have said, should not and cannot alarm anyone. What can be alarming, though, are the revolting imitations of a new art written on the order of the bureaucracy. The incongruities, falsity and ignorance of the present "Soviet" Bonapartism attempting to establish unlimited control over art — these things make impossible any artistic creativity whatsoever, the first condition for which is *sincerity.* An old engineer can perhaps build a turbine reluctantly; it would not be first-rate, precisely because it had been built reluctantly, but it would serve its purpose. But one cannot, however, write a poem *reluctantly.*

It is not by accident that Aleksei Tolstoy retreated to the end of the seventeenth century and the beginning of the eighteenth in order to gain the freedom essential to the artist.

*   *   *

Jules Romains is apparently very much concerned about it,[2] since he offers himself as a savior (Society of the Ninth of July). In one of the later books in his epic Romains seems to depict himself under the name of the writer Strigelius (I think that's the right name). This S. has the same aptitude and ability as other writers, but he has something else on top of that. His ability is not only that of a writer. He has discovered that his "ability" (genius) is universal. His capacity is greater than other people's in other fields too, in politics in particular. Hence the Society of the Ninth of July and J. R.'s book on the relations between France and Germany.

No doubt this talented writer has lost his balance a bit. He understands a good deal about politics, but rather visually, i.e., superficially. The deep social springs behind events remain hidden from him. In the sphere of individual psychology he is remarkable, but again not profound. As a writer (and even more as a politician) he is evidently lacking in *character.* He is a spectator, and not a participant. But only a participant can be a profound specta-

tor. Zola was a participant. That is why, with all his vul-
garities and lapses, he is far above Romains: deeper,
warmer, more human. J. Romains refers to himself (this
time without a pseudonym, by his own name) as *distant*
[in French]. This is true. But his *distance* [in French]
is not only optical but also moral. His moral lights allow
him to see everything only from a certain fixed distance.
That is why he seems to be too far away from little
Bastide and too close to the murderer Quinette. With a
participant, his *"distance"* changes depending on the nature
of his participation, while with a spectator it does not.
A spectator like Romains can be a *remarkable* writer,
but he cannot be a *great* writer.

*   *   *

In his novel *The Rape of Europe*—a "literary" novel,
not profound and often pretentious — Fedin[3] demonstrates
one thing: the revolution has taught (or forced) Russian
writers to pay closer attention to facts which reveal the
social dependence of one person upon another. The normal
bourgeois novel has two floors: emotions are experienced
only in the *bel-etage* (Proust!), while the people in the
basement polish shoes and take out chamber-pots. This
is rarely mentioned in the novel itself, but presupposed
as something quite natural. The hero sighs, the heroine
breathes; it follows that they perform other bodily functions too; somebody, then, has to clean up after them. I
remember reading a novel of Louys called *Amour and
Psyche*—an unusually sham and banal concoction, completed, if I am not mistaken, by the unbearable Claude
Farrere. Louys puts the servants somewhere in the nether
regions, so that his enamored hero and heroine never
see them. An ideal social system for amorous idlers and
their artists!

Essentially Fedin too is primarily interested in the people
of the *bel-etage* (in Holland), but he tries, at least in passing, to observe the psychology of the relationship between
a chauffeur and a financial magnate and between a sailor
and a shipowner. He offers no revelations, but nevertheless he does light up certain corners of those human rela-

tionships on which contemporary society rests. The influence of the October Revolution upon literature is still completely a thing of the future!

* * *

I read yesterday a novel by Victor Margueritte called *Le Compagnon*. A very feeble writer; in his banal prose one feels no trace of the great school of the French novel. His radical leanings are superficial and sentimental. This radicalism — with a lining of feminism — might not have looked bad in the age of Louis-Philippe. Now it seems completely soured. The eroticism of the novel smacks of the police blotter.

Nevertheless Mar[gueritte]'s novel does throw some light on personal and family relations in certain — and by no means the worst — bourgeois circles in France. The "hero" of the novel is a socialist. The author reproaches his hero for adopting the attitude toward women of a "bourgeois" — or rather, one should say, of a slave-owner. The polemic in *Le Populaire* on the subject of whether or not to give the franchise to women demonstrates that among the socialists, too, there reigns the same base proprietary attitude toward women that permeates the legislation and law of the country.

But even Margueritte's proposals for emancipation actually do not go beyond a separate checkbook for the wife. While in our uncouth Russia there is much barbarism, almost zoologism, in the old bourgeois cultures there are horrible encrustations of fossilized narrow-mindedness, crystallized cruelty, polished cynicism . . . What enormous upheavals, transformations, and efforts will yet be needed to raise the average man to a higher level of personality!

* * *

I have finished a novel by Leon Frapie, *La Maternelle*, a popular edition at 2 francs. I don't know this author at all. In any case he shows very courageously the backyard — and the darkest corner of the backyard — of French civilization, of Paris. The cruelty and meanness of life

strike hardest at the children, at the very smallest ones.
Frapie, then, set himself a problem of looking at present-
day civilization through the frightened eyes of the hungry
maltreated children with hereditary vices in their blood. The
narrative is not sustained artistically; there are break-
downs and failures; the heroine's arguments are at times
naive and even mannered; but the author succeeds in creating the necessary impression. He knows of no way out
and does not even seem to be looking for one. The book
is charged with hopelessness. But this hopelessness is immeasurably higher than the smug and cheap recipes of
Victor Margueritte.

*   *   *

I have been unwell, after two weeks of intensive work,
and have read several novels. *Clarisse et sa fille* by Marcel Prevost. The novel is highly virtuous, but it is the
virtue of an old cocotte. Prevost as a psychoanalyst! He
refers to himself as a "psychologist" more than once. He
also cites Paul Bourget as an authority on affairs of the
heart. [4] I remember with what well-deserved contempt, even
disgust, Octave Mirabeau spoke about Bourget. And really,
what superficial, false, and rotten literature this is!

A Russian story: *Kolkhida* by Paustovsky. The author
is evidently a sailor of the old school who took part in
the Civil War. [5] A gifted man, technically superior to the
so-called "proletarian writers." He paints nature well; you
can discern the sharp eye of a seaman. At times, in his
descriptions of Soviet life (in the Transcaucasus) he reminds one of a good gymnast with his elbows tied. But
there are some stirring pictures of work, sacrifice and
enthusiasm. Strange as it may seem, his most successful
character is an *English* sailor who finds himself stranded
in the Caucasus and is drawn into working for the cause.

The third novel — *The Great Assembly-line* by Yakov
Ilyin. This one is a pure specimen of what is called "proletarian literature," and not the worst specimen at that.
The author depicts the "romance" of a tractor factory —
how it is constructed and put in operation. There are a
great many technical problems and details, and still more

discussions about them. It is written in a comparatively lively style but it is still rather the style of a literary apprentice. In this "proletarian" work the proletariat is put *far* into the background. The foreground is taken up by the organizers, administrators, technicians, managers and — machine tools. The gulf between the upper stratum and the mass runs through the whole epic of this American assembly-line on the Volga.

The author is extremely pious about the party line; his attitude toward the leaders is permeated with official veneration. It is difficult to define either the degree of sincerity of those feelings, since they are coerced and obligatory for all, or the degree of hostility toward the Opposition. The Trotskyists do occupy a definite, although secondary, place in the novel; and the author diligently ascribes to them views borrowed from the denunciatory editorials of *Pravda*. And still, in spite of its strictly good intentions, at times the novel reads like a satire on Stalin's regime. The enormous factory is put into operation before it is finished: there are machines, but no place for the workers to live. The work is not organized; there is not enough water; anarchy reigns everywhere. It is necessary to close down the factory temporarily to make further preparations. Close down the factory? But what will Stalin say? But this was promised to the Party Congress, etc. Disgusting Byzantinism instead of businesslike considerations. The result is a monstrous squandering of manpower and — bad tractors. The author quotes Stalin's speech at the meeting of industrial administrators: "To slow down the tempos? Impossible. What about the West?" (In April, 1927, Stalin had argued that the problem of the rate of industrialization had no relation to the problem of building socialism within a capitalist encirclement: "tempo" is our "internal affair.") Consequently it is "impossible" to reduce the tempos ordered from higher up. But why is the rate of expansion given as 25, and not 40 or 75? The ordered coefficient of expansion is never reached anyway, and the price for approaching it is low quality and wearing down of workers' lives and machinery. You can see it all in Ilyin's novel, in spite of the official piety of the author . . .

Some of the details are striking. Ordzhonikidze (in the
novel) says "thou" to a worker, while the latter answers
him with "you." [6] The whole dialogue is carried on in this
style, which the author himself regards as the natural
order of things.

But the grimmest aspect of the assembly-line romance
is the absence of political rights and the lack of individuality on the part of the workers, especially the proletarian youth, who are taught only to obey. A younger engineer who rebels against the excessive assignments is reminded by the Party Committee of his recent "Trotskyism"
and threatened with expulsion. Young party members argue about why nobody in the younger generation has
done anything outstanding in any field. The disputants
console themselves with rather confused arguments.
"Couldn't it be because we are smothered?"—one of them
lets slip this remark. He is attacked by all: we don't need
freedom of discussion, we have the guidance of the party
and "Stalin's instructions." The guidance of the party—
without discussion—this is just what "Stalin's instructions"
are, and they in their turn merely constitute an empirical
summing up of the experience of the bureaucracy. The
dogma of bureaucratic infallibility suffocates the young
people by infusing their characters with servility, Byzantinism, and false "wisdom." There probably are mature
people working in hiding somewhere. But on those who
give the official coloring to the younger generation there
is the indelible imprint of immaturity.

*   *   *

The state of my health condemns me to reading novels.
I picked up a book by Edgar Wallace for the first time.
So far as I know he is one of the most popular authors
in America and England. It is hard to imagine anything
more mediocre, contemptible, and crude. Not a shade of
perception, talent, or imagination. The adventures are
piled on without any art at all, like police records laid
one on top of the other. Not for a single moment did I
feel any excitement, interest, or even simple curiosity. While
reading the book you have a feeling as if out of boredom,

for lack of anything better to do, you were drumming your fingers on a fly-specked windowpane . . .

By this book alone you can judge to what a degree enlightened England (and of course not England alone) remains a country of cultivated savages. It is the millions of Englishmen and Englishwomen who avidly and excitedly — to the point of fainting spells — gaped at the processions and solemnities of the jubilee of the royal couple, who are voracious readers of Wallace's products.

* * *

Lying in the open air, I looked through a collection of articles by the anarchist Emma Goldman with a short accompanying biography, and am now reading the autobiography of "Mother Jones" [*in English*].[7] They both came from the ranks of American working women. But what a difference! Goldman is an individualist, with a small "heroic" philosophy concocted from the ideas of Kropotkin, Nietzsche and Ibsen. Jones is a heroic American proletarian, without doubts or rhetoric, but also without a philosophy. Goldman sets herself revolutionary aims, but tries to achieve them by completely unrevolutionary means. Mother Jones always sets herself the most moderate aims: *more pay and less hours* [in English], and tries to achieve them by bold and revolutionary means. They both reflect America, each in her own way: Goldman by her primitive rationalism, Jones by her no less primitive empiricism. But Jones represents a splendid landmark in the history of her class, while Goldman signifies a departure from her class into individualistic nonexistence. I could not stomach the Goldman articles: lifeless moralizing which smacks of rhetoric, despite all its sincerity. I am reading the Jones autobiography with delight.

In her terse and completely unpretentious descriptions of strikers' battles, Jones incidentally reveals a horrifying picture of the underside of American capitalism and its democracy. It is impossible to read without shudders and curses her tales of the exploitation and maiming of young children in the factories!

*   *   *

I have finished reading the autobiography of Mother Jones. It has been a long time since I have read anything with such interest and excitement. An epic book! What unflagging devotion to the working people, what organic contempt for the traitors and careerists from among the working-class "leaders." With ninety-one years of life behind her, this woman at a Pan-American Workers' Congress held up the example of Soviet Russia. At ninety-three she joined the Farmer-Labor Party. But the main substance of her life was her participation in workers' strikes, which — in America more frequently than anywhere else — turned into civil war . . . Has this book been translated into foreign languages?

MAXIM GORKY

When Maxim Gorky died in 1936 at the age of 68, Trotsky wrote this evaluation in Norway. In the Moscow trials that soon followed, Trotsky was accused, among other crimes, of having organized a conspiracy to assassinate Stalin and other Soviet leaders and of having actually succeeded in poisoning the aged Gorky.

Gorky died when there was nothing more for him to say. This makes quite bearable the decease of a great writer who has left a deep mark on the development of the Russian intelligentsia and the Russian working class during the last forty years.

Gorky started his literary career as a tramp poet. This was his best period as an artist. From the lower depths, Gorky carried to the Russian intelligentsia the spirit of daring, the romantic bravery of people who had nothing to lose. The Russian intelligentsia was preparing to break the chains of czarism. It needed daring. It passed on its spirit to the masses.

In the events of the revolution, however, there was no

Written July 9, 1936 and published in *Bulletin of the Opposition*, number 51, July-August 1936. The first American translation appeared in *International Review*, September-October 1936.

place for a real live tramp, excepting as a participant in
robbery and pogroms. By December 1905 the Russian
proletariat and the radical intelligentsia that was bearing
Gorky on its shoulders met — in opposition. Gorky did
the honest thing. It was, in its way, a heroic effort. He
turned his face to the proletariat. The important product
of this about-face was *Mother*. A wider vista opened to the
writer, and he now dug deeper. But neither literary schooling nor political training could replace the splendid spontaneity of his first creative period. A tendency to cool
reasoning made its appearance in the ambitious tramp.
The artist began to resort to didacticism. During the years
of reaction, Gorky shared himself out almost evenly between the working class, which had then abandoned the
open political arena, and his old enemy-friend, the Russian
intelligentsia, who had now taken unto themselves a new
enthusiasm — religion. Together with the late Lunacharsky,
Gorky paid his tribute to the vogue of mysticism. As a
monument to his spiritual capitulation, we have his weak
novel *Confession*.

Deeper than any other trait in the makeup of that extraordinary self-learner was his worship of culture. It
seems that his first belated meeting with the lady had
seared him for life. Gorky lacked the necessary schooling
of thought and the historical intuition that might have enabled him to establish a convenient distance between himself and culture and would have given him the freedom
necessary for a critical estimate. In his attitude toward
culture there has always remained quite a bit of fetishism
and idolatry.

Gorky approached the war with a feeling of concern
for the cultural values of humanity. He was not so much
an internationalist as a cultural cosmopolite, though one
who was Russian to the marrow of his bones. He never
attained a revolutionary outlook on war nor a dialectical
understanding of culture. But he stood, nevertheless, heads
above the patriotic intellectual fraternity of the time.

He received the Revolution of 1917 almost in the manner
of a director of a museum of culture. He was alarmed.
He was in terror of "the savage soldiery and the workers
who would not work." He rejoined the left-wing intelli-

gentsia, who approved of a revolution but only if it was free from disorder. He met the October Revolution in the role of an outright enemy, though a passive one.

It was very hard for Gorky to get used to the victory of October. Turmoil reigned in the land. The intelligentsia hungered and suffered persecution. Culture was, or appeared to be, in danger. During those years, Gorky distinguished himself chiefly as a mediator between the Soviet power and the old intellectuals. He was their attorney in the court of the revolution. Lenin, who loved and valued Gorky, was very much afraid that the latter would fall victim to his connections and his weakness, and finally succeeded in having the writer leave the country voluntarily.

Gorky made his peace with the Soviet regime only when the "disorder" came to an end and there was evidence of an economic and cultural rise in the country. He warmly approved the great movement of the masses toward education. In gratefulness for that he even blessed, on the sly, the October overturn.

The last period of his life was undoubtedly the period of his decline. But even this decline was a natural part of his life's orbit. His tendency to didacticism received now its great opportunity. He became the tireless teacher of young writers, even schoolboys. He did not always teach the right thing but he did it with sincere insistence and open generosity that more than made up for his too inclusive friendship with the bureaucracy. Alongside with these human, a little too human, traits existed and predominated the old concern about technology, science and art. "Enlightened absolutism" gets along nicely with service to "culture." Gorky really believed that without the bureaucracy there would be no tractors, no five-year plans, and especially no printing presses and supplies of paper. He therefore forgave the bureaucracy the poor quality of the paper and even the sickening Byzantinism of the literature that was labelled "proletarian."

Most of the White emigration hated Gorky, characterizing him as a "traitor." Exactly what Gorky betrayed is not quite clear. Was he thought to be a traitor to the ideal of private property? The hatred shown to Gorky by the "former people" who once inhabited the *bel etage* is the most honorable tribute to the great man.

The Soviet press is now piling over the writer's still warm form mountains of unrestrained praise. They call him no less than a "genius." They describe him as the "greatest genius." Gorky would have most likely frowned at this kind of praise. But the press serving bureaucratic mediocrity has its criteria. If Stalin, Kaganovich and Mikoyan have been raised to the rank of genius in their lifetime, one naturally cannot refuse Gorky the epithet upon his death. Gorky will enter the history of Russian literature as an unquestionably clear and convincing example of great literary talent, not touched, however, by the breath of genius.

Of course, the dead writer is pictured now in Moscow as an unbending revolutionary and an "adamant Bolshevik." These are pure inventions of the bureaucracy. Gorky came to Bolshevism about 1905 or so, in the company of other democratic fellow travelers. He left together with them, without abandoning, however, personal friendly relations with the Bolsheviks. He entered the party only during the Soviet Thermidor. His enmity to the Bolsheviks during the October Revolution and the civil war, as well as his support of the Thermidorian bureaucracy, shows quite clearly that Gorky was never a revolutionary. True it is, however, that he was a satellite of the revolution. Bound to it by the inexorable law of gravitation, he turned about the Russian Revolution all his life. Like all satellites he had his "phases." The sun of the revolution sometimes lighted his face. Sometimes it fell on his back. But in all his phases, Gorky remained true to himself, to his peculiar, extremely rich, simple, and at the same time complicated nature. We take leave of him without a note of intimacy, without exaggerated praise, but with respect and gratefulness. The great writer and great man has left his mark on a period of history. He has helped to lay out new historic paths.

JACK LONDON'S

THE IRON HEEL

Trotsky became acquainted with The Iron Heel, *the* Looking Backward *of revolutionary socialism, through a copy which the author's daughter, Joan London, sent him. This excerpt comes from a letter he sent her.*

The book produced upon me — I speak without exaggeration — a deep impression. Not because of its artistic qualities: the form of the novel here represents only an armor for social analysis and prognosis. The author is intentionally sparing in his use of artistic means. He is himself interested not so much in the individual fate of his heroes as in the fate of mankind. By this, however, I don't want at all to belittle the artistic value of the work, especially in its last chapters beginning with the Chicago commune. The pictures of civil war develop in powerful frescoes. Nevertheless, this is not the main feature. The book surprised me with the audacity and independence of its historical foresight.

The world workers' movement at the end of the last and the beginning of the present century stood under the sign of reformism. The perspective of peaceful and uninterrupted world progress, of the prosperity of democracy and social reforms, seemed to be assured once and for

Written October 16, 1937 and appeared in *New International*, April 1945.

all. The first Russian Revolution, it is true, revived the
radical flank of the German social democracy and gave
for a certain time dynamic force to anarcho-syndicalism
in France. *The Iron Heel* bears the undoubted imprint
of the year 1905. But at the time when this remarkable
book appeared, the domination of counterrevolution was
already consolidating itself in Russia. In the world arena
the defeat of the Russian proletariat gave to reformism
the possibility not only of regaining its temporarily lost
positions but also of subjecting to itself completely the
organized workers' movement. It is sufficient to recall that
precisely in the following seven years (1907-14) the international social democracy ripened definitely for its base
and shameful role during the World War.

Jack London not only absorbed creatively the impetus
given by the first Russian Revolution but also courageously thought over again in its light the fate of capitalist
society as a whole. Precisely those problems which the
official socialism of this time considered to be definitely
buried: the growth of wealth and power at one pole, of
misery and destitution at the other pole; the accumulation
of social bitterness and hatred; the unalterable preparation of bloody cataclysms — all those questions Jack London felt with an intrepidity which forces one to ask himself again and again with astonishment: when was this
written? Really before the war?

One must accentuate especially the role which Jack London attributes to the labor bureaucracy and to the labor
aristocracy in the further fate of mankind. Thanks to
their support, the American plutocracy not only succeeds
in defeating the workers' insurrection but also in keeping
its iron dictatorship during the following three centuries.
We will not dispute with the poet the delay which can but
seem to us too long. However, it is not a question of Jack
London's pessimism, but of his passionate effort to shake
those who are lulled by routine, to force them to open
their eyes and to see what is and what approaches. The
artist is audaciously utilizing the methods of hyperbole.
He is bringing the tendencies rooted in capitalism: of
oppression, cruelty, bestiality, betrayal, to their extreme
expression. He is operating with centuries in order to mea-

sure the tyrannical will of the exploiters and the treacherous role of the labor bureaucracy. But his most "romantic" hyperboles are finally much more realistic than the
bookkeeperlike calculations of the so-called sober politicians.

It is easy to imagine with what a condescending per-
plexity the official socialist thinking of that time met Jack
London's menacing prophecies. If one took the trouble
to look over the reviews of *The Iron Heel* at that time
in the German *Neue Zeit* and *Vorwaerts,* in the Austrian
Kampf and *Arbeiterzeitung,* as well as in the other socialist
publications of Europe and America, he could easily convince himself that the thirty-year-old "romanticist" saw
incomparably more clearly and farther than all the social
democratic leaders of that time taken together. But Jack
London bears comparison in this domain not only with
the reformists. One can say with assurance that in 1907
not one of the revolutionary Marxists, not excluding Lenin
and Rosa Luxemburg, imagined so fully the ominous
perspective of the alliance between finance capital and
labor aristocracy. This suffices in itself to determine the
specific weight of the novel.

The chapter "The Roaring Abysmal Beast" undoubtedly
constitutes the focus of the book. At the time when the
novel appeared, this apocalyptical chapter must have
seemed to be the boundary of hyperbolism. However, the
consequent happenings have almost surpassed it. And
the last word of class struggle has not yet been said by
far! The "Abysmal Beast" is to the extreme degree oppressed, humiliated, and degenerated people. Who would
now dare to speak for this reason about the artist's pessimism? No, London is an optimist, only a penetrating and
farsighted one. "Look into what kind of abyss the bourgeoisie will hurl you down, if you don't finish with them!"
This is his thought. Today it sounds incomparably more
real and sharp than thirty years ago. But still more astonishing is the genuinely prophetic vision of the methods
by which the Iron Heel will sustain its domination over
crushed mankind. London manifests remarkable freedom
from reformistic pacifist illusions. In this picture of the
future there remains not a trace of democracy and peace-

ful progress. Over the mass of the deprived rise the castes of labor aristocracy, of praetorian army, of an all-penetrating police, with the financial oligarchy at the top. In reading it one does not believe his own eyes: it is precisely the picture of fascism, of its economy, of its governmental technique, its political psychology! The fact is incontestable: in 1907 Jack London already foresaw and described the fascist regime as the inevitable result of the defeat of the proletarian revolution. Whatever may be the single "errors" of the novel — and they exist — we cannot help inclining before the powerful intuition of the revolutionary artist.

A MASTERLY FIRST NOVEL:

JEAN MALAQUAIS'S

LES JAVANAIS

Trotsky wrote this article in 1939 after the appearance of Malaquais's first novel, Les Javanais, *later translated into English as* Men from Nowhere. *The magazines to which he submitted it rejected it, and after Malaquais won fame by receiving the Goncourt Prize, Trotsky, no longer feeling it necessary to call attention to Malaquais's achievement, withdrew the article from circulation.*

It is well that there is art in the world as well as politics. It is well that the potentialities of art are as inexhaustible as life itself. In a certain sense art is richer than life, for it can both overstate and understate, lay on the bright colors thickly or resort to the opposite extreme and content itself with the gray crayon, can present the same object in all its varied facets and shed a variety of light upon it. There was only one Napoleon — his reproductions in art are legion.

The Peter and Paul Fortress and other czarist prisons drew me so close to the French classics that for more than three decades thereafter I became a fairly regular reader of the more outstanding recent French fiction. Even during the years of the civil war I had a current French

Written August 7, 1939, and published in *Fourth International* (New York), January 1941, in a translation by Charles Malamuth.

novel in the car of my military train. After banishment
to Constantinople I accumulated there a modest library of
recent French fiction. It was burned with all my other
books in March 1931. However, during the last few years
my interest in novels has waned almost to the point of
extinction. Far too overwhelming were the events that rolled
over our earth and incidentally over my own head as well.
The conceits of art began to seem vapid, almost trite.
I read with interest the first few volumes of Jules Romains's
epic. But his later books, especially those that portray
the war, struck me as insipid reporting. Apparently, no
art can quite encompass war. Battle painting is for the
most part downright fatuous. But that is not all there
is to it. Just as overspicy cooking dulls the taste, so the
piling up of historical catastrophes dulls the appeal of
literature. Yet the other day I again had occasion to
repeat: it is well that there is art in the world.

Jean Malaquais, a French writer unknown to me, sent
me his book, enigmatically entitled *Les Javanais* [The
Javanese]. The novel is dedicated to Andre Gide. This
put me somewhat on guard. Gide has removed himself
too far from us, along with the epoch he reflected in his
deliberate and leisurely disquisitions. Even his latest books,
interesting though they are, read rather like human records
of the irrevocable past. But the very first few pages clearly
convinced me that Malaquais was in no way indebted
to Gide. Indeed, he is quite independent. And therein lies
his strength, especially nowadays, when all manner of
dependence has become the rule. The name Malaquais
suggested nothing to me, unless perhaps a certain street
in Paris. *Les Javanais* is his first novel; his other writings
are announced as books still "in preparation." Nonetheless,
this first book forthwith prompts the thought: Malaquais's
name is bound to be remembered.

The author is young and passionately fond of life. But
he already knows how to maintain the indispensable artistic distance between himself and life, a distance sufficient to
keep him from succumbing to his own subjectiveness. To
love life with the superficial affection of the dilettantes —
and there are dilettantes of life as well as of art — is no
great merit. To love life with open eyes, with unabating

criticism, without illusions, without embellishments, such
as it is, whatever it may offer, and even more, for what
it can come to be—that is a feat of a kind. To invest this
love of life with artistic expression, especially when this
is concerned with the very lowest social stratum—that is
a great artistic achievement.

In the south of France two hundred men extract tin
and silver from a virtually exhausted mine, owned by
an Englishman, who does not wish to spend any money
on new equipment. The country is full of persecuted foreigners—without visas, without documents, in bad with
the police. They are not in the least particular about
where they live or about safety provisions on the job,
and are ready to work for any wage at all. The mine
and its population of pariahs form a world apart, sort
of an island, which came to be called "Java," most likely
because the French are wont to describe anything incomprehensible and exotic as "Javanese."

Almost all the nationalities of Europe, and not of Europe
alone, are represented in this Java. White Russians, Poles
of unknown kidney, Italians, Spaniards, Greeks, Czechs,
Slovaks, Germans, Austrians, Arabs, an Armenian, a
Chinese, a Negro, a Ukrainian Jew, a Finn. . . . In all
this mongrel crew there is but one Frenchman, a pathetic
failure, who holds aloft the banner of the Third Republic.
In the barracks that lean against the wall of a factory
long ago gutted by fire live thirty celibates, of whom
nearly all swear in different languages. The wives of the
others, brought from all parts of the world, merely enhance the confusion of this Babel.

The Javanese pass before us, every one of them a reflection of his lost homeland, each convincing as a personality, and each (at least, apparently, without any aid
from the author) standing on his own feet. The Austrian,
Karl Mueller, yearning for Vienna while cramming up on
English conjugations; the son of Rear Admiral Ulrich von
Taupfen, Hans, himself a former naval officer and participant of the sailors' insurrection at Kiel; the Armenian
Albudizian, who for the first time in his life had his fill
of food, and even got drunk, in Java; the Russian agron-
omist Byelsky, with his half-mad wife and insane daughter;

the old miner Ponzoni who lost his sons in a mine of his native Italy and who is just as glad to talk to the wall or to a rock on the road as to the fellow working next to him; "Doctor Magnus," who left his university in the Ukraine just before graduating, so as not to live like others; the American Negro, Hilary Hodge, who every Sunday polishes his patent leather shoes, a memento of the past, but never puts them on; the former Russian shopkeeper Blutov, who says he is a former general, so as to attract customers for his future restaurant — although Blutov really dies before the action of the novel begins, leaving behind his widow, a fortune teller.

Members of broken-up families, adventurers, accidental participants of revolutions and counterrevolutions, chips of national movements and national catastrophes, refugees of all kinds, dreamers and thieves, cowards and almost-heroes, people without roots, the prodigal sons of our epoch — such is the population of Java, a "floating island tied to the Devil's tail." As Hans von Taupfen put it, "there is not one square inch on the entire surface of the globe where you might place your little foot; except for that, you are free, but only outside the border, outside all borders." The gendarme corporal Carboni, connoisseur of good cigars and fine wines, shuts his eye to the inhabitants of the island. For the time being they find themselves "outside all borders." But that does not deter them from living after their own fashion. They sleep on pallets of straw, often without undressing; they smoke heavily; drink heavily; live on bread and cheese, in order to save most of their money for wine; they seldom wash; they smell rankly of sweat, tobacco and alcohol.

The novel has no central figure and no trace of a plot. In a certain sense the author himself is the hero; but he does not appear on the scene. The story covers a period of several months; and, like life itself, consists of episodes. Notwithstanding the exoticism of the milieu, the book is far from folklore, ethnography or sociology. It is in the authentic sense a novel, a bit of life transformed into art. One might think that the author deliberately chose an isolated "island" in order all the more clearly to portray the human characters and passions. They are no less significant here than in any strata of society. These people love, hate, weep, remember, grind their teeth. Here you will find the birth and solemn baptism of a child in the family of the Pole Warski; you will find death, the despair of women, funerals; and finally, the love of a prostitute for Doctor Magnus, who until then had not known women. So touchy an episode suggests melodrama; but the author goes through the self-imposed ordeal with honor.

Through the book runs the story of two Arabs, the cousins Allahassid Ben Khalif and Daoud Khaim. Breaking the law of Mohammed once a week, they drink wine on Sundays, but modestly, only three liters, in order to save five thousand francs for themselves and return to their families in the country of Constantine. They are not real Javanese, but only temporary ones. And then Allahassid is killed in a mine landslide. The story of Daoud's attempts to get his money from the savings bank is unforgettable. The Arab waits for hours, implores, hopes, and again waits patiently. Finally his savings book is confiscated because it is made out in the name of Allahassid, the only one of the two who could sign his name. This little tragedy is told superbly!

Madame Michel, the owner of a barroom, gets rich off these people, yet wastes no love on them and despises them — not only because she does not understand their noisy chatter but also because they are too prodigal with tips, come and go with too great ease and no one knows where: frivolous people undeserving of trust. Along with the barroom, an important place in the life of Java is, of course, occupied by the nearest brothel. Malaquais describes it in detail, mercilessly, but, at the same time, in a remarkably human way.

The Javanese look at the world from below, since they themselves have been spilled on their backs to the very bottom of society; besides, at the bottom of the mine, too, the better to hew or drill the rock above them, they must lie down on their backs. That is a singular perspective. Malaquais well knows its laws and knows how to apply them. The work inside the mine is described sparingly, without tiring details but with remarkable force. No mere

artist-observer could write like that, even if he had gone
down the shaft ten times over in quest of technical details,
which writers like Jules Romains, for example, like to
flaunt. Only a former miner who has since become a great
artist can write like that.

Although social in its implications, this novel is in no
way tendentious in character. He does not try to prove
anything, he does not propagandize, as do many productions of our time, when far too many submit to orders
even in the sphere of art. The Malaquais novel is "only"
a work of art. At the same time we sense at every step
the convulsions of our epoch, the most grandiose and the
most monstrous, the most significant and the most des-
potic ever known to human history. The combination
of the rebellious lyricism of the personality with the fero-
cious epic of the era creates, perhaps, the chief fascination
of this work.

The illegal regime lasted for years. The one-eyed and
one-armed British manager, who was always drunk,
would overcome difficulties with the law by treating the
gendarme officer in charge to wine and cigars. The Javanese, without documents, continued to work in the dangerous galleries of the mine, to get drunk at Madame
Michel's, and, whenever they met the gendarmes, to hide
behind trees — just to play safe. But everything comes to
an end.

The mechanic, Karl, son of a Viennese baker, leaves
his job in the shed of his own free will, spends his time
walking under the sun on the sand of the beach, listening
to the waves of the sea and talking with the trees along
the way. Frenchmen work in the factory of a neighboring
settlement. They have their little houses with water and
electricity, their chickens, rabbits and lettuce patches. Karl,
like the majority of the Javanese, regards this settled
world without envy and with a shade of contempt. They
"have lost the sense of space but have won the sense of
property." Karl breaks off a switch and slashes the air
with it. He feels like singing. But he has no voice; so,
he whistles. Meantime, there is a cave-in underground,
and two are killed — the Russian, Malinov, who had pre-
sumably wrested Nizhni Novgorod from the Bolsheviks,

and the Arab, Allahassid Ben Khalif. Gentleman Yakovlev, a former best pupil of the Moscow Conservatory,
robs the old Russian woman, Sophia Fedorovna, widow
of the would-be general and sorceress, who had accumulated several thousand francs. By chance Karl looks in
through her open window and Yakovlev hits him on the
head with a club. Thus, catastrophe, a number of catastrophes, invade the life of Java. The desperation of the old
woman is boundless and revolting. She turns her back
on the world, answers the questions of the gendarmes
with oaths, sits on the floor without food, without sleep,
one day, two, three days, swaying from side to side in
her excrement, surrounded by a swarm of flies.

The theft calls forth a newspaper notice: where are the
consuls? Why don't they do something? Gendarme Carboni receives a circular of instruction on the necessity
of the strictest checking of foreigners. The liquor and
cigars of John Kerrigan are no longer effective. "We are
in France, Mr. Manager, and must comply with French
law." The manager is compelled to telegraph London.
The reply orders that the mine be closed. Java ceases
to exist. The Javanese disperse, to hide in other crevices.

Literary primness is foreign to Malaquais; he avoids
neither forceful expressions nor vexatious scenes. Contemporary literature, especially the French, is as a rule
more free in this respect than the old naturalists of Zola's
times, condemned by the rigorists. It would be ridiculous
pedantry to pass judgment as to whether this is good
or bad. Life has become more naked and merciless, especially since the World War, which destroyed not only
many cathedrals but also many conventions; there is
nothing else for literature to do than to adjust itself to
life.

But what a difference between Malaquais and a certain
other French writer, who made himself famous a few years
ago with a book of exceptional frankness! I am referring
to Celine. No one before him had written about the needs
and functions of the poor human body with such physiological persistence. But Celine's hand is guided by em-
bittered hurt, which descends to calumny of man. The
artist, a physician by profession, seems to have the de-

sire to convince us that the human being, obliged to dis-
charge such low functions, is in no way distinguishable
from a dog or a donkey, except perhaps by greater sly-
ness and vengefulness. This hateful attitude toward life
has clipped the wings of Celine's art: he has not gone
beyond his first book. Almost simultaneously with Celine,
another skeptic became famous — Malraux, who sought
justification of his pessimism, not below, in physiology,
but above, in the manifestations of human heroism. Malraux wrote one or two significant books. But he lacks
backbone. He is organically seeking some outside force
to lean on, some established authority. The lack of creative independence has envenomed his latest books with
the poison of falsehood and has rendered them unfit for
consumption.

Malaquais does not fear the base and the vulgar in our
nature, for, despite all, man is capable of creativeness,
of passion, of heroism — and they are far from fruitless.
Like all true optimists, Malaquais loves man for his potentialities. Gorky once said, "Man — that sounds proud!"
Perhaps Malaquais would not repeat a phrase so didac-
tic. Yet this is precisely the attitude toward man that runs
through his novel. Malaquais 's talent has two dependable
allies: optimism and independence.

I have just mentioned Maxim Gorky, another poet of
the tramps. The parallel suggests itself. I vividly remember
how the reading world was astounded by Gorky's first
great short story "Chelkash" in 1895. The young vaga-
bond emerged at once from the cellar of society into the
arena of literature as a master. In his later writings Gorky
essentially never rose above the level of his first short
story. No less does Malaquais astound one with the sure
touch of his first venture. It cannot be said of him that
he is a promising writer. He is a finished artist. In the old
schools beginners were put through cruel paces — kicks,
intimidation, taunts — so that they might receive the necessary tempering in the shortest possible time. But Malaquais, like Gorky before him, received this tempering from
life itself. It tossed them about, beat them against the earth,
chest and back, and after such a workout cast them out
into the literary arena as finished masters.

And yet how great is the difference between their epochs, between their heroes, between their artistic methods! Gorky's tramps are not the dregs of an old urban culture but the peasants of yesterday who have not yet been assimilated by the new industrial city. The tramps of capitalism's springtide, they are marked with the stamp of patriarchalism and almost of naiveté. Russia, still quite young politically, was in those days pregnant with her first revolution. Literature lived on breathless expectations and exaggerated raptures. Gorky's tramps are embellished with prerevolutionary romanticism.

A half century has not elapsed in vain. Russia and Europe have lived through a series of political earthquakes and the most terrible of wars. Great events brought with them great experiences — chiefly, the bitter experiences of defeats and disappointments. Malaquais's tramps are the product of a mature civilization. They look upon the world with less surprised, more practiced eyes. They are not national but cosmopolitan. Gorky's tramps wandered from the Baltic Sea to the Black Sea or to Sakhalin. The Javanese know no state borders; they are equally at home or equally alien in the mines of Algiers, in the forests of Canada or on the coffee plantations of Brazil. Gorky's lyricism is melodious, at times sentimental, often declamatory. Malaquais's lyricism, essentially no less intense, is more restrained in form and disciplined by irony.

French literature, conservative and exclusive, like all French culture, is slow to assimilate the new words it itself creates for the whole world, and is rather resistant to the penetration of foreign influences. True, since the war a stream of cosmopolitanism has entered French life. The French began to travel more, to study geography and foreign languages. Maurois brought to its literature the stylized Englishman, Paul Morand — the nightclubs of the world. [1] But this cosmopolitanism bears the indelible stamp of tourism. It is quite different with Malaquais. He is no tourist. He travels from country to country in a manner that meets neither with the approval of railroad companies nor the police. He has roamed in all the geographic latitudes, has worked wherever he could, was persecuted, suffered hunger and absorbed his impressions of our planet together with the atmosphere of mines, plantations and cheap barrooms, where the international pariahs generously spend their meager wages.

Malaquais is an authentic French writer; he is a master of the French technique of the novel, the highest in the world, not to mention his perfection of language. Yet he is not a Frenchman. I suspected as much while reading the novel. Not because in the tone of his narrative could be sensed a foreigner, an alien observer. Not at all. Where Frenchmen appear in the pages of his book, they are genuine Frenchmen. But in the author's approach — not only to France but to life in general — you feel a "Javanese" who has risen above "Java." This is not like the French. In spite of all the world-shattering events of the last quarter of a century, they remain too sedentary, too stable in their habits, in their traditions, to look up at the world with the eyes of a tramp.

To my letter of inquiry the author replied that he is of Polish descent. I should have guessed it without asking. The beginning of the novel is concentrated on the sketch of a Polish youth, almost a boy, with flaxen hair, blue eyes, greedy for impressions, with a hunger-drawn stomach, and with the ill-mannered habit of blowing his nose with his fingers. Such is Manek Brilya. He rides the rods of a dining car out of Warsaw with the dream of Timbuctoo. If this is not Malaquais himself, it is his brother in blood and spirit. Manek spent more than ten years wandering, learned a lot and matured, but he never dissipated his freshness of spirit; on the contrary, he accumulated an insatiable thirst for life, of which his first book is incontrovertible evidence. We await his next book. Malaquais's passport is apparently still not in good order. But literature has already conferred upon him the full rights of citizenship.

NOTES

[pages 7-15]
Introduction

1. As quoted by Max Eastman in his introduction to Leon Trotsky, *The History of the Russian Revolution*, 3 vols. (New York: Simon and Schuster, 1937), Vol. I, pp. xv.-xvi.

2. Edmund Wilson, *The Triple Thinkers* (Oxford: Oxford University Press, 1948), pp. 265, 200.

3. Rene Wellek, "The Aims, Methods and Materials of Research in the Modern Languages and Literature," *Publications of Modern Language Association (PMLA),* LXVII, 1952, p. 23.

4. Antonio Labriola, *Essays on the Materialistic Conception of History* (Chicago: Charles H. Kerr & Company, 1908), p. 204.

5. Karl Marx, *Selected Works* (New York: International Publishers, n. d.), "Letter to Heinz Starkenburg," January 25, 1894, vol. I, p. 392.

6. Ibid., "Communist Manifesto," vol. I, p. 225.

7. Leon Trotsky, *Literature and Revolution* (Ann Arbor: University of Michigan Press, 1960), p. 130.

8. Ibid., p. 163-64.

9. *Selected Works*, "A Contribution to the Critique of Political Economy," vol. I, p. 356.

10. Ibid.

11. T. S. Eliot, "A Commentary," *Criterion*, vol. XII, 1932-33, p. 247.

12. Ibid., p. 248.

13. F. R. Leavis, "Under Which King, Bezonian?" *Scrutiny*, vol. I, 1932, p. 206.

14. *Hungi Chanpao* of Peking, February 15, 1967. Quoted by Ernest Germain, "The Cultural Revolution," *International Socialist Review*, vol. 29, no. 4, July-August 1968, p. 59n.

15. Max Hayward and Leopold Labedz, eds., *Literature and Revolution in Soviet Russia, 1917-62* (Oxford: Oxford University Press, 1963), p. ix.

16. *New York Times*, February 10, 1969.

17. John Milton, *Areopagitica and Other Prose Works* (London, 1927), pp. 37-38.

18. Georg Lukacs, "Propaganda or Partisanship?" *Partisan Review*, vol. I, no. 2, 1934, p. 45.

19. Ibid., p. 42.

20. Rosa Luxemburg, "Life of Korolenko," *International Socialist Review*, vol. 30, no. 1, January-February 1969, p. 13.

From *Literature and Revolution*

1. That is, tendentious, bearing an avowed "message" or thesis.

2. The "populists" or Narodniks were intellectuals of the nineteenth century who sought to effect a revolution by a "to the people" movement, primarily to the peasantry, whom they idealized.

3. Anna Akhmatova sometime after fell silent for a long period. She resumed her writing of poetry during World War II but was denounced in 1946 by Zhdanov, Stalin's cultural satrap,

as "part nun and part harlot," and was denied publication. After Stalin's death the disapproval accorded her was eased. Today, after her death in 1966, she is granted a place of honor in Russian poetry.

Marina Tsvetaeva shortly after became an émigré but returned in 1939. She committed suicide two years later.

4. Acmeists: school of contemporary writers who sought for a neoclassical clarity in opposition to symbolism.

5. Formalists: members of a critical school which declared form to be the essence of poetry, determining the content. The formalist critics concentrated on a close analysis of the sound and meaning of the words in poetry. They constituted the leading critical opponents of Marxism of the time.

6. Aleksander Nikolaevich Ostrovsky (1823-1886): Russian realistic dramatist.

7. Shklovsky was the leading theorist of futurism as well as the chief exponent of formalism. Futurism sought to express the urgency and motion of modern life and rebelled against all traditions. Shklovsky contended the futurists were the first artists to recognize that thought and feeling are only incidental to the handling of form.

8. Rudolf Stammler (1856-1938): jurist and legal philosopher.
Nikolai Mikhailovsky (1842-1904): sociologist and political writer, leader of the Narodnik (populist) movement.

9. The New Economic Policy, under which the Soviet state permitted a limited freedom of capital in order to revive economic activity stifled by the civil war.

10. Fellow traveler: Trotsky's word for the literary intelligentsia sympathetic to the October Revolution, approving its goals but not ready to go all the way with the Bolsheviks in reaching them.

Boris Pilnyak (1894-1937) was attacked in 1929 by RAPP, the so-called Russian Association of Proletarian Writers, which was being used by the regime to hound independent writers, and was removed as chairman of the All-Russian Union of Writers. He disappeared during the period of the purges.

The "Serapion Fraternity" was a group of young writers

of whom Trotsky wrote in an earlier chapter: "The most dangerous trait of the Serapions is that they glory in their lack of principles. . . . As if an artist ever could be 'without a tendency,' without a definite relation to social life, even though unformulated or unexpressed in political terms." At the First Writers' Congress, which ushered in the period of "socialist realism," Ivanov renounced his Serapion past and announced his adherence to the "Bolshevik tendentiousness" demanded by Zhdanov in his opening address. He went on to write party-line historical novels.

11. *Kuznitsa* was a literary journal which was carrying on a campaign against the "fellow travelers" and calling for a proletarian literature. Demyan Byedny had been a member of the Communist Party and had written poetry since before the revolution. Trotsky regarded Byedny as a frequently powerful but also frequently pedestrian propagandist whose work fulfilled a unique function, but he thought that, using "the sacred old forms," he "did not and will not create a school" and was not the precursor of a proletarian literature, as *Kuznitsa* believed.

Class and Art

1. Raskolnikov had been on a diplomatic mission to Afghanistan, and so out of the way during earlier phases of this discussion. [Trans.]

2. Leonid Andreyev (1871-1919): a novelist, dramatist and short-story writer, had been hailed as "the apostle of gloom" and was, with Artzybashev, the highest paid writer of prewar Russia. A rebel but too much the misanthrope to be a revolutionist, he became increasingly conservative, fervently supported the war, attacked the revolution and crossed the border to Finland, where he died writing passionate denunciations of the Bolsheviks.

Boris Artzybashev (1878-1927): a novelist, dramatist and bohemian rebel, was highly popular before the war and inspired a cult of sex, death and despair whose disciples sometimes committed suicide. After opposing the Bolsheviks in Russia, he went to Poland and published a weekly magazine carrying on the attack.

3. Gavriil Derzhavin (1743-1816) was an early, crude Russian poet of the late eighteenth century, who wrote before the flowering of Russian literature.

4. The familiar form of Lenin's name.

5. Libedinsky: a novelist who later became an official of the RAPP.

6. Let us here quote verbatim Antonio Labriola's sharp rebuke to those simplifiers who transform Marx's theory into a sort of stencil and master key to everything: "Lazy minds," wrote the best Italian Marxist philosopher, "are readily satisfied with such crude statements. What a holiday and what gladness for all light-minded and unfastidious people: to obtain, at last, in a small summary, composed of a few propositions, the whole of knowledge and to be able to penetrate by means of just one key into all the secrets of life! To reduce all problems of ethics, aesthetics, philology, historical criticism and philosophy to a single problem, and in this way save oneself all difficulties! By this method fools could reduce the whole of history to the level of commercial arithmetic, and, finally, a new, original interpretation of Dante's work could show us *The Divine Comedy* in the light of calculations regarding pieces of cloth which crafty Florentine merchants sold for their maximum profit." There's one in the eye for certain people! [L. T.]

7. Bezymensky was later to become well known as a writer of verse on governmental policy in the pages of *Pravda*.

8. Vladimir Mayakovsky (1893-1930): the futurist poet, acclaimed the revolution and gave himself up to it. Highly popular, he read his poems to massed assemblages of workers. After his suicide in 1930, Mayakovsky, whom Trotsky in his obituary article called an "audacious spirit," was virtually canonized by the regime now that he was safely dead.

Boris Pasternak (1890-1960): futurist poet who remained silent during the Stalinist period but whose novel *Doctor Zhivago*, published abroad during "the thaw" and awarded the Nobel Prize, became a *cause celebre*.

9. Trotsky says of Andrei Byely in *Literature and Revolution*: "The interrevolutionary (1905-17) literature, which is decadent

in its mood and reach and overrefined in its technique, which
is a literature of individualism, of symbolism and of mysticism,
finds in Byely its most condensed expression. . . ."

Leopold Averbach (1903- ?) became a leader of RAPP
and then, ironically, was shot as a Trotskyite during the
purges.

10. There is a pun in the Russian: the word I have translated
as "barren," *postnaya*, begins in the same way as *Postu* (At
Our Post). [Trans.]

11. Besides this basic class interrelationship, we now have,
in connection with the growth of the bourgeoisie on the basis
of NEP, the reappearance along old, well-trodden tracks, of
bourgeois ideology which, of course, overflows into artistic
creation. It was in this very sense that I wrote in my book
that, alongside a flexible and far-seeing policy in the field
of art, we need a resolute and severe, but, of course, not petty,
censorship. This means that, besides the constant ideological
struggle for influence over the best creative elements of the
petty bourgeois peasant or "peasant-singing" intelligentsia, we
need a severe political struggle against all attempts made by
restorationists to bring the new Soviet art under bourgeois
influence. [L. T.]

12. *Rul, Dnya*: White Guard papers.

13. Ivan Andreevich Krylov (1769-1844): writer of fables.
Nikolai Vasilevich Gogol (1809-1852): humorist, short-story
writer, novelist, and dramatist.
Nikolai Alexeevich Nekrassov (1821-1877): poet and journalist.

From *Culture and Socialism*

1. The word "infest" was used by Tolstoy in *What is Art?* to
refer to the communication of emotion through art, which,
Tolstoy felt, should communicate only wholesome emotions.
It was also used by Bukharin in *Historical Materialism*, which,
Trotsky implies, pays insufficient attention to the cognitive
function of literature.

Culture and the Soviet Bureaucracy

1. Stalin, after having derided Trotsky's program for increased industrialization, abruptly adopted it when confronted with a kulak "grain strike" and embarked on a course of ruthless collectivization, the peasant opposition to which brought the country to the brink of disaster.

2. The period in the French Revolution when there was a reaction to the revolutionary Jacobins. Trotsky uses the term to refer to the period when the Soviet bureaucracy gained ascendancy.

The Future of *Partisan Review*: A Letter to Dwight Macdonald

1. The symposium was to have been on the theme "What is alive and what is dead in Marxism?" Among those invited to participate were Harold Laski, Sidney Hook, Ignazio Silone, Edmund Wilson, John Strachey and Fenner Brockway.

Art and Politics in Our Epoch

1. Andrei Vyshinsky: chief prosecutor of the Moscow trials.

2. Alexei Tolstoy (1882-1945), by birth a nobleman and distantly related to Leo Tolstoy, fought on the side of the Whites during the revolution and then settled in France. In 1921 he gave up his title of count and returned to the Soviet Union, where he became immensely popular as a novelist. The novel referred to is *Bread*, published in 1937.

3. The documentation is provided in Trotsky's *The Stalin School of Falsification.*

4. This question is fully developed in my *History of the Russian Revolution* in the chapter entitled "Legends of Bureaucracy." [L. T.] (In the University of Michigan Press edition see appendix I to volume 3, "Some Legends of the Bureaucracy.")

5. Romain Rolland (1866-1944): epic novelist, dramatist and essayist, a leading spirit of the "left" ever since his pacifist denunciation of World War I, in his later years loaned the prestige of his name to Stalinist literary congresses and manifestos. He was

a prolific letter writer, whose correspondence was later published in *Cahiers Romain Rolland.*

6. Diego Rivera (1886-1957), shortly after, succumbing to Stalinophobia, denounced President Cardenas as an "accomplice of the Stalinists" and supported a right-wing general, Almazar, in the presidential elections. Trotsky in a public statement attacked this action and declared that he could no longer have anything to do with him. When the Stalinists, however, denounced Rivera as having "sold himself to reaction," Trotsky spoke of Rivera as a "genius whose political blunderings could cast no shadow either on his art or on his personal integrity." A few years later the erratic Rivera returned penitently to the Stalinists, who received him without bringing up their previous charge of venality.

7. After Rivera completed a mural, "Man at the Crossroads," which he had been commissioned to make at Rockefeller Center, it was objected to as communist propaganda and removed. It was reconstructed at the Palace of Fine Arts in Mexico City.

Manifesto: Towards a Free Revolutionary Art

1. Garcia Oliver: Spanish anarchist leader who collaborated with the Stalinist leaders in crushing the revolutionary wing of the Loyalists.

The Independence of the Artist: A Letter to Andre Breton

1. Edouard Daladier, (1884-1970), who had been the head of the Radical Party during the time of its Popular Front alliance with the Socialist and Communist parties, as premier in 1938 signed the Munich Pact. He was to outlaw the Communist Party after the war with Germany began. Interned by the Vichy government in 1940, he was sent in 1943 to a fascist prison in Germany fulfilling Trotsky's prediction, and was liberated in 1945.

2. Ilya Ehrenburg (1891-1967): novelist, journalist and noted war correspondent during World War II, was most skillful at meeting the demands made upon writers by Stalin. During the purge of the "cosmopolitans" after the war, he was apparently the only writer of Jewish origin of any prominence who survived. After Khrushchev's exposure of Stalin, however, Ehren-

burg hailed the relaxation of controls in his novel *The Thaw,* gave information about the purges in his memoirs and cautiously called for greater freedom for writers.

3. The reference is to Henri Barbusse (1873-1935), French war novelist, pacifist, Stalinist and organizer of the World Congress against War and Fascism, who actually did write biographies of Christ and Stalin.

Tolstoy: Poet and Rebel

1. Max Nordau (1849-1923): a Hungarian writer whose works were in vogue. In his novel *Degeneration* Nordau sought to show a connection between genius and degeneration.

Samuel Smiles (1812-1904): Scotch author of popular works on self-improvement which preached the Victorian "gospel of work" and individual enterprise.

Cesare Lombroso (1836-1909): Italian criminologist, who held that criminals generally exhibit certain physical and mental traits that are due partly to atavism and partly to degeneration.

2. The journalist M. O. Menshikov began by writing articles on humanist morality but in the 1890s became a mouthpiece for reaction and anti-Semitism.

Baron Wilhelm Hammerstein was a reactionary German Reichstag deputy and the editor of an anti-Semitic newspaper.

3. Swiss landscape painter.

4. Frederic Bastiat (1801-1850): French economic journalist who advocated free trade and attacked socialism, which he equated with the other forms of state economic controls that he opposed.

5. The reference is to the governmental repression following the unsuccessful Revolution of 1905.

On Tolstoy's Death

1. Piotr Arkadevich Stolypin became the premier shortly after the unsuccessful revolution of 1905. Under his regime thousands were executed and exiled, giving Russia the peace of the graveyard. Stolypin was assassinated in 1911.

Churchill as Biographer and Historian

1. Lord Frederick Birkenhead (1872-1930) was a leading Tory, a close personal friend of Churchill's and, like him, a member of Lloyd George's wartime coalition government.

Arnold Bennett's novel *Lord Raingo* portrayed members of the coalition cabinet.

2. Brest-Litovsk was the scene of peace negotiations initiated in December 1917, following the revolution in Russia, the Bolshevik appeal to all warring nations for a general peace conference, the Allied rejection of this appeal, and the German armistice with the new Soviet government.

The Bolshevik leadership was divided on the policy to be pursued at Brest-Litovsk. The largest group, led by Bukharin, wanted to wage a "revolutionary war" of self-defense against imperial Germany. Both Lenin and Trotsky believed this was impossible for exhausted and war-weary Russia. Lenin wanted to prolong negotiations as long as possible but finally sign whatever treaty the Germans insisted on. Trotsky was for prolonging and using the negotiations as a forum to unmask the predatory war aims of the German government, and when the showdown came, declaring that as far as the Soviet government was concerned the war was over and it was demobilizing its army, but would not sign the robber treaty; then if the German army resumed hostilities, the Soviet government should sign the treaty, thus demonstrating to the world that it was doing so under the coercion of superior force.

Trotsky's policy had a double aim — to promote revolutionary antiwar propaganda in Germany, and to convince the workers in the Allied countries, whose leaders were saying the Bolsheviks were German agents, that the Soviets were only yielding to superior force.

After some hesitation about this "no war, no peace treaty" tactic, the Germans launched a military attack on February 18, 1918. The Bolshevik leaders met the night before to debate what to do if the Germans resumed hostilities. Lenin moved that in such a case the negotiators should sign the treaty. Trotsky voted with Lenin for this, his support enabling Lenin to prevail over the "revolutionary war" faction. The Bolshevik negotiators returned to Brest-Litovsk and signed the treaty, whose terms were now even stiffer, without even deigning to read it.

After Lenin's death, the facts were falsified by Stalin as part of his anti-Trotskyism campaign. The dispute over Brest-Litovsk was now said to have been principally between Lenin and Trotsky, and Trotsky, the chief negotiator, was accused of having acted contrary to party and government instructions. See the documentation in Trotsky's book, *The Stalin School of Falsification*.

The Suicide of Vladimir Mayakovsky

1. Alexander Blok (1880-1921): a symbolist poet, was regarded by aesthetes as the type of the pure artist although, says Trotsky in *Literature and Revolution*, Blok himself "did not speak of pure art, and did not place poetry above life." To the surprise of these aesthetes, Blok acclaimed Mayakovsky, the avowed partisan of the revolution.

2. Both Alexander Serafimovich and Fyodor Gladkov (1883-1958) participated in revolutionary activity before the war, were among the first writers to adhere to the Bolshevik regime and were the authors of novels that were highly praised when they appeared.
   Vissarion Grigorievich Belinsky (1811-1848): highly influential literary critic of the early nineteenth century, whose support of advanced and socially critical writers affected the course of Russian literature.

3. Sergei Malashkin, a writer of the twenties now fallen into deserved obscurity, combined political conformity to the Stalinist apparatus and its credo of "proletarian literature" with a flair for pornography. His *Moon on the Right-Hand Side* was the literary sensation of 1927, with its morbidly pornographic scenes of the escapades of demoralized Komsomol elements. [Trans.]

The Strangled Revolution: Andre Malraux's *The Conquerors*

1. Michael Borodin (1884-1953): a Russian Communist who was a political advisor to the Chinese Nationalist government and is a character in *The Conquerors*.

2. Stanley Baldwin (1867-1947): British Tory prime minister.
   Ramsay MacDonald (1866-1937): prime minister first of the Labour government and then of the "National government."

3. Raymond Poincare (1860-1934): reactionary prime minister of several governments.

Edouard Herriot (1872-1957): leader of the Radical Socialist Party.

Leon Blum (1872-1950): leader of the Socialist Party.

These three were representatives of parties from right to left which supported French imperialism.

Celine and Poincare: Novelist and Politician

1. As minister of justice during the French Revolution, Georges Danton (1759-1794) expressed its fighting spirit, refusing to withdraw the government from Paris when the Prussians advanced against it.

2. Emil Ludwig (1881-1948): German journalist and biographer of contemporary statesmen and historical figures.

French troops occupied the Ruhr in 1923 when the German government was unable to pay the heavy reparations provided for in the Treaty of Versailles. In response to passive resistance in the mines and factories, the occupation forces carried out mass arrests and an economic blockade which further shattered the economy.

3. Heinrich Bruening (1885-1970): the head of the German government, who, in the midst of a severe financial crisis that further depressed a deteriorating economy, appealed to France and England for financial assistance.

4. Silvio Pellico (1789-1854) was an Italian patriot and revolutionist of the nineteenth century. His classic account of his suffering as a political prisoner of the Austrians was written in a simple, direct style.

5. The Union-General was a combine which sought unsucessfully in the 1880s to defeat the entrenched banks and their political representatives.

The Panama Canal Company, as was revealed in the early 1890s after it went bankrupt, bribed many great figures of the journalist world and approximately one hundred senators and deputies.

The highest circles of the army were involved in the frame-up of Dreyfus in the late 1890s.

Rochette was a financier who in 1911 used government influence to put off an investigation into his shady business affairs.

Serge Stavisky was a shyster, whose bankruptcy in the 1930s revealed once more the connections between crooked business, journalism and politics.

6. Peret was involved in the scandal when, after the provincial banks controlled by the Oustric interests collapsed, it was discovered that Oustric had been financed by the Bank of France, which accepted as collateral bills drawn with sleight of hand by one Oustric company upon another.

7. Auguste Blanqui (1805-1881): socialist revolutionist, who was many times imprisoned for long terms but continued his political activity.

Critical Jottings

1. Francois Mauriac (1885-1970): liberal Catholic novelist.

2. Jules Romains (1885-   ): French novelist, poet and dramatist, author of the epic novel *Men of Good Will,* whose twenty-seven volumes cover the historical scene of the period from 1908 to 1933.

"It" refers to the social order, which Trotsky just stated "has hopelessly undermined itself" and will "collapse with a stench."

3. Konstantin Fedin (1892-   ) began his long literary career as a " fellow traveler" in the 1920s.

4. Both Marcel Prevost (1862-1941) and Charles Bourget (1852-1935) were elderly novelists who wrote stories about young women.

5. Konstantin Paustovsky was not a sailor, as Trotsky infers, but as an editor of *The Seaman,* a newspaper published in the port city of Odessa by the Sailors' Union for Russian and foreign seamen, he became intimately acquainted during the civil war years with seamen and the sea. Paustovsky distinguished himself in the years after World War II by the boldness of his opposition to governmental restrictions.

6. Grigori Ordzhonikidze (1886-1937) was a political associate of Stalin.

"Thou" is the familiar form, used with social inferiors; "you" is the polite form, used toward superiors.

7. Emma Goldman (1869-1940): the American anarchist, was deported to the Soviet Union — Russia was her birthplace — in 1919 for obstructing the draft. Rejecting the Soviet regime, she went to England and then to Canada and Spain, dying on a trip to Canada in 1940.

Sometime after she lost her husband and four children in a yellow fever epidemic, Mary Jones (1830-1930), the daughter of an Irish rebel and the wife of a staunch union man, became a militant labor agitator and organizer for the rest of her long life. Going to the coal mine towns of Pennsylvania and West Virginia and to the other places where labor was in combat, she was undeterred by guns or jails and became a living legend as "Mother" Jones.

A Masterly First Novel: Jean Malaquais's *Les Javanais*

1. Andre Maurois (1885-1967): a liaison officer to the British army during World War I, wrote a highly popular war novel, *The Silence of Colonel Bramble,* about Englishmen and went on to write romanticized biographies of English historical figures.

Paul Morand served as a diplomatic attaché in London, Rome and Madrid. His *Open All Night* (1922) and *Closed All Night* (1923) were collections of short stories which shuttle from one capital of postwar Europe to another, with a dizzying, hectic effect.

NAME INDEX